CASEBOOK SERIES

JANE AUSTEN: *Emma* (Revised) David Lodge
JANE AUSTEN: *'Northanger Abbey' & 'Persuasion'* B. C. Southam
JANE AUSTEN: *'Sense and Sensibility', 'Pride and Prejudice' & 'Mansfield Park'*
  B. C. Southam
BECKETT: *Waiting for Godot* Ruby Cohn
WILLIAM BLAKE: *Songs of Innocence and Experience* Margaret Bottrall
CHARLOTTE BRONTE: *'Jane Eyre' & 'Villette'* Miriam Allott
EMILY BRONTE: *Wuthering Heights* (Revised) Miriam Allott
BROWNING: *'Men and Women' & Other Poems* J. R. Watson
CHAUCER: *The Canterbury Tales* J. J. Anderson
COLERIDGE: *'The Ancient Mariner' & Other Poems* Alun R. Jones & W. Tydeman
CONRAD: *'Heart of Darkness', 'Nostromo' & 'Under Western Eyes'* C. B. Cox
CONRAD: *The Secret Agent* Ian Watt
DICKENS: *Bleak House* A. E. Dyson
DICKENS: *'Hard Times', 'Great Expectations' & 'Our Mutual Friend'* Norman Page
DICKENS: *'Dombey and Son' & 'Little Dorrit'* Alan Shelston
DONNE: *Songs and Sonnets* Julian Lovelock
GEORGE ELIOT: *Middlemarch* Patrick Swinden
GEORGE ELIOT: *'The Mill on the Floss' & 'Silas Marner'* R. P. Draper
T. S. ELIOT: *'Prufrock', 'Gerontion' & 'Ash Wednesday'* B. C. Southam
T. S. ELIOT: *The Waste Land* C. B. Cox & Arnold P. Hinchliffe
T. S. ELIOT: *Plays* Arnold P. Hinchliffe
HENRY FIELDING: *Tom Jones* Neil Compton
E.M. FORSTER: *A Passage to India* Malcolm Bradbury
WILLIAM GOLDING: *Novels 1954–64* Norman Page
HARDY: *The Tragic Novels* (Revised) R. P. Draper
HARDY: *Poems* James Gibson & Trevor Johnson
HARDY: *Three Pastoral Novels* R. P. Draper
GERARD MANLEY HOPKINS: *Poems* Margaret Bottrall
HENRY JAMES: *'Washington Square' & 'The Portrait of a Lady'* Alan Shelton
JONSON: *Volpone* Jonas A. Barish
JONSON: *'Every Man in his Humour' & 'The Alchemist'* R. V. Holdsworth
JAMES JOYCE: *'Dubliners' & 'A Portrait of the Artist as a Young Man'* Morris Beja
KEATS: *Odes* G.S. Fraser
KEATS: *Narrative Poems* John Spencer Hill
D.H. LAWRENCE: *Sons and Lovers* Gamini Salgado
D.H. LAWRENCE: *'The Rainbow' & 'Women in Love'* Colin Clarke
LOWRY: *Under the Volcano* Gordon Bowker
MARLOWE: *Doctor Faustus* John Jump
MARLOWE: *'Tamburlaine the Great', 'Edward II' & 'The Jew of Malta'* J. R. Brown
MARLOWE: *Poems* Arthur Pollard
MAUPASSANT: *In the Hall of Mirrors* T. Harris
MILTON: *Paradise Lost* A. E. Dyson & Julian Lovelock
O'CASEY: *'Juno and the Paycock', 'The Plough and the Stars' & 'The Shadow of a
  Gunman'* Ronald Ayling
EUGENE O'NEILL: *Three Plays* Normand Berlin
JOHN OSBORNE: *Look Back in Anger* John Russell Taylor
PINTER: *'The Birthday Party' & Other Plays* Michael Scott
POPE: *The Rape of the Lock* John Dixon Hunt
SHAKESPEARE: *A Midsummer Night's Dream* Antony Price
SHAKESPEARE: *Antony and Cleopatra* (Revised) John Russell Brown
SHAKESPEARE: *Coriolanus* B. A. Brockman

Shakespeare's Early Tragedies

Richard III, *Titus Andronicus* and *Romeo and Juliet*

A CASEBOOK

EDITED BY

NEIL TAYLOR

and

BRYAN LOUGHREY

MACMILLAN

First published 1990 by
MACMILLAN PRESS LTD
Houndmills, Basingstoke, Hampshire RG21 6XS
and London
Companies and representatives
throughout the world

ISBN 0–333–42489–1 hardcover
ISBN 0–333–42490–5 paperback

A catalogue record for this book is available
from the British Library.

10   9   8   7   6   5   4   3
03   02   01   00   99   98   97

Printed in Hong Kong

CONTENTS

GENERAL EDITOR'S PREFACE

The Casebook series, launched in 1968, has become a well-regarded library of critical studies. The central concern of the series remains the 'single-author' volume, but suggestions from the academic community have led to an extension of the original plan, to include occasional volumes on such general themes as literary 'schools' and genres.

Each volume in the central category deals either with one well-known and influential work by an individual author, or with closely related works by one writer. The main section consists of critical readings, mostly modern, collected from books and journals. A selection of reviews and comments by the author's contemporaries is also included, and sometimes comment from the author himself. The Editor's Introduction charts the reputation of the work or works from the first appearance to the present time.

Volumes in the 'general themes' category are variable in structure but follow the basic purpose of the series in presenting an integrated selection of readings, with an Introduction which explores the theme and discusses the literary and critical issues involved.

A single volume can represent no more than a small selection of critical opinions. Some critics are excluded for reasons of space, and it is hoped that readers will pursue the suggestions for further reading in the Select Bibliography. Other contributions are severed from their original context, to which some readers may wish to turn. Indeed, if they take a hint from the critics represented here, they certainly will.

A. E. DYSON

INTRODUCTION

Shakespeare's contemporaries regarded the three plays covered by this volume as tragedies. (At least, each was so described on the title page of its First Quarto and in the relevant title within the First Folio of 1623.) Tragedy, in the formulations it was given by Elizabethan theorists, recounts the falls of eminent men and offers a number of moral lessons. If Kings are Tyrants they will be punished, which implies that there is divine justice. On the other hand, life is entirely unpredictable. There is a contradiction in the argument here, but then tragedy is an enactment of painfully contradictory facts.

Tragedy leads to contradictory responses too. Medieval accounts of tragic falls preach the need for resignation in the face of suffering. Such a lesson encourages the somewhat negative conclusion that the world should be held in contempt as a mere vale of tears. Those who suffer most spectacularly are those who expose themselves to trouble by seeking worldly success. But the Elizabethans came to see a positive significance in suffering as well, and this derived in part from their interest in the plays of the Roman dramatist Seneca, who seemed to be asserting the *nobility* of suffering.

Seneca was, as Joost Daalder puts it, 'the only *tragic* dramatist at all familiar to most Elizabethans.'[1] By 1581 all his plays were readily available in English translations, and a play like Thomas Kyd's *The Spanish Tragedy* (1589) displays the influence of his sensationalism and declamatory style. His influence on Shakespeare's early tragedies was strongly advocated by late nineteenth- and early twentieth-century scholars but in the last fifty years a counter-case has also been put. For example, in 1936, Willard Farnham was arguing that

Before Christian Europe could produce Shakespeare it needed to evolve slowly its own Gothic sense of tragic form and content . . . [and] experience something of the same vision out of which the earlier classic world had produced tragedy.

(*The Medieval Heritage of Elizabethan Tragedy*, Berkeley, p. 3)

Farnham went on to describe a native tradition of both dramatic and non-dramatic moralising literature (including not only tales of famous falls and treatments of the theme of Contempt in verse and prose, but Morality Plays as well) which, to his satisfaction, provided the structure and ethos of Elizabethan tragedy.

Irving Ribner, in his *Patterns in Shakespearean Tragedy* (London, 1960), attempted to reconcile the Senecan and indigenous cases. For him, *Titus Andronicus*, *Richard III* and *Romeo and Juliet* are highly imitative of Senecan tragedy but seek to grasp 'the life-journey of man in conflict with evil' (p. 12). *Titus Andronicus* is like the Morality Plays in that it shows a virtuous man's fall through deception. *Richard III* describes the rise and fall of a deliberately evil man but ends with the cleansing of the social order and employs throughout a universalising ritual technique learnt from the Moralities. *Romeo and Juliet* tells of a hero and heroine whose youthful vulnerability and folly is symbolic of the human condition. Whether or not he makes his case a persuasive one, Ribner typifies much of the criticism of the last thirty years in that he believes Shakespeare wrote all three of these plays, considers each of them worthy of serious attention, and questions the notion of a single formula for 'Shakespearean Tragedy'.

The notion that Shakespearean Tragedy is a distinct sub-genre was given its most famous and influential expression by A. C. Bradley. By the late nineteenth century the critical term *tragedy* had acquired an immense spiritual and ideological significance. In 1904, A. C. Bradley was writing of the Shakespearean tragic hero that he represented 'the full power and reach of the soul' and 'a type of the mystery of the whole world'. As for tragedy itself, it was 'the typical form of this mystery, because that greatness of soul which it exhibits oppressed, conflicting and destroyed, is the highest existence in our view'.[2]

One effect of this development was that these three plays, almost certainly written during the period 1591–1595 (when Shakespeare was in his late twenties and early thirties), had now to live in the shadow of supposedly profounder tragedies written later in his career. Bradley himself played a key role in this process of discrimination. Indeed, he virtually ignored all three plays in his famous lectures on *Shakespearean Tragedy*. *Romeo and Juliet*, he explained, may have been a 'pure tragedy', but it was immature. *Richard III* was *not* pure tragedy. *Titus Andronicus* was neither mature nor pure.[3]

Underlying Bradley's thinking about tragedy is an assumption that the word has a universal and eternal meaning. If such were the case, then after 2,500 years of effort we might indeed be able to identify the essence of 'pure tragedy', isolate the best examples of the genre and dismiss the rest. But an historical approach to the word undermines such a proposition. As Raymond Williams has argued, the tradition of tragic theory since Aristotle is characterised by change rather than stability.[4] Bradley's ideas inevitably reflected the nature of the culture within which he was writing. Such diverse factors as the cult of the hero, the popularity of the naturalistic novel, and the growth of humanism as an alternative to religious faith, contributed to the particular emphases in Bradley's notion of what constitutes 'pure tragedy'.

We may also wish to distance ourselves from Bradley when he uses such terms as 'maturity' and 'immaturity'. His usage is, of course, only part of the widespread wish since Coleridge to conceive of literature as a living organism subject to growth and decay. But why should we be bullied by a metaphor? Does it not give a spurious authority to highly subjective judgements? And when a critic evaluates a work of literature as displaying 'maturity', are we really being told any more than that the author's ideas about life have happened to coincide with those of the critic?

Richard III

The critical response to *Richard III* has been dominated by a discussion of its eponymous 'hero' and also by a debate about the success or failure of its structure. As early as 1700 these two issues were implicitly taken up by Colly Cibber (1671–1757) when he made a radical adaptation of the play. His version held the stage, despite Samuel Phelps's attempt in 1845 to restore Shakespeare's text, until 1870. He cuts the play drastically, retaining only about a third of Shakespeare's lines, incorporates bits of other Shakespeare plays and adds a thousand or so lines of his own. Margaret, Clarence, Hastings and Edward are omitted entirely, Buckingham, Rivers, Grey and Vaughan are reduced in significance, and eight whole scenes go by the board. The resulting play concentrates relentlessly on Richard himself, and in particular on his feelings and the feelings of his victims (both areas which Cibber 'wrote up'). He is effectively isolated, an unsympathetic and inexplicable moral phenomenon without the ironical placing of history or divine providence.

George Steevens* wrote in 1793 that he regarded Cibber's adaptation as 'judicious' and was relieved that it omitted Clarence's dream 'and other undramatick incumbrances'. Charles Lamb,* on the other hand, considered Cibber's version 'wretched' (letter to Robert Lloyd, 26th June 1801) and one therefore assumes that his comments derive from a study of the printed text. He detected an ambivalence in Shakespeare's portrait of Richard: 'He set out to paint a *monster*, but his sympathies produced a *Man*'. For Lamb, Richard was a man with a knowledge of the human heart and, above all, an 'habitual jocularity',[5] and Lamb was full of admiration for his genius, and his mounting spirit. Georg Gottfried Gervinus* approved the prominence which Shakespeare gives to Richard. It provides an intellectual unity, for everything else in the play is organised in relation to the brutality which is Richard's character. Hermann Ulrici,* another mid-nineteenth-century German, appears to be condemning the play for what he regards as an artistic defect— the want of 'drastic animation' in the first four acts ('On the one side we have only power and energy, on the other only submission and impotence'). But the resulting portrait of Richard is a study in tyranny. And this, he asserts, is the historical significance of the whole drama, its presentation of 'the historico-political phenomenon of selfishness in its worst form'. Similarly, R. G. Moulton* finds in the centrality of the character study of Richard the artistic and moral integrity of the play. Like Lamb, Edward Dowden* finds himself admiring Richard's 'daring experiment of choosing evil for his good'. This recognition of a paradoxical ambivalence in our response to Richard is at the heart of much criticism of the play in the twentieth century too.

An ambivalence is already built into the play's structure, for it presents an immediate problem of generic location. The editors of the First Folio called it a tragedy but inserted it into the section occupied by the history plays. R. G. Moulton, writing in 1885, regarded it as a sort of Christianised Greek Tragedy, arguing that Shakespeare had transformed the world of history into 'an intricate design of which the recurrent pattern is Nemesis'.[6] Sixty years later, Lily B. Campbell felt that it succeeded in being simultaneously history and tragedy, even though Shakespeare was 'writing without a clear distinction between these genres in mind'.[7]

* The authors whose critical material is included in the relevant section of this Casebook are indicated by an asterisk.

But tragic form is surely under strain in this play. It may indeed be regarded as the culmination of a tragic process which begins with *Richard II* and occupies the whole cycle of eight English history plays. And one of the statements they all seem to be making is the tragic one that hopes and ambitions fade and achievements are lost. But could Shakespeare afford to let such a statement emerge when he is supposed to be celebrating the 'Tudor Myth'? Isn't the victory of Richmond, the grandfather of Queen Elizabeth I, necessarily *comic* in the formal sense? And if we return to the character of the 'hero', can we take him seriously? Isn't Richard too much of both the comedian and the monster? Has he the human representativeness, the dignity, the capacity for moral insight and growth, which many critics have demanded from a tragic figure?

These issues are raised by A. P. Rossiter.* Rossiter saw himself as mounting a challenge to the dominant reading of the play as 'moral history', of which E. M. W. Tillyard* is the most famous exponent. The assault on Tillyard's books and the 'Elizabethan World Picture'[8] has been conducted with some intensity in recent years. The accusations against Tillyard are, firstly, that his account is usually over-simplified and reductive and, secondly, that his own political assumptions inform his readings of the plays. In the case of *Richard III* Tillyard asserted that 'in spite of the eminence of Richard's character the main business of the play is to complete the national tetralogy and to display the working out of God's plan to restore England to prosperity' (*Shakespeare's History Plays* (London), p. 199). Richard is indeed the instrument of God's ends but Shakespeare's instrument is Richmond who makes a 'full declaration of the principle of order, thus giving final and unmistakable shape to what, though largely implicit, had been all along the animating principle of the tetralogy' (ibid., p. 201).

Rossiter chooses to attack Tillyard's wish to see the play as ultimately unproblematic. Rossiter not only finds in the play rather more than the Tudor myth and the Christian principle of history but is conscious that his response is always ambivalent. Shakespeare has converted the Senecan tyrant into a creature with another nature, deriving from the native Morality tradition—the 'diabolic humorist'. The play's unity derives from the central paradoxes that (a) we must find Richard morally ugly but are nevertheless seduced by his 'volcanic Renaissance energies', his stage personality and histrionic skill, and (b), while we recognise God's agency in Richard's killing and may even lack Christian charity to those whom he destroys, 'God's will. . . . sickens us'. Rossiter stops short, however, of drawing conclusions about Shakespeare's attitude to his material: Shakespeare, he says, is not debunking or disproving the Tudor myth, indeed he is not *proving* anything, preferring to pass the responsibility to us of interpreting 'relatives, ambiguities, irony'. When he talks of the play as being comic history rather than moral history he seems to be using 'comic' as a term denoting tone rather than form. When he talks of the play as 'a process thoroughly dialectical' he seems to be using the phrase formalistically rather than politically. For Rossiter, perhaps because of the prevalent ideas of the American New Criticism in the post-war period (the lecture was first delivered in 1953), irony and paradox are seemingly acceptable structures in themselves, complete in their uncompletedness.

For all that Rossiter is interested in considering *Richard III* as an experiment in 'comic history', it is implicit in his discussion that the play is tragic ('Early it may be; but the play is a triumphant contrivance in a manner which cannot properly be compared with that of any other tragedy'). Furthermore, the emphasis he puts on both Richard himself and the ambivalence of our attitude to him encourages a reading which conceives of Richard as a tragic hero.

Peter Reynolds* takes as his topic the theatrical presentation of Richard as hero. He argues against what he regards as the dominant reading of the part, a reading which dates back to Cibber and received further authorisation in Laurence Olivier's 1955 film version of the play. This theatrical tradition makes of Richard a matinee idol whose star-quality finally overrides all moral considerations. Reynolds not only questions the authority of that tradition by proposing an alternative reading but tries to explore the significances of other characters who occupy the stage, even when they are silent.

Even so, Reynolds still concentrates on one man, Richard. Irene G. Dash* begins her reading by exploring the significance of a woman, Margaret – a woman whom Cibber and Olivier chose entirely to omit from their versions of the text. Those directors who cut the part of Margaret conventionally argue that the play is too long and something has to go; that the play lacks unity, and concentration on Richard supplies it; and that, without a knowledge of the earlier plays in the tetralogy, an audience is at a loss to understand Margaret's contribution. Dash alerts us to the fact that the directorial decision to silence Margaret only reinforces the larger wish of a male-dominated society (both the society portrayed by the play and the society in which the play is performed) to render women silent, and therefore powerless. She then goes on to consider the other women in the play, arguing that Shakespeare's text 'challenges the idea of woman's innate inferiority' and reveals him to be a proto-feminist.

Titus Andronicus

Despite the absence of his name on their First Quartos, *Richard III* and *Romeo and Juliet* have always been accepted as being by Shakespeare. However, *Titus Andronicus* is a different matter. Francis Meres listed it as one of Shakespeare's tragedies in 1598, but most readers during the next three centuries regarded it as shocking and inept and doubted whether the great man could have been responsible for such a piece of work. Even the editor of the 1984 *Oxford Shakespeare* edition of the play felt the need to devote nine pages of his Introduction to the question of authorship before concluding, 'I believe that the evidence I have presented points to the conclusion that *Titus Andronicus* is entirely by Shakespeare'.[9]

Whether or not it was by Shakespeare, the critical assault on *Titus Andronicus* has been pretty wholesale. Edward Ravenscroft* called *Titus Andronicus* 'a heap of Rubbish'. 'Rubbish' suggests he was attacking its content, but his scorn was actually directed at its form (hence 'heap'). However, Lewis Theobald* was appalled by the plot and the diction, and Samuel Johnson* and August Wilhelm Schlegel* by the barbarous incidents and shallow sensationalism. What grudging praise pre-twentieth-century critics offered focused on details of language or characterisation. Johnson found the style 'not always inelegant' and Schlegel admitted that, in addition to some beautiful lines and bold images, there were occasional original and affecting features in the presentation of Titus and Aaron.

The turning point in the play's critical fortunes came in 1943, when Hereward T. Price wrote a detailed defence against three hundred years of abuse ('The Authorship of *Titus Andronicus*', *Journal of English and Germanic Philology*, 42 (1943), pp. 55–81). According to Price, the author of this experimental play is Shakespeare and his stagecraft is 'excellent'. Price finds the structure entirely coherent: it is, he claims, a political play organised around a central hero, Rome. Its harshness is intentional, an attempt to be Senecan.

Subsequent criticism has tended to extend the case for the defence. The accusation that the play is crudely sensational has been countered by the claim made by Eugene M. Waith that Shakespeare was attempting to create 'admiration', i.e. wonder, an effect which Sidney had argued tragedy sets out to induce.[10] (Waith has published a series of important essays on the play but because his *Oxford Shakespeare* edition (cited above) with its valuable introductory essay, is readily available we have not felt it necessary to include any of his work in this volume.) Despite a good number of reservations, recent criticism has seen in the play a substantial advance on earlier English tragedies.

The essays collected in this volume reflect the new high valuation of the play. In an eclectic essay drawing on a wide range of current ideas about the play, Michael Hattaway* attributes to Shakespeare an attempt to explore all possible theatrical effects, 'juxtaposing . . . great images or ceremonies and fusing them into a whole that cannot be explained from the shape of the narrative or by development of character'. Picking up M. C. Bradbrook's idea that the play is a pageant,[11] he argues that its structure is visual rather than literary.

By contrast, Albert H. Tricomi* focuses on the play's language. He analyses how Shakespeare strives to exhaust the vocabulary as well as the events of tragedy, forcing the play's figurative language to imitate the literal events of the plot. According to Tricomi, Shakespeare is interested in 'the gulf between metaphoric descriptions of events and the irrefutable realities they purport to communicate' and the play '"exposes" the euphemisms of metaphor . . . rejecting it as a device that tends to dissipate the unremitting terrors of the tragedy'.

G. K. Hunter's* essay explores *Titus Andronicus* and *Romeo and Juliet* as formulations of tragic experience, finding not just differences in their visions of the human condition, but interesting similarities in their dramatic structures. (He even extends this second concern to point the parallel, in their use of the forest, of *Titus Andronicus* with another early play, *A Midsummer Night's Dream*.) The essay provides a bridge to *Romeo and Juliet*, therefore, but is finally concerned with the nature of *Titus Andronicus* and, in particular, the affirmation of a value-system which 'sternly suppresses self' in the interest of the family. The tomb of the Andronici is seen as being at the centre of the play, symbolising as it does the sense of selfhood held by the family which is the centre and soul of Rome. 'Interment in the tomb validates the efforts of the life preceding, and ensures

the continuity of past, present and future under the same standards
of civilisation'. Like Rossiter in his reading of *Richard III*, neither
Hattaway nor Hunter is persuaded by a providentialist interpretation
of *Titus Andronicus*. Hunter uses the contrast with *Romeo and Juliet* to
assess the centrality of evil in *Titus Andronicus*: in *Romeo and Juliet*, he
argues, evil is simply the conflict between the houses of the
Montagues and Capulets, and not only can this non-political conflict
give way to the pressure for stability and concord and peace but its
function in the play is structural—to force attention on the love
story which is at the heart of the play. By contrast, the conflict of
houses in *Titus Andronicus* is central, political, and representative of
a universal conflict between the personal will to evil 'deeply
implanted in human nature' and the need to resist man's bestiality
in the name of civilisation.

Romeo and Juliet

Charles Gildon's* comments typify the eighteenth-century response
to *Romeo and Juliet*. He is pleased by the degree to which the play
seems to present 'pure unsophisticated Nature' and irritated by the
degree to which Shakespeare, under the malign influence of Petrarch,
has given the hero and heroine lines which are 'not natural'. Even
Samuel Taylor Coleridge* is caught up in this conflict. The Nurse
is a wonderfully realistic portrait of a nurse, but 'Capulet and
Montague not unfrequently talk a language only belonging to the
poet'. Johnson had liked the way Shakespeare was prepared to
attempt the conversation of young *gentlemen*. Coleridge chooses to
emphasise the play's expression of *youthfulness* rather than gentility,
and does so because he finds in youth and spring what he found in
all Shakespeare's plays, a unifying principle.

At first, some of William Hazlitt's* phrases seem commonplace:
'This play presents a beautiful *coup-d'oeil* of the progress of human
life'; 'Youth is the season of love . . . for it knows no end of its
enjoyments or its wishes'. But, in fact, they are part of a most
sensitive and eloquent commentary on the play. The first provides
his own perception of the play's truth and unity. The second is more
than a variant on Coleridge's theme: it leads into an original (and
uncannily modern) exploration of pleasure and desire. Similarly
G. W. F. Hegel's* association of Romeo and Juliet with spring
flowers budding in a cruel month is a necessary ingredient in his

own theory of tragedy, whereby a clash of principles (a beautiful love planted in alien soil) finds narrative resolution in death and affective resolution in our paradoxical sense of *unhappy blessedness*.

Nor is the ending the only original aspect of *Romeo and Juliet*'s construction. The tragic outcome arises, according to most interpret-ations, from individuals' momentary impulsiveness, from longstand-ing inter-family feuding, or from bad luck and unfortunate coincidences, rather than from Character or Fate. Furthermore, counter to commonly-held principles of tragic composition, the play's setting is narrowly domestic, its topic adolescent love, its tone frequently flippant and bawdy, and its hero and heroine relatively low-born. In his essay on the two plays, G. K. Hunter contrasts what he calls the 'hysterically bleak view of human potential' in *Titus Andronicus* with the almost comic world of domestic Verona in *Romeo and Juliet*. This latter insight is developed and extended in Susan Snyder's* essay. Her proposition is that 'Unlike all Shakespeare's other tragedies, *Romeo and Juliet* becomes, rather than is, tragic. . . . Action and characters begin in the familiar comic world and are then transformed, or discarded, to compose the shape of tragedy'. This is not a new perception but Snyder explores it very thoroughly and persuasively, locating the change in genre at the moment of Mercutio's sudden, violent death.

M. M. Mahood* shifts our attention from the macro-structure of *Romeo and Juliet* to its micro-structure. She addresses herself to Shakespeare's use of puns in Shakespeare's most punning play. But this seemingly unambitious tactic is part of a grander strategy, a means of focusing on what she regards as the play's most fundamental questions. Is the ending one of frustration or of fulfilment? Does Death choose the lovers or do they elect to die? Mahood insists that the play should not be read as a *Liebestod*. It is not a simple statement about our desire for a tragic love. The play incorporates but places such an idea, making us feel that death neither thwarts nor saves the lovers. There is, she claims, a tragic equilibrium, including and transcending such feelings.

If, for Mahood, the play's meanings were focused in its puns, for T. J. L. Cribb* the ultimately dominating figure becomes oxymoron, 'ironically concealing truth behind apparent contradiction'. Cribb wishes to read the play as a theatrical experiment in a very unorthodox kind of religion, Renaissance Platonism. The paradox of neo-Platonism is its insistence that, while the ultimate Reality of the divine might appear to be the antithesis of the mundane reality of the physical world, there is a 'glow of divinity, shining in beautiful bodies, like the image of God' (Ficino) and 'the amatory life. . . . by sensible beauties, excites in the soul a remembrance of the intellectual' (Pico). Thus, erotic passion is the *via amoris* to the divine. The play's unity is the fact that it is informed by 'a particular set of values or ideas, principally embodied in the lovers', an intense idealism, combined with intense emotion founded on real desire. Shakespeare takes the unhappy story of the two young lovers as suitable for a serious stage tragedy because, in neo-Platonic thought, the lover has the dignity of a hero. The death of the lovers is the triumph of life in death, a consummation.

According to Ribner, the Shakespeare of the early tragedies was 'learning his craft, adapting and changing the traditional Senecan devices of the late 1580s, and in each instance creating at least something. . . . entirely new'.[12] In other words, Shakespeare was experimenting. The word 'experimental' proves an attractive way of coping with all these tragedies, for it nicely accommodates the early date of composition and a sense of unease about the achieved quality of the product, while also managing to suggest that each play is courageous and interesting. Experiment, in other words, is the acceptable face of impurity and immaturity.[13]

The phrase 'experimental tragedy' has emerged as a solution to what these critics have perceived as the problematic nature of the plays. But the plays present problems for directors as much as they do for critics, and the solution has sometimes been to go for 'experimental productions'. Every theatrical realisation of a dramatic text is inevitably an interpretation of that text, and some directors have experimented with the text in the spirit of new trends in literary criticism.

Titus Andronicus provides at least one good example of this procedure. Although the least performed of all Shakespeare's plays, its acceptance into the canon has meant that The Royal Shakespeare Company gives it the occasional production, even if the decision to mount it seems to be taken with reluctance. (In 1981, for example, it appeared in a cruelly mutilated text—John Barton had lopped off 850 lines—and then only as part of a double bill with the almost equally unpopular *Two Gentlemen of Verona*.) The particular problems it presents are the crudity of its stage horrors and the artificiality of its speeches.

Jane Howell faced these problems head-on in her BBC Television version of *Titus Andronicus*, broadcast in Great Britain for the first time on 27th April 1985. She introduced a mediating agent into the cast – Young Lucius, a bespectacled child who witnessed all the horrors perpetrated by the adults of Rome. She may have felt that Shakespeare's play was pornographic in its portrayal of violence and that Lucius could provide a critical perspective upon it. Alternatively, she may have believed that the stylisation of the play's language and characterisation was part of Shakespeare's own strategy for distancing his audience from that violence, but that when the play was translated into the naturalistic medium of television she needed a televisual device to reproduce that original effect. (Like some of the comedies (one thinks particularly of *Love's Labour's Lost*), *Titus Andronicus* is concerned with the nature of discourse, and feminist readings stress that Lavinia, raped and rendered speechless, acts as an emblem of the denial of woman's identity and voice in a male-dominated society.)

Jane Howell also directed *Richard III* for BBC Television on 23rd January 1983. Unlike *Titus Andronicus*, this play has always been popular with audiences and since 1900 it has already received over fifty professional productions in the theatre and eight on television or in the cinema. The problem which directors of *Richard III* face is the same one which critics such as Rossiter have debated at length: the relationship between Richard and the less-individualised historical material of the play. Cibber's solution had been to create a scene-stealing protagonist and allow him to dominate the action, and Olivier's film version follows in this tradition. Howell argued, however, 'It's not a play about a single man. It's a play about a society'.[14] Like Peter Reynolds*, in his essay on 'Acting Richard III', she wished to resist the theatrical tradition of treating Richard as the heroic villain. To this end she cast a relatively unknown actor in the name part and set the production in a crude wooden structure which was meant to suggest a derelict building site such as might be found in the terrorist-torn Belfast of the 1980s. Her play began with Richard scrawling his own name on a wall, as if he were a hooligan and Shakespeare's text so much graffiti. This Richard was no worse (and no better) than any other of the characters caught up in a process of social and historical turbulence.

Romeo and Juliet may appear to be the least problematic of these texts. Only *Hamlet* can claim to have been performed more often on the stage, there have been twenty-three screen versions and the play remains a favourite with teachers and examiners. When treated as a celebration of youthful romantic love, as in Zeffirelli's classic film version of 1968, it does indeed appear to present few interpretative problems. But the twentieth century has nevertheless developed an ambivalent attitude towards the claims of romantic love. Its continuing popularity as a literary theme is evidenced by the success of escapist romantic fiction. But romantic love can be regarded as an opium of the people, a false consciousness which encourages passive acceptance of the brutal social forces which determine our lives. Such a view seems implicit in Michael Bogdanov's 1986 RSC production of *Romeo and Juliet* which placed romantic love within the context of an aggressive capitalist society. Taking their cue from a Mafioso Prince Escalus, the Montagues (fading aristocrats) and Capulets (*nouveaux riches*) behaved brutally and hypocritically towards the young lovers. But while they were victims of their society, Romeo and Juliet were also implicated in it. They were the products of modern western culture. They wore fashionable clothes, lived the *dolce vita* and lacked any distinctive character as individuals. Mercutio was merely a drunk, and Tybalt drove round in an Alfa Romeo. To close the play, the Prince read out (insincerely) a version of the opening chorus. Then everyone posed for the press so that, as Stanley Wells wrote at the time, the lovers' tragedy could become a media event.[15] Romeo and Juliet were then revealed as golden statues, melted down as it were into money. The young and their story had been sold to the highest bidder, Mammon.

NOTES

1. Introduction to Jasper Heywood's translation of *Thyestes* (London, 1982) p. xxvi.

2. 'The Substance of Shakespearean Tragedy', *Shakespearean Tragedy* (London, 1904; 1957 edition), pp. 14, 16.

3. Ibid. Introduction to 1957 edition, pp. xiv–xv.

4. *Modern Tragedy* (London, 1979 ed.), p. 60.

5. This phrase comes from his 8th January 1802 *Morning Post* review of G. F. Cooke in the part, so Cibber has probably interfered.

6. *Shakespeare as a Dramatic Artist* (Oxford, 1885), p. 108.

7. *Shakespeare's Histories: Mirrors of Elizabethan Policy* (Cambridge, 1947), p. 306.

8. In particular, Tillyard's *The Elizabethan World Picture* (London, 1943) and *Shakespeare's History Plays* (London, 1944).

9. Eugene M. Waith, p. 20.

10. 'The Metamorphosis of Violence' in *Titus Andronicus*'. *Shakespeare Survey 10* (1957), pp. 39–47.

11. *Shakespeare and Elizabethan Poetry* (London, 1951; 1964 edition), p. 101.

12. I. Ribner, *Patterns in Shakespearean Tragedy* (London, 1960) p. 14.

13. For example, Albert Tricomi regards the peculiar nature of *Titus Andronicus*'s figurative language as 'a significant dramatic experiment', and Susan Snyder describes *Romeo and Juliet* as an 'experimental tragedy'.

14. *Richard III*, The BBC TV Shakespeare (London, 1983), p. 30.

15. Review in *The Times Literary Supplement*, 25th April 1986, p. 448.

PART ONE

Early Criticism (1687–1943)

RICHARD III

George Steevens (1793)

I most cordially join with Dr Johnson and Mr. Malone in their opinions [that *Richard III* was over-valued]; and yet perhaps they have overlooked one cause of the success of this tragedy. The part of Richard is perhaps beyond all others variegated, and consequently favourable to the judicious performer . . . a Burbage, a Garrick, and a Henderson. . . . Yet the favour with which this tragedy is now received must also in some measure be imputed to Mr. Cibber's reformation of it, which generally considered, is judicious: for what modern audience would patiently listen to the narrative of Clarence's Dream, his subsequent expostulation with the murderers, the prattle of his children, the soliloquy of the scrivener, the tedious dialogue of the citizens, the ravings of Margaret, the gross terms thrown out by the Duchess of York on Richard, the repeated progress to execution, the superfluous train of spectres, and other undramatick incumbrances. . . ?

SOURCE: Extract from *The Plays of William Shakespeare*, 4th edition (1793).

Charles Lamb (1801; 1802)

I am possessed with an Admiration of the genuine Richard, his genius, and his mounting spirit, which no consideration of his cruelties can depress. Shakespear has not made Richard so black a Monster, as is supposed. Wherever he is monstrous, it was to conform to vulgar opinion. But he is generally a Man. Read his most exquisite address to the Widowed Queen to court her daughter for him, the topics of maternal feeling, of a deep knowledge of the heart, are such as no monster could have supplied. Richard must have *felt*, before he could feign so well; tho' ambition choked the good seed. I think it the most finished piece of Eloquence in the world; of *persuasive* Oratory, far above Desmosthenes, Burke, or any man. – Far exceeding the courtship of Lady Anne. – *Her* relenting is barely natural after all; the more perhaps S's merit to make *impossible* appear *probable*, but the *Queen's consent* . . . is *probable*. . . . This observation applies to many other parts. All the inconsistency is, that Shakespeare's better Genius was forced to struggle against the prejudices, which made a monster of Richard. He set out to paint a *monster*, but his human sympathies produced a *Man* –

Are you not tired with this *ingenious* criticism? I am. . . .

Richard itself is wholly metamorphosed in the wretched *Acting play* of that name, which you will see: altered by *Cibber* –.

SOURCE: Letter to Robert Lloyd, 26 June 1801; in Joan Coldwell (ed.), *Charles Lamb on Shakespeare* (Colin Smythe, Gerrards Cross, 1978), pp. 17–18.

[Richard's] *habitual jocularity*, the effect of buoyant spirits, and a elastic mind, rejoicing in its own powers, and in the success of its machinations. This quality of unrestrained mirth accompanies *Richard*, and is a prime feature in his character. It never leaves him; in plots, in stratagems, and in the midst of his bloody devices, it is perpetually driving him upon wit, and jests, and personal satire, fanciful allusions, and quaint felicities of phrase. It is one of the chief artifices by which the consummate master of dramatic effect has contrived to soften the horrors of the scene, and to make us contemplate a bloody and vicious character with delight. No where, in any of his plays, is to be found so much of sprightly colloquial dialogue, and soliloquies of genuine humour, as in *Richard*.

SOURCE: Extract from 'G. F. Cooke in "Richard the Third"', *Morning Post*, 8 January 1802; in Coldwell, p. 21.

Hermann Ulrici   (1846)

As in life, so in the play, he [Richard] in reality stands *alone*. All the other personages (chiefly women and children, or single subjects) are in no way his equals, and are powerless against the whole royal power which is on his side. The destructive force of his tyranny, the violence of his unmitigated selfishness and wickedness, accompanied as they are by intellect, wit, and eloquence, have no organic counterpoise. On the one side we have only power and energy, on the other only submission and impotence. The principle of interaction, which is so important in life and in history, retires far into the background; not till the fifth act is the tyrant opposed by a real and worthy adversary in the person of Richmond. Accordingly, the drama is wanting in drastic animation; the action (that which is actually done or which happens) proceeds but slowly compared with others of Shakespeare's plays, and what does happen suffers from an internal uniformity; it is ever but the consequence of the same oppressive tyranny, ever the same victory of the same power, by the same means.

However, on the one hand, it must be remembered the nature of tyranny is outward peace, *i.e.* rigidity and uniformity, the unnatural accumulation of all the weight in the one scale, want of organic interaction and co-operation in the several parts, and hence the highest stage of decay in the organism of the state; and this was necessarily the consequence of a period like that of the reign of Henry VI. It is the description of the nature of *tyranny* that forms the historical significance of the whole drama, and here, as everywhere, the truly *historical* conception coincides with the truly *poetical* character of the representation. Therefore, on the other hand, it cannot be denied that the poet, by this very artistic defect, has contrived to render the meaning of the whole the more vivid, the clearer and the more forcible. Tyranny is the historico-political phenomenon of selfishness in its worst form, *i.e.* reckless love of dominion which tramples upon all rights and all laws, as well as upon all human ties; hence it is evil in its highest possible consummation. The individual *I* arrogates to itself the full dominion over all the powers of the mind, over all worldly possessions, and over the weal and woe in the life of all others; the individual man, with his finite power, presumes not only to direct a whole nation and its fate, but to be its fate himself. This is the meaning of Richard's words, 'I am myself alone', the motto of the perfect tyrant, and it at the same time expresses his full, clear consciousness of his own nature. Richard is quite aware that he is a tyrant, he *knows* it, and *wills* it; this was required by Shakespeare's view of life, which is far removed from the thought that man is a *mere* instrument in the hand of a higher power. This is the reason and significance of the reflections which Richard is perpetually making upon himself and his own nature, and which have been censured as unnatural. But such soliloquies essentially belong to the character of the tyrant, according to the conception of modern times; Richard soliloquises in order to gain a clear insight into his own nature, his vocation, his aims, plans and actions, for, in his weird loneliness, he cannot hold communion with others. . . .

But the attainment of the object at which Richard had aimed, proves the turning-point in his fortunes; for tyranny cannot of course *maintain* anything, inasmuch as it is essentially destruction and annihilation, and accordingly cannot even maintain its own existence.

SOURCE: Extract from *Shakespeare's Dramatic Art*, 3rd edition, 1876 (1st edition, 1846), translated by L. D. Schmitz (London, 1889), vol. ii, pp. 276–79.

Georg Gottfried Gervinus   (1849)

The poet has taken the characteristics from the chronicle, but in the chief point he has made a thorough alteration. The chronicle seems to give hypocrisy to Richard as his nature, and to exhibit cruelty in him rather as a cold work of policy; but the poet has made the inclination to brutality innate in him, and hypocrisy, on the contrary, a chosen means for his ambition. . . .

Once this character is established and its central point perceived, the central point and the idea of the piece is also apprehended; for Richard fills the center entirely. This exclusively prominent position of Richard and his highly tragic nature, has given to this history the character rather of a pure tragedy; just as in Shakespeare's freest tragedies, all the persons of the piece are arranged with an inner relation to the principal figure and to the principal idea of the piece, whilst usually the peculiarity of historical plays was, that the events and facts were distributed among more extensive groups of acting characters, who stand not throughout in that close connection exhibited by the characters of pieces designed at will and fettered by no historical material.

SOURCE: Extract from *Shakepeare* (1849), translated by F. E. Bunnett (London, 1863) vol. i, p. 375.

Edward Dowden (1875)

... all that Richard achieves tends to his own supremacy. Nevertheless, the central characteristic of Richard is not self-seeking or ambition. It is the necessity of releasing and letting loose upon the world the force within him (mere force in which there is nothing moral), the necessity of deploying before himself and others the terrible resources of his will. . . . Richard is of the diabolical (something more dreadful than the criminal) class. He is not weak, because he is single-hearted in his devotion to evil. Richard does not serve two masters. . . . He has fierce joy, and he is an intense believer – in the creed of hell. And therefore he is strong. He inverts the moral order of things, and tries to live in this inverted system. He does not succeed; he dashes himself to pieces against the laws of the world which he has outraged. Yet . . . we cannot refrain from yielding a certain tribute of admiration to the . . . malefactor, who ventures on the daring experiment of choosing evil for his good.

SOURCE: Extract from *Shakspere: a Critical Study of His Mind and Art* (London, 1875), p. 187.

R. G. Moulton   (1885)

Viewed as a study in character the play leaves in us only an intense craving for Nemesis: when we turn to consider the plot, this presents to us the world of history transformed into an intricate design of which the recurrent pattern is Nemesis.

> SOURCE: Extract from *Shakespeare as a Dramatic Artist* (Oxford, 1885), p. 108.

Henry James   (1897)

The attempt to make real or even plausible a loose, violent, straddling romance like *Richard III* – a chronicle for the market-place, a portrait for the house wall – only emphasises what is coarse in such a hurly-burly and does nothing for what is fine. It gives no further lift to the poetry and adds a mortal heaviness to the prose. The thing suffers (till it positively howls) from everything to which, in fiction – the fiction of the theatre or any other – the present general cultivation of a closer illusion exposes it. The more it is painted and dressed, the more it is lighted and furnished and solidified, the less it corresponds or coincides, the less it squares with our imaginative habits. By what extension of the term can such a scene as Richard's wooing of Lady Anne be said to be represented? We can only use the word to mean that Sir Henry Irving shows his experience and his art. It leaves us doggedly defying any actress whatever to give a touch of truth, either for woe or for weal, to the other figure of the situation – leaves us weltering, at this and to the great majority of the other moments, in a sea of weak allowances from which we at last scramble ashore with (for all spoil of the wreck,) a sore sense that the more Shakespeare is 'built in' the more we are built out.

> SOURCE: Extract from a review of Sir Henry Irving as Richard III in *Harper's Weekly*, 23 January 1897.

TITUS ANDRONICUS

Edward Ravenscroft (1687)

READER, I think it a greater theft to Rob the dead of their Praise than the Living of their Money: That I may not appear Guilty of such a Crime, 'tis necessary I should acquaint you, that there is a Play in Mr *Shakespeare's* Volume under the name of *Titus Andronicus*, from whence I drew part of this. I have been told by some anciently conversant with the Stage, that it was not Originally his, but brought by a private Author to be Acted, and he only gave some Master-touches to one or two of the Principal Parts or Characters; this I am apt to believe, because 'tis the most incorrect and indigested piece in all his Works; It seems rather a heap of Rubbish than a Structure.

> SOURCE: Extract from Preface to *Titus Andronicus, or The Rape of Lavinia . . . A Tragedy, Alter'd from Mr Shakespeare's Works* (1687).

Lewis Theobald (1730)

There is something so barbarous and unnatural in the fable, and so much trash in the diction, even beneath the three parts of *Henry VI*, that I am very much inclined to believe it was not one of our Author's own compositions but only introduced by him and honoured with some of his masterly touches.

> SOURCE: Observation of 24th February 1730, in John Nicols (ed.), *Illustrations of the Literary History of the Eighteenth Century*, vol. II (1817), p. 512.

Samuel Johnson   (1765)

... the colour of the stile is wholly different from that of the other plays, and there is an attempt at regular versification, and artificial closes, not always inelegant, yet seldom pleasing. The barbarity of the spectacles, and the general massacre which are here exhibited, can scarcely be conceived tolerable to any audience.

SOURCE: Extract from *The Plays of William Shakespeare* (1765).

August Wilhelm Schlegel   (1815)

Titus Andronicus ... is framed according to a false idea of the tragic, which by an accumulation of cruelties and enormities, degenerates into the horrible, and yet leaves no deep impression behind. ...

In detail there is no want of beautiful lines, bold images, nay, even features which betray the peculiar conception of Shakespeare. Among these we may reckon the joy of the treacherous Moor at the blackness and ugliness of his child begot in adultery; and in the compassion of *Titus Andronicus*, grown childish through grief, for a fly which had been struck dead, and his rage afterwards when he imagines he discovers in it his black enemy, we recognize the future poet of *Lear*.

SOURCE: Extracts from lectures in *A Course of Lectures on Dramatic Art and Literature*, translated by John Black (London, 1815), vol. 2, pp. 253–55.

H. T. Price   (1943)

Titus . . . resembles Shakespeare's other work, both comedy and tragedy, in that it is built upon the principle of contrast. We have the contrasting pairs or groups: Titus–Aaron, Lavinia–Tamora, Saturninus–Bassianus, the sons of Titus–the sons of Tamora. . . . On the one hand we have courage, stern probity, honour, but also stubbornness, hardness, and stupidity, on the other hand, slipperiness, trickiness, intrigue, the lie, foulness of every sort . . . *Titus* is a political play, and Shakespeare is the most political of all dramatists . . . *Titus* centres round an affair of state, and its hero is no particular person but it is Rome itself. All the characters are viewed in their relation to Rome. . . .

Titus alone of Shakespeare's tragic heroes never arrives at healing self-knowledge. At the beginning of the play we hope that Titus will succeed against his enemies; at the end we wish that he had not. But we must not forget the task that Shakespeare has set himself. He is writing a Senecan play according to the rules, that is to say, a play in which the hero is a man who inexorably pursues revenge and who dies in the act of taking it. Such a plan leaves no room for change of character. . . .

Shakespeare, following the mood of his time, wrote a complete Senecan tragedy, an experiment of unity in harshness and gross cruelty. He makes almost everything harsh, the language, the characters, the incidents. Where he appears to be relenting towards mildness, that is only an artistic device to make the harshness appear all the harsher . . . [Furthermore] irony permeates the play so thoroughly. . . .

The horrors of the play are undesirable. But if scholars would refrain from still harping upon these horrors and would instead consider the play on its merits as an excellent piece of stagecraft, they might see in it something not unworthy of the young Shakespeare.

SOURCE: Extract from 'The Authorship of *Titus Andronicus*', *Journal of English and Germanic Philology* 42 (1943), pp. 70–80.

ROMEO AND JULIET

Charles Gildon   (1710)

There are in it many Beauties of the Manners, and Sentiments, and Diction. The Character of *Mercutio* is pleasant and uniform; that of *Tybalt* always *equal*; as indeed they all are; the Nurse is a true Comic Character, tho' some of our *Chit-chat* Poets wou'd look on it as Farce or low Comedy. . . .

Whether Passion be so pregnant of Similes as *Romeo* and *Juliet* everywhere give us I dare not determine, since to say that all they speak is not natural wou'd be to provoke too many that admire it as the Soul of Love. . . .

The Scene betwixt *Romeo* and *Juliet* when he is in the Garden and she at her Window, tho' it contain many things that will not join with Probability, and tho' perhaps *Shakespeare*, like *Cowley*, was a little corrupted by reading *Petrarch*, that modern Debaucher of Poetry into *Conceits* and *Conundrums*, yet the Fancy is every where so fine and Nature so agreeably painted that we are pleas'd with the very *Fucus* and perswade our selves that it is pure unsophisticated Nature. . . .

> SOURCE: Extracts from *Remarks on the Plays of Shakespeare*, in *The Works of Mr William Shakespeare*, vol. 2 (1710), p. 371, in B. Vickers (ed.), *Shakespeare: The Critical Heritage*, vol. 2, pp. 253–54.

Samuel Johnson   (1765)

This play is one of the most pleasing of our Author's performances. The scenes are busy and various, the incidents numerous and important, the catastrophe irresistibly affecting, and the process of the action carried on with such probability, at least with such congruity to popular opinions, as tragedy requires.

Here is one of the few attempts of *Shakespeare* to exhibit the conversation of gentlemen, to represent the airy sprightliness of juvenile elegance.

SOURCE: Extract from *The Plays of William Shakespeare* . . . (1765), vol. vii, p. 135.

Samuel Taylor Coleridge (1811–12; ?1813)

Mercutio is a man possessing all the elements of a poet: the whole world was, as it were, subject to the law of association. Whenever he wishes to impress anything, all things become his servants for the purpose: all things tell the same tale, and sound in unison. This faculty, moreover, is combined with the manners and feelings of a perfect gentleman, himself utterly unconscious of his powers. By his loss it was contrived that the whole catastrophe of the tragedy should be brought about: it endears him to Romeo, and gives to the death of Mercutio an importance which it could not otherwise have acquired.

I say this in answer to an observation, I think by Dryden [Hawkes's note: 'This is an alleged remark of Shakespeare, which Dryden quotes in order to differ with it (*The Conquest of Granada, Part Two*, Defence of the Epilogue). . . .'] (to which indeed Dr Johnson has fully replied), that Shakespeare having carried the part of Mercutio as far as he could, till his genius was exhausted, had killed him in the third act to get him out of the way. What shallow nonsense! As I have remarked, upon the death of Mercutio the whole catastrophe depends; it is produced by it. The scene in which it occurs serves to show how indifference to any subject but one, and aversion to activity on the part of Romeo, may be overcome and roused to the most resolute and determined conduct. Had not Mercutio been

rendered so amiable and so interesting, we could not have felt
so strongly the necessity for Romeo's interference, connecting it
immediately, and passionately, with the future fortunes of the lover,
and his mistress.

But what am I to say of the Nurse? . . . Let any man conjure up
in his mind all the qualities and peculiarities that can possibly
belong to a nurse, and he will find them in Shakespeare's picture of
the old woman. . . .

Thus in the Nurse you have all the garrulity of old age, and all
its fondness; for the affection of old age is one of the greatest
consolations of humanity. I have often thought what a melancholy
world this would be without children, and what an inhuman world
without the aged.

You have also in the nurse the arrogance of ignorance with the
pride of meanness at being connected with a great family. You have
the grossness, too, which that situation never removes, though it
sometimes suspends it; and arising from that grossness, the little
low vices attendant upon it, which, indeed, in such minds are
scarcely vices.

. . . in this tragedy the poet is not, as I have hinted, entirely
blended with the dramatist – at least, not in the degree to be
afterwards noticed in *Lear, Hamlet, Othello,* or *Macbeth*. Capulet and
Montague not unfrequently talk a language only belonging to the
poet, and not so characteristic of, and peculiar to, the passions of
persons in the situations in which they are placed. . . .

SOURCE: Extracts from a report by J. P. Collier of a lecture given
by Coleridge (1811–12), in T. Hawkes, *Coleridge's Writings on
Shakespeare* (New York, 1959), pp. 140–56.

A *unity of feeling* pervades the whole of his plays. In *Romeo and Juliet*
all is youth and spring – it is youth with its follies, its virtues, its
precipitancies; it is spring with its odours, flowers, and transiency –
the same feeling commences, goes through, and ends the play. The
old men, the Capulets and Montagues, are not common old men;
they have an eagerness, a hastiness, a precipitancy – the effect of
spring. With Romeo his precipitate change of passion, his hasty
marriage, and his rash death are all the effects of youth. With Juliet

love has all that is tender and melancholy in the nightingale, all that is voluptuous in the rose, with whatever is sweet in the freshness of spring; but it ends with a long deep sigh, like the breeze of the evening. This unity of character pervades the whole of his dramas.

SOURCE: Extract from notes for a lecture on Shakespeare (?1813), in Hawkes, p. 112 (op. cit.).

William Hazlitt (1817)

Romeo and Juliet are in love, but they are not love-sick. Every thing speaks the very soul of pleasure, the high and healthy pulse of the passions: the heart beats, the blood circulates and mantles throughout. . . .

He has founded the passion of the two lovers not on the pleasures they had experienced, but on all the pleasures they had *not* experienced. All that was to come of life was theirs. At that untried source of promised happiness they slaked their thirst, and the first eager draught made them drunk with love and joy. They were in full possession of their senses and their affections. Their hopes were of air, their desires of fire. Youth is the season of love, because the heart is then first melted in tenderness from the touch of novelty, and kindled to rapture, for it knows no end of its enjoyments or its wishes. Desire has no limit but itself. . . . The only evil that even in apprehension befalls the lovers is the loss of the greatest possible felicity; yet this loss is fatal to both, for they had rather part with life than bear the thought of surviving all that had made life dear to them. . . .

This play presents a beautiful *coup-d'oeil* of the progress of human life. In thought it occupies years, and embraces the circle of the affections from childhood to old age. Juliet has become a great girl, a young woman since we first remember her a little thing in the idle prattle of the nurse, Lady Capulet was about her age when she became a mother, and old Capulet somewhat impatiently tells his younger visitors,

> I've seen the day,
> That I have worn a visor, and could tell
> A whispering tale in a fair lady's ear,
> Such as would please: 'tis gone, 'tis gone, 'tis gone.

Thus one period of life makes way for the following, and one generation pushes another off the stage.

SOURCE: Extract from *Characters of Shakespeare's Plays* (London, 1817), pp. 136–41.

G. W. F. Hegel   (c. 1829)

[Take] the case of Romeo and Juliet. The ground on which these tender blossoms have been planted is alien to their nature; we have no alternative left us but to lament the pathetic transiency of such a beautiful love, which, as some tender rose in the vale of this world of accident, is broken by rude storms and tempests, and the frangible reckonings of noble and well-meaning devices. This pitiful state of our emotions is, however, simply a feeling of reconciliation that is painful, a kind of *unhappy blessedness* in misfortune.

SOURCE: Extract from *The Philosophy of Fine Art*, translated by F. P. B. Osmaston (London 1920) vol. iv, in A. and H. Paolucci (eds.), *Hegel On Tragedy* (New York, 1962), p. 91.

PART TWO

Modern Criticism

Richard III
Titus Andronicus
Romeo and Juliet

RICHARD III

E. M. W. Tillyard   *Richard III* and the Tudor Myth   (1944)

In spite of the eminence of Richard's character the main business of the play is to complete the national tetralogy and to display the working out of God's plan to restore England to prosperity.

In its function of summing up and completing what has gone before, *Richard III* inevitably suffers as a detached unit. Indeed it is a confused affair without the memory of Clarence's perjury to Warwick before Coventry, of Queen Margaret's crowning York with a paper crown before stabbing him at Wakefield, and of the triple murder of Prince Edward at Tewkesbury. The play can never come into its own till acted as a sequel to the other three plays. . . . I advisedly include all four plays, because, though for immediate understanding of incident a memory of *3 Henry VI* is sufficient, there are many links with the other two parts. Thus *Richard III*, after the temporary boredom of *3 Henry VI*, regains the interest, so powerful in *2 Henry VI*, in the massive scene of political intrigue: for instance in Act I Scene iii, where Richard makes trouble with the queen and her relations and Queen Margaret appears, to curse all; or in Act III Scene vii, where Richard is jockeyed into the throne. In the first of these there is even a direct reference back to *2 Henry VI*. Margaret, advancing to the front of the stage where Richard and Queen Elizabeth's kindred have been quarrelling, says:

> Hear me, you wrangling pirates, that fall out
> In sharing that which you have pill'd from me.

This is the metaphor York had used in his first soliloquy in *2 Henry VI*. Only now the position has changed, and it is the house of Lancaster that watches the Yorkists fighting over the spoil. With *1 Henry VI* the resemblances are closer and different, and they have to do with the plot. Both *1 Henry VI* and *Richard III*, unlike the other plays, contain an outstanding character having a Frenchwoman as his chief opponent. Talbot stands for order and Richard for its contrary, chaos, and whereas Joan prospers in her efforts to humiliate England, Margaret through her curses unwittingly creates the unity of the land she has so terribly injured. Again, in *1 Henry VI* the nobles are wantonly disunited, while in *Richard III* they are schooled by their sufferings into a unity otherwise unattainable. When there is already so much evidence that Shakespeare wrote his tetralogy deliberately and academically and that he was deeply influenced by the Morality tradition with its medieval passion for equivalences, it is not pressing things to assert that Shakespeare fully intended the above cross-references between the first and last plays of his series.

However, the greatest bond uniting all four plays is the steady political theme: the theme of order and chaos, of proper political degree and civil war, of crime and punishment, of God's mercy finally tempering his justice, of the belief that such had been God's way with England.

I noticed that in each part of *Henry VI* there was some positive, usually very formal or stylized reference to the principle of order. In *1 Henry VI* there was the scene of Talbot doing homage to his king, in *2 Henry VI* the blameless conduct of Iden and his perfect contentment with his own station in life, in *3 Henry VI* Henry's pathetic longing for the precisely ordered life of a shepherd. In *Richard III* Shakespeare both continues this technique by inserting the choric scene of the three citizens, and at the end of the play comes out with his full declaration of the principle of order, thus giving final and unmistakable shape to what, though largely implicit, had been all along the animating principle of the tetralogy. His instrument, obviously and inevitably, is Richmond; and that this instrument should be largely passive, truly an instrument (hence likely to be overlooked or made little of by the modern reader), was also inevitable in the sort of drama Shakespeare was writing. In the tremendous evolution of God's plans the accidents of character must not be obtruded. Every sentence of Richmond's last speech, today regarded as a competent piece of formality, would have raised the Elizabethans to an ecstasy of feeling. Richmond gets everything right and refers to all the things they minded about. He is conventionally pious, his first words after the victory being, 'God and your arms be prais'd, victorious friends'; just as Talbot after his capture of Rouen had said 'Yet heavens have glory for this

victory'. Then he thinks of the immediate problems and asks about
the dead. Hearing of them, he begins his last speech,

> Inter their bodies as becomes their birth,

and thereby implies: after thanks to God, the keeping of due degree
on earth. And again he duplicates Talbot, who in the same scene,
after thanking God, said

> let's not forget
> The noble Duke of Bedford late deceas'd,
> But see his exequies fulfill'd in Roan.

Then, after degree, mercy:

> Proclaim a pardon to the soldiers fled
> That in submission will return to us.

And lastly an oath, taken with full religious solemnity and duly
observed, and the healing of the wounds of civil war, with an
insensible and indeed very subtle transfer of reference from the
epoch of Bosworth to the very hour of the play's performance,
from the supposed feelings of Richmond's supporters to what
Shakespeare's own audience felt so ardently about the health of
their country. The reference to father killing son and son killing
father served at a single stroke both to recall the battle of Towton
and to take the audience out of the Wars of the Roses to the wider
context of civil wars in general: to Israel, France, and Germany; to
the writers of chronicles and the Homilies[1]; to what they had heard
endlessly repeated on the subject by fireside or in tavern.

> And then, as we have ta'en the sacrament,
> We will unite the White Rose and the Red.
> Smile heaven upon this fair conjunction,
> That long have frown'd upon their enmity!
> What traitor hears me and says not amen?
> England hath long been mad and scarr'd herself:
> The brother blindly shed the brother's blood;
> The father rashly slaughter'd his own son;
> The son, compell'd, been butcher to the sire.
> All this divided York and Lancaster,
> Divided in their dire division,
> O now let Richmond and Elizabeth,
> The true succeeders of each royal house,

By God's fair ordinance conjoin together;
And let their heirs, God, if thy will be so,
Enrich the time to come with smooth-fac'd peace,
With smiling plenty and fair prosperous days.
Abate the edge of traitors, gracious Lord,
That would reduce these bloody days again,
And make poor England weep in streams of blood.
Let them not live to taste this land's increase
That would with treason wound this fair land's peace.
Now civil wars are stopp'd, peace lives again:
That she may long live here God say amen.

An Elizabethan audience would take the dramatist's final amen
with a transport of affirmation.

But Richmond's final speech not only voiced popular opinion, it
showed Shakespeare fulfilling his old debt to Hall[2], when he
invested the very practical and politic match between Richmond
and Elizabeth with a mysterious and religious significance. True,
Shakespeare quite omits the Tudors' ancient British ancestry; but
his references to the marriage are in the very spirit of Hall's title,
The Union of the two noble and illustre Families of Lancaster and York, and
his statement in his preface of the 'godly matrimony' being 'the final
end of all dissensions titles and debates'. Nor is this the only place in
the play that sends us back to Hall and Tudor conceptions of history.
There are some rather queer lines in III. i, where Edward V,
Richard, and Buckingham talk about oral and written tradition.
They serve to bring out Edward's precociousness but they also take
us into the centre of contemporary opinions on history. Edward,
before the Tower, asks if Julius Caesar built it. Buckingham tells
him that Julius Caesar began it; and Edward asks:

> Is it upon record, or else reported
> Successively from age to age, he built it?

Buckingham answers it is 'upon record', and Edward goes on:

> But say, my lord, it were not register'd,
> Methinks the truth should live from age to age,
> As 'twere retail'd to all posterity,
> Even to the general all-ending day.

His words take us to the familiar medieval and renaissance context
of fame: its capriciousness, its relation to all history and to all time.
And he goes on to a more specifically historical commonplace:

> That Julius Caesar was a famous man.
> With what his valour did enrich his wit,
> His wit set down to make his valour live.
> Death makes no conquest of this conqueror,
> For now he lives in fame though not in life.

It was a stock saying in discussions on history that Caesar provided both the material of history and its memorial. Shakespeare was telling his audience that they must put his tetralogy among other solemn documents of history, that he is striving to continue the high tradition of Polydore[3] and Hall.

Above, I put the theme of *Richard III* partly in terms of God's intentions. As it is usual to put it in terms of Richard's character, I had better expand my thesis. But it is a delicate matter. People are so fond of Shakespeare that they are desperately anxious to have him of their own way of thinking. A reviewer in the *New Statesman* was greatly upset when I quoted a passage in *Measure for Measure* as evidence that Shakespeare was familiar with the doctrine of the Atonement: he at once assumed I meant that Shakespeare believed the doctrine personally. And if one were to say that in *Richard III* Shakespeare pictures England restored to order through God's grace, one gravely risks being lauded or execrated for attributing to Shakespeare personally the full doctrine of prevenient Grace according to Calvin. When therefore I say that *Richard III* is a very religious play, I want to be understood as speaking of the play and not of Shakespeare. For the purposes of the tetralogy and most obviously for this play Shakespeare accepted the prevalent belief that God had guided England into her haven of Tudor prosperity. And he had accepted it with his whole heart, as later he did not accept the supposed siding of God with the English against the French he so loudly proclaimed in *Henry V*. There is no atom of doubt in Richmond's prayer before he falls asleep in his tent at Bosworth. He is utterly God's minister, as he claims to be:

> O Thou, whose captain I account myself,
> Look on my forces with a gracious eye;
> Put in their hands thy bruising irons of wrath,
> That they may crush down with a heavy fall
> The usurping helmets of our adversaries.
> Make us thy ministers of chastisement,
> That we may praise thee in the victory.
> To thee I do commend my watchful soul,
> Ere I let fall the windows of mine eyes.
> Sleeping and waking, O, defend me still.

In the same spirit Shakespeare drops hints of a divine purpose in
the mass of vengeance that forms the substance of the play, of a
direction in the seemingly endless concatenation of crime and
punishment. In *3 Henry VI*, York at Wakefield, Young Clifford at
Towton, Warwick at Barnet, and Prince Edward at Tewkesbury
die defiantly without remorse. In *Richard III* the great men die
acknowledging their guilt and thinking of others. Clarence, before
his murderers enter, says:

> O God, if my deep prayers cannot appease thee,
> But thou wilt be aveng'd on my misdeeds,
> Yet execute thy wrath in me alone:
> O spare my guiltless wife and my poor children.

Edward IV, near his death, repents his having signed a warrant for
Clarence's death and while blaming others for not having restrained
him blames himself the most:

> But for my brother not a man would speak,
> Nor I, ungracious, speak unto myself
> For him, poor soul. The proudest of you all
> Have been beholding to him in his life;
> Yet none of you would once plead for his life.
> O God, I fear thy justice will take hold
> On me and you and mine and yours for this.

The Duchess of York, who once rejoiced when her family prospered,
now in humility acknowledges the futility of ambitious strife.

> Accursed and unquiet wrangling days,
> How many of you have mine eyes beheld.
> My husband lost his life to get the crown,
> And often up and down my sons were toss'd,
> For me to joy and weep their gain and loss.
> And, being seated and domestic broils
> Clean overblown, themselves, the conquerors,
> Make war upon themselves: blood against blood,
> Self against self. O, preposterous
> And frantic outrage, end thy damned spleen.

All this penitence cannot be fortuitous; and it is the prelude to
forgiveness and regeneration. But the full religious temper of the
play only comes out in the two great scenes in the last third of the
play: the lamentations of the three queens after Richard has

murdered the princes in the Tower, and the ghosts appearing to
Richard and Richmond before Bosworth. These are both extreme
and splendid examples of the formal style which should be considered
the norm rather than the exception in the tetralogy. Both scenes are
ritual and incantatory to a high degree, suggesting an ecclesiastical
context; both are implicitly or explicitly pious; and both are archaic,
suggesting the prevalent piety of the Middle Ages. The incantation
takes the form not only of an obvious antiphony like Queen
Margaret's balancing of her own woes with Queen Elizabeth's –

> I had an Edward, till a Richard kill'd him;
> I had a Harry, till a Richard kill'd him;
> Thou hadst an Edward, till a Richard kill'd him;
> Thou hadst a Richard, till a Richard kill'd him –

but of a more complicated balance of rhythmic phrases and of varied
repetitions, as in the Duchess of York's self-address:

> Blind sight, dead life, poor mortal living ghost,
> Woe's scene, world's shame, grave's due by life usurp'd,
> Brief abstract and record of tedious days,
> Rest thy unrest on England's lawful earth,
> Unlawfully made drunk with innocents' blood.

The piety in this scene is implicit rather than explicit, and the two
passages just quoted will illustrate it. Queen Margaret is thinking
of Richard's crimes and the vengeance he will incur, yet by repeating
a phrase in four successive lines she expresses unconsciously the
new and fruitful unity that God is to construct out of Richard's
impartial wickedness. The Duchess's mention of England's *lawful*
earth is in itself an assertion of the principle of order and an implicit
prayer for a juster age. The medievalism and its accompanying
suggestion of piety comes out in Margaret's great speech to Elizabeth,
itself an example of incantation and antiphony. She refers to her
prophecies made earlier in the play and now fulfilled.

> I call'd thee then vain flourish of my fortune.
> I call'd thee then poor shadow, painted queen;
> The presentation of but what I was;
> The flattering index of a direful pageant;
> One heav'd a-high, to be hurl'd down below;
> A mother only mock'd with two sweet babes;
> A dream of what thou wert, a breath, a bubble,

> A sign of dignity, a garish flag,
> To be the aim of every dangerous shot;
> A queen in jest, only to fill the scene.
> Where is thy husband now? where be thy brothers?
> Where are thy children? wherein dost thou joy?
> Who sues to thee and cries 'God save the queen'?
> Where be the bending peers that flatter'd thee?
> Where be the thronging troops that follow'd thee? –
> Decline all this and see what now thou art:
> For happy wife a most distressed widow;
> For joyful mother one that wails the name;
> For queen a very caitiff crown'd with care;
> For one being sued to one that humbly sues;
> For one that scorn'd at me now scorn'd of me;
> For one being fear'd of all now fearing one;
> For one commanding all obey'd of none.
> Thus hath the course of justice wheel'd about
> And left thee but a very prey to time;
> Having no more but thought of what thou wert
> To torture thee the more being what thou art.

The speech takes us back to the Middle Ages; to the laments of the fickleness of fortune, to the constant burden of *Ubi sunt*, and to the consequent contempt of the world. It contains the same matter as the verses attributed to St Bernard, of which the following is a specimen in Elizabethan translation:

> Where is that Caesar now, whose high renowmed fame
> Of sundry conquests won throughout the world did sound?
> Or Dives rich in store and rich in richly name,
> Whose chest with gold and dish with dainties did abound?
> Where is the passing grace of Tully's pleading skill?
> Or Aristotle's vein, whose pen had wit and will?

Or still more apt, because narrowing the general passing of the great to the loss of a single person's treasures, is the complaint of Henryson's Cressida:

> Quhair is thy garding with thir greissis gay
> And fress flouris, quhilk the quene Floray
>   Had paintit plesandly in every pane,
> Quhair thou was wont full merily in May
> To walk and tak the dew be it was day
>   And heir the merle and mavis mony ane;
>   With ladyis fair in carrolling to gane
> And see the royal rinkis in their array
>   In garmentis gay garnishit on every grane?[4]

The scene of the ghosts of those Richard has murdered follows immediately on Richmond's solemn prayer, quoted above. It is essentially of the Morality pattern. Respublica or England is the hero, invisible yet present, contended for by the forces of heaven represented by Richmond and of hell represented by Richard. Each ghost as it were gives his vote for heaven, Lancaster and York being at last unanimous. And God is above, surveying the event. The medieval strain is continued when Richard, awaking in terror, rants like Judas in the Miracle Plays about to hang himself. The scene, like Richmond's prayer and his last speech, is very moving. It may have issued from Shakespeare's official self, from Shakespeare's identifying himself with an obvious and simple phase of public opinion. But the identification is entirely sincere, and the opinion strong and right, to be shared alike by the most sophisticated and the humblest. The scene becomes almost an act of common worship, ending with Buckingham's assertion:

> God and good angels fight on Richmond's side;
> And Richard falls in height of all his pride.

And just because he participates so fully, because he holds nothing of himself back, Shakespeare can be at his best, can give to his language the maximum of personal differentiation of which he was at the time capable. This differentiation he achieves, not as in some of the other great places in the play by surprising conjunctions of words or new imagery but by subtle musical variations within a context of incantation. He seems indeed to have learnt and applied the lessons of Spenser. At the same time the substance of what each ghost says is entirely appropriate to the speaker and by referring back to past events in the tetralogy serves to reinforce the structure of the plot. There may be better scenes in Shakespeare, but of these none is like this one. Of its kind it is the best.

That the play's main end is to show the working out of God's will in English history does not detract from the importance of Richard in the process and from his dominance as a character. And it is through his dominance that he is able to be the instrument of God's ends. Whereas the sins of other men had merely bred more sins, Richard's are so vast that they are absorptive, not contagious. He is the great ulcer of the body politic into which all its impurity is drained and against which all the members of the body politic are

united. It is no longer a case of limb fighting limb but of the war of
the whole organism against an ill which has now ceased to be
organic. The metaphor of poison is constantly applied to Richard,
and that of beast, as if here were something to be excluded from the
human norm. Queen Margaret unites the two metaphors when she
calls him 'that poisonous hunch-back'd toad' and that 'bottled
spider', the spider being proverbially venomous.

In making Richard thus subservient to a greater scheme I do not
deny that for many years now the main attraction of the play has
actually been Richard's character in itself, like Satan's in *Paradise
Lost*. Nor was this attraction lacking from the first. Indeed it
antedates the play, going back to More's *History of Richard III*[5],
which was inserted with trifling modifications into Hall's chronicle
and repeated thence by Holinshed.[6] Shakespeare in singling out
Richard III and later Henry V for special treatment as characters
is not therefore departing from tradition but following closely his
own main teacher of the philosophy of history, Hall.

One would like to think of Shakespeare hailing More (through
Hall) as a kindred spirit and using his charm as an inspiration.
Actually, though Shakespeare accepts More's heightened picture of
Richard as an arch-villain, he can very coolly reject the episodes of
which More made much. He quite omits Edward's wonderful speech
on his death bed and the most moving scene of all, the Archbishop
persuading Queen Elizabeth to give up her younger son out of
sanctuary. It may be however that More's abundant sense of humour
encouraged Shakespeare to add to Richard that touch of comedy
that makes him so distinguished a villain. His aside after he has
gone on his knees to ask his mother's blessing is very much in
More's spirit:

> *Duchess:* God bless thee, and put meekness in thy mind,
>   Love, charity, obedience, and true duty.
> *Richard:* Amen; and make me die a good old man.
>   That is the butt-end of a mother's blessing:
>   I marvel why her grace did leave it out.

A number of people have written well on the character of Richard:
in one place or another all has been said that need be said. It
remains now to think less in terms of alternatives and to include
more than is usually done in Richard's character, even at the
sacrifice of consistency. Lamb, for instance, who in his brief

references raised most of the pertinent questions, wants to exclude the melodramatic side:

Shakespeare has not made Richard so black a monster as is supposed. Wherever he is monstrous, it was to conform to vulgar opinion. But he is generally a Man.

Actually Shakespeare was already at one with vulgar opinion and willingly makes him a monster. But only in some places; in others he keeps him human. Similarly we need not choose between Richard the psychological study in compensation for physical disability and Richard the embodiment of sheer demonic will, for he is both. It is true that, as Lamb notes, Richard in the allusions to his deformity

mingles . . . a perpetual reference to his own powers and capacities, by which he is enabled to surmount these petty objections; and the joy of a defect *conquered*, or *turned* into an advantage, is one cause of these very allusions, and of the satisfaction, with which his mind recurs to them.

But Dowden also is right when he says of Richard that

his dominant characteristic is not intellectual; it is rather a daemonic energy of will. . . . He is of the diabolical class. . . . He is single-hearted in his devotion to evil. . . . He has a fierce joy, and he is an intense believer, – in the creed of hell. And therefore he is strong. He inverts the moral order of things, and tries to live in this inverted system. He does not succeed; he dashes himself to pieces against the laws of the world which he has outraged.

It might be retorted that the above distinction is superfluous, because an extreme manifestation of demonic will can only arise from the additional drive set in motion by an unusual need to compensate for a defect. But the point is that Shakespeare does actually make the distinction and that Richard, within the limits of the play, is psychologically both possible and impossible. He ranges from credibly motivated villain to a symbol, psychologically absurd however useful dramatically, of the diabolic.

This shift, however, is not irregular. In the first two scenes, containing his opening soliloquy, his dealings with Clarence, his interruption of the funeral of Henry VI with his courtship of Ann Nevil, he is predominantly the psychological study. Shakespeare here builds up his private character. And he is credible; with his humour, his irony, and his artistry in crime acting as differentiating agents, creating a sense of the individual. After this he carries his established private character into the public arena, where he is more than a match for anyone except Queen Margaret. Of her alone he is afraid; and her curse establishes, along with the psychologically probable picture just created, the competing and ultimately victorious picture of the monstrosity, the country's scapegoat, the vast impostume of the commonwealth. She makes him both a cosmic symbol, the 'troubler of the poor world's peace', and sub-human, a 'rooting hog', 'the slave of nature and the son of hell'. She calls on him the curse of insomnia, which later we find to have been fulfilled. Clearly this does not apply to the exulting ironic Richard: *he* must always have slept with infant tranquillity. Thus Margaret's curse is prospective, and though he continues to pile up the materials for the construction of his monstrosity, it is the credible Richard, glorying in his will and his success in compensating his disabilities, who persists till the end of the third act and the attainment of the throne. Thenceforward, apart from his outburst of energy in courting Queen Elizabeth for her daughter's hand, he melts from credible character into a combination of sheer melodrama villain and symbol of diabolism. His irony forsakes him; he is unguarded not secretive in making his plans; he is no longer cool but confused in his energy, giving and retracting orders; he *really* does not sleep; and, when on the eve of Bosworth he calls for a bowl of wine because he has not 'that alacrity of spirit nor cheer of mind that I was wont to have', he is the genuine ancestor of the villain in a nineteenth-century melodrama calling for whisky when things look black. Then, with the ghosts and his awakening into his Judas-like monologue, psychological probability and melodramatic villainy alike melt into the symbol of sheer denial and diabolism. Nor does his momentary resurrection at Bosworth with his memorable shout for a horse destroy that abiding impression. That a character should shift from credible human being to symbol would not have troubled a generation nurtured on Spenser. Richard in this respect resembles one of Spenser's masterpieces, Malbecco, who from a realistic old cuckold is actually transformed into an allegorical figure called Jealousy.

Finally we must not forget that Richard is the vehicle of an orthodox doctrine about kingship. It was a terrible thing to fight the ruling monarch, and Richard had been crowned. However, he was so clearly both a usurper and a murderer that he had qualified as a tyrant; and against an authentic tyrant it was lawful to rebel.

Richmond, addressing his army before Bosworth, makes the point absolutely clear:

> Richard except, those whom we fight against
> Had rather have us win than him they follow.
> For what is he they follow? truly, gentlemen,
> A bloody tyrant and a homicide;
> One rais'd in blood and one in blood establish'd;
> One that made means to come by what he hath
> And slaughter'd those that were the means to help him. . .
> One that hath ever been God's enemy.
> Then if you fight against God's enemy,
> God will in justice ward you as his soldiers;
> If you do sweat to put a tyrant down,
> You sleep in peace, the tyrant being slain.

And Derby, handing Henry the crown after the battle, calls it 'this long-usurped royalty'.

I have indicated in outline the course of the play: the emerging of unity from and through discord, the simultaneous change in Richard from accomplished villain to the despairing embodiment of evil. Shakespeare gives it coherence through the dominant and now scarcely human figure of Queen Margaret: the one character who appears in every play. Being thus a connecting thread, it is fitting that she give structural coherence to the crowning drama. As Richard's downfall goes back to her curse, so do the fates of most of the characters who perish in the play go back to her curses or prophecies in the same scene, I. iii. Nor are her curses mere explosions of personal spite; they agree with the tit-for-tat scheme of crime and punishment that has so far prevailed in the tetralogy. She begins by recalling York's curse on her at Wakefield for the cruelty of her party to Rutland and the penalty she has paid; and then enumerates the precisely balanced scheme of retribution appointed for the house of York:

> If not by war, by surfeit die your king,
> As ours by murder, to make him a king.
> Edward thy son, which now is Prince of Wales,
> For Edward my son, which was Prince of Wales,
> Die in his youth by like untimely violence.
> Thyself a queen, for me that was a queen,
> Outlive thy glory like my wretched self.

Curses on minor characters follow, but Richard, as befits, has a speech to himself. His peculiar curse is the gnawing of conscience, sleeplessness, and the mistake of taking friends for enemies and enemies for friends. I have spoken of the sleeplessness above, how it could not apply to the Richard of the first three acts. Similarly it is not till Bosworth that the curse of thinking his enemies friends comes true. We are meant to think of it when Richmond says in lines quoted above that 'those whom we fight against had rather have us win than him they follow'. The man with the best brain in the play ends by being the most pitifully deceived. . . . Margaret in her last lines before she goes out unconsciously forecasts the larger theme of the plays. Talking of Richard she says:

> Live each of you the subjects to his hate,
> And he to yours, and all of you to God's.

Margaret does not realize that this grouping of Yorkists against Richard will unite them to the Lancastrians similarly opposed, and that the just vengeance of God had even then given way to his mercy.

In style the play is better sustained than its predecessor. There is less undifferentiated stuff, and the finest pieces of writing (as distinguished from the finest scenes) are more dramatic. The quiet concentration of the Duchess of York's last words to Richard is beyond anything in the other three plays:

> Either thou wilt die, by God's just ordinance,
> Ere from this war thou turn a conqueror,
> Or I with grief and extreme age shall perish
> And never look upon thy face again.
> Therefore take with thee my most heavy curse;
> Which, in the day of battle, tire thee more
> Than all the complete armour that thou wear'st!
> My prayers on the adverse party fight;
> And there the little souls of Edward's children
> Whisper the spirits of thine enemies
> And promise them success and victory.
> Bloody thou art, bloody will be thy end;
> Shame serves thy life and doth thy death attend.

Richard's plotting with Buckingham and his acquisition of the throne though strongly organized must have tired Shakespeare. There are even signs of strain in the last stage of the process when

Richard appears between the two bishops; the verse droops somewhat. After this (and it is here that Richard begins his change of nature) the vitality flags, except in patches, till the great scene when the three queens get together to join in lamentation. The courting of Elizabeth for her daughter is a prodigious affair, but not at all apt at this point. It leads nowhere; for in the very next scene (IV. 5) Elizabeth is reported to have consented to her daughter's union with Richmond. Are we to think that Elizabeth had outwitted Richard and had consented, only to deceive? This is so contrary to the simple, almost negative character of Elizabeth and so heavily ironical at Richard's expense that I cannot believe it. A better explanation is that Elizabeth was merely weak and changeable and that Richard's comment on her as she goes from him, having consented,

> Relenting fool and shallow, changing woman,

was truer than he thought, forecasting the second change. It is fitting that Richard, having been so often ironical at the expense of others, should himself be the occasional victim of the irony of events. Even so, the scene is far too elaborate and weighty for its effect on the action. Indeed I suspect an afterthought, a mistaken undertaking to repeat the success of the earlier scene of courtship. It would have been better to have gone quickly on to the great finale of the ghosts and of Bosworth, to that consummate expression, achieved here once and for all, of what I have ventured to call Shakespeare's official self.

SOURCE: Extract from *Shakespeare: History Plays* (London, 1944), pp. 199–214.

NOTES

(All except Note 4 have been added by the Editors.)

1. The *Books of Homilies* were collections of doctrinal statements of the Church of England (published in 1547 and 1563) appointed to be read in churches.

2. Edward Hall (1498–1547), author of *The Union of the two noble and illustre Families of Lancastre and York* (1548).

3. Polydore Vergil (*c.*1470–*c.*1555) was an Italian scholar who came to England in 1501 and was commissioned six years later to write a history of

England for Henry VII – *Polydori Vergilii Urbinatis Anglicae Historiae Libri xxvi* (1534).

4. 'Where is your garden with its gay lawn and fresh flowers, which Queen Flora has painted delightfully in every bed; where you used to walk so merrily in May and take the dew before daylight, and hear all the blackbirds and thrushes; where you used to go singing with fair ladies and see the throng of courtiers dressed in gay colours?'

5. Sir Thomas More (1478–1535) wrote an unfinished history of Richard III in 1513.

6. Raphael Holinshed (died c.1582), author of *Chronicles of England, Scotland and Ireland* (2nd edn, 1587).

A. P. Rossiter   Angel with Horns   (1961)

'Let's write "good angel" on the devil's horn' – *Measure for Measure*, II.iv.16

In the Second Part of *Henry IV* (III. i.) the King and Warwick are talking away the midnight, or the King's insomnia; and the King remembers how Richard spoke like a prophet of the future treachery of the Percies. Warwick replies that those who look for rotations in history can indeed appear to be prophets:

> There is a history in all men's lives,
> Figuring the nature of the times deceas'd;
> The which observ'd, a man may prophesy,
> With a near aim, of the main chance of things
> As yet not come to life, who in their seeds
> And weak beginnings lie intreasured.
> Such things become the hatch and brood of time.

Richard, he explains, had observed 'the necessary form' of the events he had seen happen; and from that he could 'create a perfect guess' of some that were to ensue as 'the hatch and brood of time'.

Men have always looked for such a predictability in history: it gives the illusion of a comfortably ordered world. They have also often read – and written – historical records to show that the course of events has been guided by a simple process of divine justice, dispensing rewards and punishments here on earth and seeing to it that the wicked do *not* thrive like the green bay-tree (as the Psalmist thought), and that virtue is not 'triumphant only in theatrical performances' (as the humane Mikado put it: being a Gilbertian Japanese, not an Elizabethan Christian). The story-matter of the Henry VI plays and of *Richard III* accepted both of these comforting and comfortable principles.

When I say 'story-matter' I mean what the Chronicles gave the author (or authors) of these four plays, and I wish to remain uncommitted as to whether their *plots* (and especially that of *Richard III*) work entirely within those reassuring limitations.

I am averse to source-study, as material for lectures. Yet sad experience of human nature (and perhaps of historians) leads me to remind you how the Richard III myth ('*story*') came to reach Shakespeare. In the play, you remember, the Bishop of Ely, Morton, plots with Buckingham and runs away to join Richmond (Henry Tudor). He duly became one of Henry's ministers; and Thomas More grew up in his houschold – and later wrote the life of Richard III. It would only be human if Morton recounted all the worst that was ever said of the master he had betrayed: it is not surprising that Edward Hall should accept More's account, in writing his vast book on the 'noble and illustre families of Lancastre and York'; and still more human that Raphael Holinshed (whom no one could call a historian) should copy extensively from Hall – and so leave room for all those since Horace Walpole who have had doubts about the historical character of this terrible monarch and the events of his times.

To think that we are seeing anything like sober history in this play is derisible naïvety. What we are offered is a formally patterned sequence presenting two things: on the one hand, a rigid Tudor *schema* of retributive justice (a sort of analogy to Newton's Third Law in the field of moral dynamics: 'Action and reaction are equal and apposite'); and, on the other, a huge triumphant stage-personality, an early old masterpiece of the art of rhetorical stage-writing, a monstrous being incredible in any sober, historical scheme of things – Richard himself.

I will talk about the first, first. The basic pattern of retributive justice (or God's vengeance) is well enough illustrated in Holinshed, in the passage telling how Prince Edward (Henry VI's son and Margaret's) was murdered at the Battle of Tewkesbury. The Prince

was handed over to Edward IV on the proclamation of a promise
that he would not be harmed; he was brought before the King,
asked why he 'durst so presumptuously enter into his realm' and
replied courageously 'To recover my father's kingdom and heritage'
(and more to that purpose) – but let Holinshed say the rest:

At which words king Edward said nothing, but with his hand thrust him
from him, or (as some saie) stroke him with his gantlet; whom incontinentlie,
George duke of Clarence, Richard duke of Glocester, Thomas Greie
marquesse Dorcet, and William lord Hastings, that stood by, suddenlie
murthered; for the which cruell act, the more part of the dooers in their
latter daies dranke of the like cup, by the righteous justice and due
punishment of God.

There you have the notional pattern, in little, of the whole
framework of *Richard III*: Clarence – 'false, fleeting, perjur'd Clarence'
(who took the sacrament to remain true to Henry VI of Lancaster
and deserted him); Gray – one of the group of Queen Elizabeth
Woodeville's relations, who fall to Richard and Buckingham next
after Clarence; Hastings, who says he will see 'this crown of mine
hewn from its shoulders/Before I see the crown so foul misplaced'
(on Richard's head) – and *does* (if a man can be said to see his own
decapitation). Holinshed really understates the matter in writing
'the more part of the dooers . . . dranke of the like cup'; for of those
he names, everyone did. On the one hand, that is what *Richard III*
is about: what it is composed of. A heavy-handed justice commends
the ingredients of a poisoned cup.

This notional pattern of historic events rigidly determined by a
mechanical necessity is partly paralleled by, partly modified by, the
formal patterns of the episodes (or scenes) and the language. By
'formal patterns' I mean the unmistakably iterated goings-on in
scenes so exactly parallel that if the first *is* passable on a modern
stage as quasi-realistic costume-play stuff, the second (repeating it
always *more* unrealistically) cannot be. The two wooing-scenes
(Richard with Anne and Elizabeth) are the simplest case; but in the
lamentation-scenes – where a collection of bereft females comes
together and goes through a dismal catalogue of *Who was Who* and
Who has lost Whom (like a gathering of historical Mrs Gummidges[1],
each 'thinking of the old 'un' with shattering simultaneity) – there,
even editors have found the proceedings absurd; and readers difficult.
When Queen Margaret, for example, says;

> I had an Edward, till a Richard kill'd him;
> I had a husband, till a Richard kill'd him:
> Thou hadst an Edward, till a Richard kill'd him;
> Thou hadst a Richard, till a Richard kill'd him.
>   (IV. iv. 40–3)

a reader may *just* keep up (and realize that the last two are the Princes in the Tower, so that Queen Elizabeth is being addressed); but when the Duchess of York takes up with

> I had a Richard too, and thou didst kill him;
> I had a Rutland too, thou holp'st to kill him,

it is likely that you are lost, unless your recollection of *Henry VI* and the ends of Richard, Duke of York and his young son (Edmund) is unusually clear.

It is not only the iteration of scene that is stylized: the stiffly formal manipulation of echoing phrase and sequence of words within the scenes is even more unrealistic. A closely related parallelism exists in the repeated occurrence of a sort of 'single line traffic' in sentences: the classicist's *stichomythia*. One speaker takes from the other exactly the same ration of syllables, and rejoins as if under contract to repeat the form of the given sentence as exactly as possible, using the maximum number of the same words or their logical opposites, or (failing that) words closely associated with them. I describe the game pedantically, because it *is* an exact and scientific game with language, and one of the graces and beauties of the play Shakespeare wrote. If we cannot accept the 'patterned speech' of *Richard III*, its quality must remain unknown to us. 'Early work' is an evasive, criticism-dodging term. Early it may be; but the play is a triumphant contrivance in a manner which cannot properly be compared with that of any other tragedy – nor of any history, except *3 Henry VI* (where the manner takes shape, and particularly in III. ii.) and *King John* (which is not half so well built or integrated as this).

I have emphasized the stylization of verbal patterning (with its neatly over-exact adjustments of stroke to stroke, as in royal tennis), because the sequence of most of the important events offers very much the same pattern. I might remark, in passing, that these verbal devices were offering to the Elizabethans an accomplished English equivalent to the neat dexterities they admired in Seneca (a point made by T. S. Eliot years ago; though he did not examine how the dramatic ironies of the action run in parallel with these counter-stroke reversals of verbal meaning, and form a kind of harmony). But we miss something more than Shakespeare's rhetorical game of tennis if merely irritated by, e.g.:

> *Anne:*   I would I knew thy heart.
> *Richard:*   'Tis figured in my tongue.
> *Anne:*   I fear me, both are false.
> *Richard:*   Then never man was true.

Those reversals of intention (*heart-tongue; false-true*) are on precisely the pattern of the repeated reversals of human expectation, the reversals of events, the anticipated reversals (foreseen only by the audience), which make 'dramatic irony'. The patterned speech of the dialogue – the wit that demonstrates that a sentence is but a cheveril glove, quickly turned the other way – is fundamentally one with the ironic patterns of the plot. 'Dramatic irony' here is verbal *peripeteia*.

You will see that simply exemplified if you read Buckingham's speech at the beginning of Act II, where he calls a curse on himself if ever he goes back on his reconciliation with the Queen (and is quite specific about it); then turn straight to his last lines in v. i., when he is on the way to execution: 'That high All-seer, which I dallied with.' He has got exactly what he asked for. He did not mean the words he used, but they have been reversed into actuality, in exactly the same way as verbal terms are reversed in the tennis-court game of rhetoric.

The same irony plays all over *Richard III*. It lurks like a shadow behind the naïvely self-confident Hastings; it hovers a moment over Buckingham when Margaret warns him against 'yonder dog' (Richard), and, on Richard's asking what she said, he replies, 'Nothing that I respect, my gracious lord' (I. iii. 296) – and this at a time when Buckingham is under no threat whatsoever.

Its cumulative effect is to present the personages as existing in a state of total and terrible uncertainty. This is enhanced if we know the details of what comes into the play from *3 Henry VI*, but is there even if we know only a few bare essentials of what has gone before. We need to know who Margaret is; how Lancaster has been utterly defeated, and King Henry and his son murdered; how Clarence betrayed his King and returned to the Yorkists; and how Richard, his younger brother, has already marked him as his immediate obstruction on his intended way to the crown. We need to know too that the Duchess of York is mother to that unrewarding trio, Edward IV, Clarence, Gloucester; that Edward IV has married an aspiring commoner, Elizabeth Grey (*née* Woodeville); and that she has jacked up her relations into nobility. Beyond those half-dozen facts we do not need back-reference to *3 Henry VI* for any but the finer points – so far as the essential ironics of the plot go.

Far more important than these details is the simple over-riding principle derived from the Tudor historians: that England rests under a chronic curse – the curse of faction, civil dissension and fundamental anarchy, resulting from the deposition and murder of the Lord's Anointed (Richard II) and the usurpation of the House of Lancaster. The savageries of the Wars of the Roses follow logically (almost theologically) from that; and Elizabeth's 'All-seeing heaven, what a world is this!' says but half. It is a world of absolute and hereditary moral ill, in which *everyone* (till the appearance of Richmond-Tudor in Act v) is tainted with the treacheries, the blood and the barbarities of civil strife, and internally blasted with the curse of a moral anarchy which leaves but three human *genera*: the strong in evil, the feebly wicked and the helplessly guilt-tainted (such as the Princes, Anne – all those despairing, lamenting women, whose choric wailings are a penitential psalm of guilt and sorrow: England's guilt, the individual's sorrow). The 'poor painted Queen's' 'What a world' needs supplementing with the words of the pessimistically clear-sighted Third Citizen:

> All may be well; but, if God sort it so,
> 'Tis more than we deserve or I expect. (II. iii. 36)

I have in effect described the meaning of the framework of the play: presented it as 'moral history', to be interpreted in abstract terms. But the play itself is also a symphonic structure which I can only describe in terms of music: a rhetorical symphony of five movements, with first and second subjects and some Wagnerian *Leitmotifs*. The play-making framework is Senecan revenge, the characterization largely Marlovian; but the orchestration is not only original, but unique. It can be sketched like this.

The first movement employs five 'subjects': Richard himself, his own overture; the wooing-theme (to be repeated in the fourth movement); Richard among his enemies (repeating the duplicity with which he has fooled Clarence); Margaret's curse; and the long dying fall of Clarence. It occupies the whole of Act I.

The second movement includes Act II. and scenes i.–iv. of Act III. It begins with the King's feeble peace-making – in which Buckingham invites his curse – and its other subjects are: a lamentation after the King's death (repeated in the fourth movement); the fall of the curse on Rivers, Grey and Vaughan (when the curse is remembered), and on Hastings (the curse briefly recalled again). The future subject of Richard's moves against the Princes is introduced between-whiles.

The third movement cuts across the Act-divisions and runs from III. v. to IV. iii. Its main subject is the Gloucester-Buckingham plot for the crown, with the magnificently sardonic fooling of the London *bourgeoisie* with a crisis-scare, a brace of bishops, and the headline-story that here is a highly respectable unlibidinous monarch for decent England. On its success, Anne is called to be Queen, and thus to meet the curse she herself called on Richard's wife before he wooed her in that humour and won her (the first movement is here caught up). Buckingham now makes himself one of Richard's future victims by showing reluctance for the plot against the Princes, and Richard throws him off with a snub. The Princes are dealt with (the account of Forrest and Deighton echoing that of the murderers of Clarence, one of whom had a temporary conscience); and Richard concludes with a brisk summary and prospectus:

> The sons of Edward sleep in Abraham's bosom,
> And Anne my wife hath bid this world good night;

and so, since Richmond plans to marry 'young Elizabeth, my brother's daughter,' 'To her go I, a jolly thriving wooer'. (Richard's last jocularity). The movement ends with the first murmurs of Richmond. Previously there has been slipped in the trivial-sounding prophecy about 'Rugemount', besides Henry VI's prophecy (IV. ii. 99 f.). The flight of the Bishop of Ely (Morton) really troubles Richard.

The fourth movement brings down the curse on Buckingham (v. i. is obviously misplaced, so the movement runs from IV. iv. to v. i. inclusive). Mainly it repeats themes heard before: with a long lamentation-scene (the Blake-like weeping Queens); a repetition of Margaret's curse with the curse of Richard's mother added; the second wooing-scene; the subject of Nemesis repeated by Buckingham. In it the sound of Richmond's advance has become clearer; and Richard's self-command and certainty begin to waver.

The fifth movement is all at Bosworth: the fall of the curse on Richard himself. There is the dream-prologue of the procession of contrapuntal Ghosts (including all those so qualified from the four previous movements) and, like all ghosts, they are reminiscent and repetitive. The play ends with the epilogue to the Wars of the Roses – spoken by Queen Elizabeth's grandfather – calling a blessing on the English future, and inverting the opening lines of Richard's prologue:

> Now is the winter of our discontent
> Made glorious summer . . .

The deliberateness of this highly controlled workmanship needs but little comment. I shall take up a single musical phrase: one that intertwines its plangent undertones throughout the whole symphony, a true *Leitmotif*.

At first sight, Clarence's dream (i. iv. 9 f.) appears to contribute little to the play, nothing to the plot; and it may seem a rhetorical indulgence, even if we accept Mr Eliot's judgement that it shows 'a real approximation in English to the magnificence of Senecan Latin at its best. . . . The best of Seneca has here been absorbed into English.'[2] But first recollect the setting. Clarence has been sent to the Tower, by the machinations of the Queen's party (so he thinks), and he is confident that his brother Richard will stand good friend to him. He believes Richard's worried 'We are not safe, Clarence; we are not safe'; cannot possibly see the ironical joke Richard is cracking with himself; has no idea that he has been first on Richard's list since that moment in *3 Henry VI* (v. vi. 84) when his brother muttered, 'Clarence, beware; thou keep'st me from the light'.[3] (A line that follows a passage predetermining the gulling of both Clarence and Anne to follow:

> I have no brother, I am like no brother;
> And this word 'love', which greybeards call divine,
> Be resident in men like one another,
> And not in me! I am myself alone.)

Clarence had not been there to hear that: knows nothing of the typically sharp reversal of Richard's solemnly hypocritical fooling now with:

Go tread the path that thou shalt ne'er return.
Simple, plain Clarence, I do love thee so
That I will shortly send thy soul to heaven,
If heaven will take the present at our hands. (I. i. 117–20)

Clarence has his nightmare in the Tower: a vision prophetic of doom, and thick with curdled guilt. He dreams that Richard blunderingly knocks him overboard from a vessel; he drowns; goes to hell; and his guilt-sick mind spews up its own evil;

Keeper: Awak'd you not in this sore agony?
Clarence: No, no, my dream was lengthen'd after life.
        O, then began the tempest to my soul!
        I pass'd, methought, the melancholy flood
        With that sour ferryman which poets write of,
        Unto the kingdom of perpetual night.
        The first that there did greet my stranger soul
        Was my great father-in-law, renowned Warwick,
        Who spake aloud 'What scourge for perjury
        Can this dark monarchy afford false Clarence?'
        And so he vanish'd. Then came wand'ring by
        A shadow like an angel, with bright hair
        Dabbled in blood, and he shriek'd out aloud
        'Clarence is come – false, fleeting, perjur'd Clarence,
        That stabb'd me in the field by Tewkesbury.
        Seize on him, Furies, take him unto torment!'
                              (I. iv. 42–57)

It is as fine a passage in that style as English can offer: calculated to leave its solemn music in even half-attentive ears. In the second movement of the play (II. ii. 43 f.), Queen Elizabeth announces the King's death:

If you will live, lament; if die, be brief,
That our swift-winged souls may catch the King's,
Or like obedient subjects follow him
To his new kingdom of ne'er-changing night.

It is scarcely a proper-wifely expectation of the fate of her husband's spirit: but the echo of 'Unto the kingdom of perpetual night' is the effect intended, not Elizabeth's notions. The actors who put together the Q. text of 1597 showed that they appreciated, if clumsily, the author's intention. They made it 'To his new kingdom of perpetuall rest': catching the echo rightly, while missing the point.

The same 'dark monarchy' awaits all these people: they are the living damned. That is the translation of this echo-technique of *Leitmotifs*; and why I call the play's anatomy 'musical'. Nor is that all: the phrase returns again. But before I come to that, remark how Hastings philosophizes on his fall at the end of the second movement:

> O momentary grace of mortal men,
> Which we more hunt for than the grace of God!
> Who builds his hope in air of your good looks
> Lives like a drunken sailor on a mast,
> Ready with every nod to tumble down
> Into the fatal bowels of the deep. (III. iv. 98–103)

We have heard that surging rhythm before. And with it the feeling of being aloft, in air, unbalanced: the rhythm of Clarence dreaming:

> As we pac'd along
> Upon the giddy footing of the hatches,
> Methought that Gloucester stumbled, and in falling
> Struck me, that thought to stay him, overboard
> Into the tumbling billows of the main. (I. iv. 16–20)

Pattern repeats pattern with remarkable exactitude. 'Into the fatal bowels of the deep' is where the giddy Hastings also goes. 'O Lord, methought what pain it was to drown' might be extended to all these desperate swimmers in the tide of pomp and history. The elaboration of the dream is no mere exercise in fine phrase on Latin models: it offers a symbol of choking suspense above black depths (the ocean, and perpetual night) which epitomizes the 'momentary grace' of all these 'mortal men' and women. And the sea as figure of 'the destructive element' appears again in Elizabeth's lines in the second wooing-scene:

> But that still use of grief makes wild grief tame,
> My tongue should to thy ears not name my boys
> Till that my nails were anchor'd in thine eyes;
> And I, in such a desp'rate bay of death,
> Like a poor bark, of sails and tackling reft,
> Rush all to pieces on thy rocky bosom. (IV. iv. 229–34)

'Bay' of death suggests also an animal at bay; just plausibly relevant, since Richard (the boar) would be at bay when she *could* scratch his eyes out. But the repetition of the rather too emphatic anchors and the eyes from Clarence's dream is much more striking.

You will find a further echo of the 'night-motif' in the last movement. Richard suspects Stanley (confusingly also called Derby), and reasonably so: for he was husband to the Countess of Richmond, Henry Tudor's mother, the famous Lady Margaret Beaufort; and therefore keeps his son, George Stanley, as hostage. Before Bosworth, he sends a brisk message to warn the father of the black depths beneath the son; and again Shakespeare sounds his doom-music from the Clarence sequence:

> bid him bring his power
> Before sunrising, lest his son George fall
> Into the blind cave of eternal night. (v. iii. 60–2)

Need I remark that Clarence was 'George' too, and lightly called that by Richard when he was afraid that King Edward might die before he signed his brother's death-warrant?

> He cannot live, I hope, and must not die
> Till George be packed with post-horse up to heaven.
>
> (I. ii. 145)

I could further exemplify the play's tight-woven artistry by taking up that very remarkable prose-speech on 'conscience' by Clarence's Second Murderer (I. iv. 133 f.), and following the word into Richard's troubled mind in Act v. before Margaret's curse attains its last fulfilment. But to reduce attention to Richard himself in his own play, beyond what I am already committed to by my insistence on taking the play as a *whole* (as a dramatic pattern, not an exposition of 'character'), would be to do it – and Shakespeare – an injustice.

Richard Plantagenet is alone with Macbeth as the Shakespearian version of the thoroughly bad man in the role of monarch and hero; he is unique in combining with that role that of the diabolic humorist. It is this quality which makes it an inadequate account to say that the play is 'moral history', or that the protagonists are the personality of Richard and the curse of Margaret (or what it stood for in orthodox Tudor thinking about retributive justice in history) – for all that these opposed 'forces' *are* central throughout. The first movement establishes both, and emphatically. First, Richard, stumping down the stage on his unequal legs, forcing his hitched-up left shoulder and his withered arm on us, till we realize that *this* is what the 'winter of our discontent' in *3 Henry VI* has produced, *this* the proper 'hatch and brood of time'; and then, Richard established, his cruel and sardonic effectiveness demonstrated on Clarence and Anne, there arises against his brazen Carl Orff-like music the one voice he quails before (if but slightly): the sub-dominant notes of Margaret and her prophecy of doom, to which the ghosts will walk in the visionary night before Bosworth. It is a conflict between a spirit and a ghost: between Richard, the spirit of ruthless will, of daemonic pride, energy and self-sufficiency, of devilish gusto and *Schadenfreude* (he *enjoys* wickedness even when it is of no practical advantage to his ambitions or to securing himself by murder: it may be only wickedness in *words*, but the spirit revealed is no less evilly exultant for that); and the ghost, as I call her – for what else is Margaret, Reignier's daughter picked up on a battlefield by Suffolk and married to that most etiolated of Shakespeare's husbands, Henry VI, but the living ghost of Lancaster, the walking dead, memorializing the long, cruel, treacherous, bloody conflict of the years of civil strife and pitiless butchery?

You can, of course, see more there if you will. Make her the last stage or age of woman-in-politics: she who has been beautiful, fiercely passionate, queenly, dominating, master of armies, *generalissima*; now old, defeated, empty of everything but fierce bitterness, the illimitable bitterness and rancour of political zeal. What did Yeats write of *his* equivalent symbol? It is in *A Prayer for my Daughter*. For her he prays:

> An intellectual hatred is the worst,
> So let her think opinions are accursed.
> Have I not seen the loveliest woman born
> Out of the mouth of Plenty's horn,
> Because of her opinionated mind
> Barter that horn and every good
> By quiet natures understood
> For an old bellows full of angry wind?

Margaret is that, if you like; but, not to go beyond Shakespeare, I cannot but think that when the old Duchess of York sits down upon the ground for the second lamentation-scene (to tell 'sad stories of the death of kings'), the *author's* mind ran more upon Margaret as he wrote:

> Dead life, blind sight, poor mortal living ghost, . . .
> Brief abstract and record of tedious days,
> Rest thy unrest on England's lawful earth,
> Unlawfully made drunk with innocent blood.

> (IV. iv. 26, 28–30)

Here Shakespeare devises a new variation on the Senecan visitant from another world howling for revenge, by making the spectre nominal flesh and blood; the tune of the Dance of Death to which all dance to damnation is played by Margaret; and one aspect of the play is our watching the rats go into the Weser, compelled by that fatal tune.

But Richard himself is not simply the last and most important (and worst) of the victims – if those justly destroyed can be called 'victims'. That is just where the label 'moral history' is inadequate. For Richard has grown a new dimension since his abrupt and remarkable development in *3 Henry VI*: he has become a wit, a mocking comedian, a 'vice of kings'[4] – but with a clear inheritance from the old Vice of the Moralities: part symbol of evil, part comic devil, and chiefly, on the stage, the generator of roars of laughter at wickednesses (whether of deed or word) which the audience would immediately condemn in real life. On the one hand, his literary relations with the Senecan 'Tyrant' . . . are clear enough; as they are with the Elizabethan myth of 'the murderous Machiavel' . . . enough has been written on them. But only the medieval heritage – from the comic devils with their *Schadenfreude*, and the Vice as comic inverter of order and decency – can fully explain the new Richard of this apparent sequel to the *Henry VI* series.

I have said that the Christian pattern imposed on history gives the simple plot of a cast accursed, where all are evil beings, all deserve punishment. Look then, with a believing Tudor eye, and ought you not to *approve* Richard's doings? *Per se*, they are the judgement of God on the wicked; and he

> *Ein Teil von jener Kraft*
> *Die stets das Böse will, und stets das Gute schafft.*[5]

But that is not all. Richard's sense of humour, his function as clown, his comic irreverences and sarcastic or sardonic appropriations of things to (at any rate) *his* occasions: all those act as underminers of our assumed naïve and proper Tudor principles; and we are on his side much rather because he makes us (as the Second Murderer put it) 'take the devil in [our] mind', than for any 'historical-philosophical-Christian-retributional' sort of motive. In this respect a good third of the play is a kind of grisly *comedy*; in which we meet the fools to be taken in on Richard's terms, see them with his mind, and rejoice with him in their stultification (in which execution is the ultimate and unanswerable practical joke, the absolutely final laugh this side of the Day of Judgement). Here, Richard is a middle-term between Barabas, the Jew of Malta (*c.* 1590) and Volpone (1606). He inhabits a world where everyone deserves everything he can do to them; and in his murderous practical joking he is *inclusively* the comic exposer of the mental shortcomings (the intellectual and moral deformities) of this world of beings depraved and besotted. If we forget to pity them awhile (and he does his best to help us), then his impish spirit urges us towards a positive reversal of 'Christian charity' until the play's fourth movement (which is when the Elizabethan spectator began to back out, I take it) – or even beyond that point.

An aspect of Richard's appeal, which has, I fancy, passed relatively unexamined,[6] is one that we can be confident that William Shakespeare felt and reflected on. I mean the appeal of the actor: the talented being who can assume every mood and passion at will, at all events to the extent of making others believe in it. Beyond question, all our great actors have regarded the part as a fine opportunity. The extent to which the histrionic art (as Shakespeare thought and felt about it) contributed to the making of this great stage-figure is to me more interesting.

The specific interest here is the *power* that would be in the hands of an actor consummate enough to make (quite literally) 'all the world a stage' and to work on humanity by the perfect simulation of every feeling: the appropriate delivery of every word and phrase that will serve his immediate purpose; together with the complete dissimulation of everything that might betray him (whether it be his intentions, or such obstructive feelings as compunction, pity or uncertainty of mind). This appears at once when Gloucester first takes shape as the man self-made to be King, in the long soliloquy in *3 Henry VI* (iii. ii. 124 f.). The closing lines are specifically on histrionic genius:

> Why, I can smile, and murder whiles I smile,
> And cry 'Content!' to that which grieves my heart,
> And wet my cheeks with artificial tears,
> And frame my face to all occasions.
>
> (ibid. 182–5)

And then, after a little bragging prospectus on his intended deadli-ness, he ends:

> I can add colours to the chameleon,
> Change shapes with Protheus for advantages,
> And set the murderous Machiavel to school.
> Can I do this, and cannot get a crown?
> Tut, were it farther off, I'll pluck it down.
>
> (ibid. 191–5)

M. R. Ridley notes here that 'Machiavelli . . . seems to have been to the Elizabethans a type of one who advocated murder as a method of cold-blooded policy.'[7] It is true that that marks off one point of difference between the 'Senecan' tyrant-villainy (which is primarily for revenge) and the 'Machiavellian' (which is for power, or self-aggrandizement . . . though I do not think that the distinction can be maintained, if you read Seneca. But surely Ridley's note misses the point, in its context? What the 'Machiavel' allusion represents is, I believe, Shakespeare's recognition that the programme set before the Prince in *Il Principe* is one that demands exactly those histrionic qualities I have just described: a lifelong, unremitting vigilance in relentless simulation and impenetrable deception. There, precisely, lies the super-humanity of the Superman. The will-to-power is shorn of its effective power without it. He is an *artist* in evil.

Now Richard in his own play shows this power – these powers – to perfection. Except to the audience, he is invisible; but the audience he keeps reminded not only of his real intentions, but equally of his actor's artistries. The bluff plain Englishman, shocked at ambitious go-getters and grievingly misunderstood, is perfectly 'done' before the Queen's relations:

> Because I cannot flatter and look fair,
> Smile in men's faces, smooth, deceive, and cog,
> Duck with French nods and apish courtesy,
> I must be held a rancorous enemy.
> Cannot a plain man live and think no harm
> But thus his simple truth must be abus'd
> With silken, sly, insinuating Jacks?
>
> (I. iii. 47–53)

A little later, it is: 'I am too childish-foolish for this world' (ibid., 142); and even: 'I thank my God for my humility' (II. i. 72).

Then, left to himself and the audience, after egging on all their quarrels:

> But then I sigh and, with a piece of Scripture,
> Tell them that God bids us do good for evil.
> And thus I clothe my naked villainy
> With odd old ends stol'n forth of holy writ,
> And seem a saint when most I play the devil.
> (I. iii. 334–8)

The stage-direction, '*Enter two Murderers*', caps this nicely. It is not simply that Richard is a hypocrite and (like other stage-villains) tells us so. The actor's technique of 'asides' is the essence of his chuckling private jokes – made to 'myself alone'. (You might say that Shakespeare is giving not merely 'the acting of drama', but also 'the drama of consummate *acting*'.)

The same reminders, nudging the audience's attention, appear in his swift-switched actual asides: e.g., his thoroughly unholy reception of his mother's blessing, spoken as he gets up off his dutiful knees:

> Amen! And make me die a good old man!
> That is the butt end of a mother's blessing;
> I marvel that her Grace did leave it out.
> (II. ii. 109–11)

Or, again, we have Richard's insinuating equivocations in talking to the prattling little Princes; in one of which he acknowledges his theatrical-historical legacy from the Moralities: 'Thus, like the formal vice, Iniquity,/I moralize two meanings in one word.' (III. i. 82–3). Over and above this there is that striking passage (III. v. 1–11) where he and Buckingham are working up a crisis (appearing ill-dressed in old rusty armour, as if they had armed in desperate haste), when Richard specifically inquires whether Buckingham can 'do the stage-tragedian':

Richard: Come, cousin, canst thou quake and change thy colour,
  Murder thy breath in middle of a word,
  And then again begin, and stop again,
  As if thou wert distraught and mad with terror?
Buckingham: Tut, I can counterfeit the deep tragedian;
  Speak and look back, and pry on every side,
  Tremble and start at wagging of a straw,
  Intending deep suspicion. Ghastly looks
  Are at my service, like enforced smiles;
  And both are ready in their offices
  At any time to grace my stratagems.

It is all sardonically jocular; but nothing shows more clearly the artist's delight in his craft: call it illusion or deception, it makes no odds. It is this dexterity that his other rapid reversals of tone keep us aware of; whether he is half-amazedly rejoicing in his conquest of Anne, or poking unfilial fun at his mother (a performance more shocking to Elizabethans than to our more child-foolish days).

Yet again, there is that admirable moment when the Londoners are being fooled into believing that he must be persuaded to be king; when Buckingham pretends to lose patience, with 'Zounds, I'll entreat no more.' And Richard, bracketed aloft with two Bishops, is distressed: 'O, do not swear, my lord of Buckingham' (III. vii. 220). (It is like the moment in *Eric, or Little by Little*[8] (ch. 8) when Eric refers to the usher as a 'surly devil'; and the virtuous Russell exclaims: 'O Eric, that is the first time that I have heard you swear.') It is this unholy jocularity, the readiness of sarcastic, sardonic, profane and sometimes blasphemous wit, the demonic gusto of it all, which not only wins the audience over to accepting the Devil as hero, but also points us towards the central paradox of the play. And, through that, to a full critical awareness of its unity: with a few remarks on which I shall conclude.

To begin with Richard. On the face of it, he is the demon-Prince, the cacodemon born of hell, the misshapen toad, etc. (all things ugly and ill). But through his prowess as actor and his embodiment of the comic Vice and impish-to-fiendish humour, he offers the false as more attractive than the true (the actor's function), and the ugly and evil as admirable and amusing (the clown's game of value-reversals). You can say, 'We don't take him seriously.' I reply, 'That is exactly what gets most of his acquaintances into Hell: just what the devil-clown relies on.' But he is not only this demon incarnate, he is in effect God's agent in a predetermined plan of divine retribution: the 'scourge of God'.[9] Now by Tudor-Christian historical principles, this plan is *right*. Thus, in a real sense, Richard is a King who 'can do no wrong'; for in the pattern of the justice of divine retribution on the wicked, he functions as an avenging angel. Hence my paradoxical title, 'Angel with Horns.'

The paradox is sharpened by what I have mainly passed by: the repulsiveness, humanely speaking, of the 'justice'. God's will it may be, but it sickens us: it is as pitiless as the Devil's (who is called in to execute it). The contrast with Marlowe's painless, dehumanized slaughterings in *Tamburlaine* is patent.

This overall system of *paradox* is the play's unity. It is revealed as a constant displaying of inversions, or reversals of meaning: whether we consider the verbal patterns (the *peripeteias* or reversals of act and intention or expectation); the antithesis of false and true in the histrionic character; or the constant inversions of irony. Those verbal capsizings I began by talking about, with their deliberate reversals to the opposite meaning in equivocal terms, are the exact correlatives of both the nature of man (or man in power: Richard) and of the nature of events (history); and of language too, in which all is conveyed.

But, start where you will, you come back to history; or to the pattern made out of the conflict of two 'historical myths'. The orthodox Tudor myth made history God-controlled, divinely prescribed and dispensed, to move things towards a God-ordained perfection: Tudor England. Such was the *frame* that Shakespeare took. But the total effect of Shakespeare's 'plot' has quite a different effect from Halle: a very different meaning. Dr. Duthie may write, 'But there is no doubt that Shakespeare saw history in the same light as Halle saw it.'[10] I say there *is* doubt. Dover Wilson has nothing to offer but what he summarizes from Moulton, but his last sentence points my doubting way: 'it appears, to me at least, unlikely that Shakespeare's "main end" in *Richard III* was "to show the working out of God's will in English history".'[11] (The quotation he is discussing is from Tillyard's *Shakespeare's History Plays* (1944), p. 208.) He can go no further because his own limitations on *Henry IV* inhibit his ever observing that the comic Richard has no more place in Halle's scheme than Falstaff has.

The other myth is that of Richard the Devil-King: the Crookback *monstrum deforme, ingens*[12] whom Shakespeare *found* as a ready-made Senecan tyrant and converted into a quite different inverter of moral order: a ruthless, demonic comedian with a most un-Senecan sense of humour and the seductive appeal of an irresistible gusto, besides his volcanic Renaissance energies. They are themselves demoralizing: *Tapfer sein ist gut*[13] is the antithesis of a Christian sentiment.

The outcome of this conflict of myths was Shakespeare's display of constant inversions of meaning; in all of which, two systems of meaning impinge and go over to their opposites, like the two 'ways' of the cheveril glove. This applies equally to words and word-patterns; to the actor-nature; to dramatic ironies; and to events, as the hatch and brood of time, contrasted with opposite expectations.

As a result of the paradoxical ironic structure built from these inversions of meaning – built above all by Richard's demonic appeal – the naïve, optimistic, 'Christian' principle of history, consoling and comfortable, modulates into its opposite. The 'Christian' system of retribution is undermined, counter-balanced, by historic irony. (Do I need to insist that the coupling of 'Christian' and 'retribution' itself is a paradox? That the God of vengeance is *not* a Christian God; that his opposite is a God of mercy who has no representation in this play. If I do, I had better add that the so-called 'Christian' frame is indistinguishable from a pagan one of Nemesis in which the 'High all-seer' is a Fate with a cruel sense of humour.)

But do not suppose I am saying that the play is a 'debunking of Tudor myth', or that Shakespeare is disproving it. He is not 'proving' anything: not even that 'Blind belief is sure to err/And scan his works in vain' (though I think that is *shown*, nevertheless). Contemporary 'order'-thought spoke as if naïve faith saw true: God was above God's Englishmen and ruled with justice – which meant summary vengeance. This historic myth offered absolutes, certainties. Shakespeare in the Histories always leaves us with relatives, ambiguities, irony, a process thoroughly dialectical. Had he entirely accepted the Tudor myth, the frame and pattern of order, his way would have led, I suppose, towards writing *moral history* (which is what Dr. Tillyard and Dr. Dover Wilson and Professor Duthie have made *out* of him). Instead, his way led him towards writing *comic history*. The former would never have taken him to tragedy: the latter (paradoxically) did. Look the right way through the cruel-comic side of Richard and you glimpse Iago. Look back at him through his energy presented as evil, and you see Macbeth. And if you look at the irony of men's struggles in the nets of historic circumstance, the ironies of their pride and self-assurance, you will see Coriolanus; and you are past the great tragic phase and back in history again.

Source: 'Angel with Horns' in *Angel With Horns; and Other Shakespearian Lectures* (London, 1961), pp. 1–21.

NOTES

(Reorganised and renumbered and some added by Editors.)

1. A character in Charles Dickens's *David Copperfield*. [Eds]

2. T. S. Eliot, *Selected Essays* (London, 1932), p. 90: reprinted from Introduction to *Seneca His Tenne Tragedies* (London, 1927).

3. This contradicts R. G. Moulton, *Shakespeare as a Dramatic Artist* (London, 1985), p. 92, who says Richard is *not* 'ambitious' (as Macbeth is): 'never found dwelling upon the prize in view'. This presumes a complete disconnection between *3 Henry VI* and *Richard III*. No such assumption is acceptable nowadays – nor was it sensible even then.

4. *Richard III*, 3.2.155–6. [Eds]

5. 'A part of that Power which always wills evil and yet always brings about good.' (Goethe's *Faust*).

6. J. Middleton Murry, *Shakespeare* (London, 1936), pp. 125–6, quotes the theatrical metaphors and remarks briefly on the conception of Richard as an actor.

7. New Temple edition (London, 1935) p. 140.

8. F. W. Farrar, *Eric, or Little by Little* (London, 1858). [Eds]

9. This phrase is Christopher Marlowe's: *Tamburlaine the Great: Part Two*, 5.3.248. [Eds]

10. G. I. Duthie, *Shakespeare* (London, 1951), p. 118.

11. *Richard III* (New Cambridge edition, Cambridge, 1954), p. 45.

12. The full quotation is from Virgil, 'Monstrum, horrendum, informe, ingens cui lumen ademptum': A monster, horrible, unshapely, gigantic, and eyeless. [Eds]

13. 'To be bold is good.'

Irene G. Dash   The Paradox of Power in *Richard III*   (1981)

> Am I a queen in title and in style,
> And must be made a subject to a duke?
> (*2 Henry VI*, ɪ.iii.48–49)

Queens and duchesses stalk through these plays, commanding, ordering, sweeping officiously in and out of the English court, but also walking alone, powerless – for they are women. Married to men of power, these women rule by fiat. They dazzle when in power, arouse sadness and terror when out. In their experiences, in the uncertainty of their power, women recognize the anomalousness of their own lives. When, near the close of this tetralogy, Margaret, the deposed, widowed Queen turns to her alter ego, Elizabeth, and mocks, 'Vain flourish of my fortune. . . . A queen in jest, only to fill the scene' (*Richard III*, iv.iv.82,91), the elder woman has begun to achieve self-knowledge. The ambiguous and uncertain limits of her own power have taught her the condition of women. For she has, at moments, reached the zenith of power, but she stands now powerless. In exaggerated form, her experience and those of the queens and duchesses in these plays illustrate the dilemma of most women. Sexual politics molds their lives, distorts their perspectives, and damages their relationships with women as well as men. Kate Millett defines sexual politics as the process by which women have been socialized into accepting the values of a patriarchal society where men control 'every avenue of power'.[1] She then describes the destruction of a woman's self-esteem by this system, observing that it leads to woman's 'self-hatred and self-rejection, a contempt both for herself and for her fellows – the result of that continual, however subtle, reiteration of her inferiority which she eventually accepts as a fact'.[2]

Shakespeare presents a range of women in this tetralogy, one of whom, Margaret, provides the overall arch, giving this boldly spreading group of dramas a unity. Although she does not dominate any single play, she links the works from the end of *I Henry VI* through *Richard III*, provides continuity, and allows one to observe how women must contend with the power structure in a patriarchy. Not included in this chapter are Joan of Aire and the Countess of Auvergne, two women prominent in *1 Henry VI*. Rather, the women chosen for discussion interact with one another and reveal Shakespeare's gift for reiterating elements in women's experiences and yet showing the individuality of each life.[3] Shakespeare dramatizes the meaning of power for women – its nearness and infinite distance. By creating portraits of women who are mature and thoughtful, he also challenges the idea of woman's innate inferiority and shows how sexual politics destroys her ability to see life whole.

Married to wielders of power, these women find weakness, greed, and incompetence and they wonder at the validity of the system. Nevertheless, they must accept it. Discovering the powerlessness of their titular authority, the women become angry, irrational, self-doubting, self-denigrating and, ultimately denigrating of all women. Unlike Hermione and Paulina of *The Winter's Tale*, these queens and duchesses have great difficulty liking or sympathizing with others of their sex. In an attempt to cope with powerlessness, they imitate the actions of the men. Margaret Fuller, in the nineteenth century, logically explained:

> Ye cannot believe it, men; but the only reason why women ever assume what is more appropriate to you, is because you prevent them from finding out what is fit for themselves. Were they free, were they wise fully to develop the strength and beauty of Woman; they would never wish to be men, or man-like. The well-instructed moon flies not from her orbit to seize on the glories of her partner. No; for she knows that one law rules, one heaven contains, one universe replies to them alike.[4]

Shakespeare's characters, too, have difficulty 'finding out what is fit for them', as he illustrates through the material he chooses to dramatize and the limited options he allows the women.

Margaret, who spans the tetralogy, falls in love, marries, becomes a mother, and, later, a widow. Unlike most women, however, she becomes a queen. Endowed with power and confronted by powerful enemies, she arouses an extra measure of hatred and contempt. Her sorrows and joys, her vulnerability to sexual approaches and derisive slurs on her womanliness: these she shares with others of her sex. Her right to exercise power and to lead armies – these are hers alone. During the course of the plays, the handsome young woman of *1 Henry VI* becomes the Cassandra-like older woman of *Richard III*, foreseeing the doom of those who mock her. To acquire this skill, however, Margaret must make mistakes, be trapped by her vanity and ambition, react unwisely to personal affronts when deciding on political moves, and come to understand the ambiguities of her position as a woman and political figure. . . .

In *Richard III*, four widows walk the stage: Margaret, Elizabeth, the Duchess of York, and Anne. If women are confused by the meaning of power when they are young, being wooed or acting as wives to men of power, they realistically discover its meaning when they become widows. They learn that their husbands were not only the source of their power, but worse still, of their identity. How does a woman cope with this discovery, this becoming a nonperson? Shakespeare offers four versions in *Richard III*, from the simple acceptance of her status by the Duchess of York to the anxious search for new patterns by Elizabeth, who first entered this tetralogy when, as a widow suing for rights to her husband's lands, she

discovered her powerlessness for the first time. Saved by her wit
and beauty, she then moved from powerlessness to power. Like
Margaret earlier, she became a queen and the mother of princes.
When, in *Richard III*, the pattern repeats itself, Elizabeth seeks more
substantial answers.

Her experience continues to mirror Margaret's despite deviations.
Elizabeth's husband, instead of being murdered by Richard, dies,
his illness aggravated by Richard's histrionics. Instead of losing one
son and heir to the throne, she loses two. Instead of being childless
at the end of the play, she remains a mother with surviving children.
Instead of being a widow of a defeated monarch, she is widow of a
man who was in power. But it little matters. Like Margaret,
Elizabeth too loses power, discovering the strength of the patriarchal
system. Finally, near the play's close, she seeks alternatives. Shakespeare offers a tentative glimpse at women supporting women,
women relying on women, women bonding – even if in bitterness –
with women.

To do this, the dramatist alters history and creates one of
the most interesting studies in the play – he retains Margaret.
Historically, she never returned to England after the deaths of her
son and husband. Moreover, she died before the time of the action
of this play. According to the chronicles, she roamed the French
court, a woman in mourning for the rest of her life:

And where in the beginning of her tyme, she lyved like a Quene, in the
middel she ruled like an empresse, toward thende she was vexed with
troble, never quyet nor in peace, & in her very extreme age she passed her
days in Fraunce, more lyke a death then a lyfe, languishyng and mornyng
in continuall sorowe, not so much for her selfe and her husbande, whose
ages were almost consumed and worne, but for the losse of prince Edward
her sonne (whome she and her husband thought to leve, both overlyver of
their progeny, and also of their kyngdome) to whome in this lyfe nothyng
coulde be either more displeasant or grevous.[5]

Shakespeare not only brings her back to England but gives her an
important role in the play. She acts as narrative voice; she is seer
and sibyl, predicting the doom of those responsible for the deaths of
her son and husband; but she is also a dynamic woman, an
anomalous character, roaming the palace of a rival monarch,
expressing her opinions in positive language, sneering at York's
unattractive progeny who now control power. Having lost all, she
fears no one.

Margaret, who weaves in and out of this tetralogy, the only woman character whose growth we observe from youth to old age, may also have challenged Shakespeare as a creative artist. Knowing that she walked through the court in France, a person in constant mourning, he might have wanted to project this image on the stage. Would such a woman have learned anything? Would she have grown? How might she have handled life, alone, in a hostile environment? Finally, has she made any breakthrough in self-knowledge; did she learn anything about herself as a woman?

Before she enters, Shakespeare introduces her principal antagonist, Richard, the title character. He defines the power and powerlessness of women in the first scene of *Richard III*. Introduced in soliloquy, he confides his plans to reach the throne despite the mass of relatives standing between him and his objective. 'I am determined to prove a villain' (i.i.30), he proclaims, baring his plot to frame his brother Clarence. When the latter enters, en route to prison, Richard immediately blames a woman for Clarence's present fate. 'Why, this it is, when men are rul'd by women' (62), Richard asserts, implying Queen Elizabeth's evil influence on Edward. Misogyny runs wild, for Clarence easily agrees, adding Mistress Shore's name to those who 'rule' the King. Before the scene closes, a third woman is mentioned. Richard, again in soliloquy, admits,

> . . . I'll marry Warwick's youngest daughter.
> What though I kill'd her husband and her father?
> The readiest way to make the wench amends
> Is to become her husband and her father.
>   (i.i.153–56)

Moments later Anne, the play's third widow, walks on following the coffin of King Henry, her father-in-law, and taking it to burial. Asking the pall bearers to 'set down' their 'honourable load' (i.ii.i), Anne delivers a long set speech of mourning explicitly cursing the murderer, Richard. She then orders the pallbearers to resume the trek to the place of burial. Richard, unobserved, interferes, countermanding her order. 'Stay, you that bear the corse, and set it down' (33). At their attempt to continue, Richard threatens with his sword. They obey. Graphically, this scene illustrates Richard's power and Anne's powerlessness. Helpless to challenge him physically, she attempts to disarm him with words. She seeks to force her will. Scorn, hatred, vehemence, curses: all fall from her lips. Little anticipating the aim of his confrontation, she is astonished and completely bewildered when Richard offers marriage.

Historically, Richard pursued Anne for two years before winning her. Shakespeare compresses this into one scene, choosing a moment when she is most confused and emotionally most unstable. In a long protracted courtship, their debates – her responses to his persistent claims – would have to be developed so that the many variables in personality could influence the decision. When compressed into a single scene, his duplicity and her confusion must be apparent at once. Some critics believe that the scene offers an opportunity to prove Richard's extraordinary ability.[6] More recently critics have become aware of the psychological vulnerability of a person at a time of emotional crisis such as the loss of a husband and a father-in-law.[7]

First Richard tries flattery, but Anne resists, assuring him that she would scratch her beauty with her nails (i.ii.126) if she thought it were the cause of the death of her husband or father-in-law. Then Richard, the consummate actor, offers her his sword and 'lays his breast open' for her to kill him. He challenges her in a style that she cannot fathom. Untrained in the use of the sword, unwilling to take a human life, Anne reacts as a normal human being might, especially someone who has not been initiated into the games of war and murder. Although Richard continues 'Nay, do not pause: for I did kill King Henry – / But 'twas thy beauty that provoked me' (179–80), she drops the sword. But Richard's words are really superfluous. All of her training as a woman assures him success. Men are trained to kill. Women are not. Here, against a defenceless person, in a time of uncertain peace, to kill the brother of the King would be insanity as well as suicide.

Richard then poses a false dichotomy for her: 'Take up the sword again, or take up me' (i.ii.183). He leaves her no option; she must either kill him or accept him as her husband. Caught between suspicion and her training as a woman, Anne can do no more than say, 'Arise, dissembler! Though I wish thy death, / I will not be thy executioner' (184–85). Still she does not acquiesce to marriage. The key interchange between them occurs moments later when Richard offers 'Then bid me kill myself' (186) but refuses to accept her words, 'I have already' (187). Instead, he then questions the honesty of her original intention. 'That was in thy rage. / Speak it again' (187–88) he challenges, promising to kill himself for love. Anne's agonized words, 'I would I knew thy heart' (192) are spoken by many of the characters throughout the play. No one knows Richard's 'heart' – his intention – until it is too late. For a woman being wooed, however, the price is particularly high – not friendship or allegiance, but marriage.

Although Richard congratulates himself on his success – 'To take her in her heart's extremest hate, / With curses in her mouth, tears in her eyes' (i.ii.231–32) – Shakespeare here creates a situation in which a manipulative liar has the best chance of success, a moment when his prey is most confused. Richard's timing, audacity, overwhelming flattery, and histrionics with the sword are beyond Anne's ability to cope. She belongs with such characters as Ophelia, who is conforming, obedient, docile, 'feminine'. Historically, having resisted Richard for two years, she may have had more of the strength of a Margaret or an Elizabeth. She may also have had as few options as they did, being sought by the persistent brother of the King. But rather than repeat a pattern already twice told, Shakespeare creates another type of woman, caught in a different situation, and reacting on a level not yet dramatized in this tetralogy. The man she must confront is the man who boasted in the previous play:

> Why, I can smile, and murther whiles I smile,
> . . . .
> Deceive more slily than Ulysses could,
> . . . .
> Change shapes with Proteus for advantages,
> . . . .
> Can I do this, and cannot get a crown?
> Tut, were it farther off, I'll pluck it down.
> (*3 Henry VI*, iii.ii.182–95)

Richard applies his abilities, skills, and techniques to convince Anne.

Critics have been harsh in their evaluation of her. August W. Von Schlegel, the nineteenth-century German scholar, writes that 'Anne disappears without our learning anything further respecting her: in marrying the murderer of her husband she had shown a weakness almost incredible'.[8] William Richardson, in the eighteenth century, concludes that 'She is represented by Shakespeare of a mind altogether frivolous; incapable of deep affection; guided by no steady principles of virtue. . . ; the prey of vanity, which is her ruling passion'. As Richardson continues, he not only says that Richard understands her perfectly but that she is a character of 'no rational or steady virtue, and consequently of no consistency of character'. He even suggests that it is 'resentment, rather than grief, which she expresses'.[9] Georg Gervinus, the nineteenth-century German literary historian, offers a more balanced appraisal, however, when he writes, 'We must take into account the extraordinary degree of dissimulation, which deceives even experienced men', noting also how stereotypical a portrait Shakespeare creates in Anne by having her delight in saving 'such a penitent'.[10]

Anne appears in only one other scene, and that without Richard. Now married, she hopes to visit her nephews – the heirs apparent – held in the tower by her husband. Unlike her historical prototype, she admits:

> Lo, ere I can repeat this curse again,
> Within so small a time, my woman's heart
> Grossly grew captive to his honey words,
> And prov'd the subject of mine own soul's curse.
>
> (iv.i.77–80)

She is self-deprecating, and blames herself for her fate. Her conventionality is perhaps best testified to by the fact that she survives in all versions of the play. In Colley Cibber's version, Richard even tries to tempt her to commit suicide.[11] In a recent production at the Cort Theatre starring Al Pacino, she appears so cold, self-righteous, and vindictive that audiences applaud Richard's success.[12] There, although the text that remains is Shakespeare's, the cuts are reminiscent of Cibber's popular eighteenth-century work.

On the other hand, the one woman who most frequently disappears from productions is the one who challenges Richard, the least conventional woman – Margaret. Cibber set the pattern in 1700 when he eliminated her from his text. Since then, his version with its heavy emphasis on the male 'star' role has seldom left the stage. But even when Shakespeare's text is used, Margaret frequently disappears or loses most of her lines. For example, in a Phelps 1845 prompt-book, she no longer functions as an individual, cursing the many members of the court, but acts rather as a choral voice of doom.[13] Very similar cutting appears in a 1964 typescript of the play.[14] She is also absent from Laurence Olivier's film version and from the Pacino 1979 production.[15] Comparing the Cibber version with Shakespeare's play, Arthur Colby Sprague writes that:

the more obviously memorable episodes ... have survived. ... But
Margaret is gone and Clarence and Hastings and Edward: the price paid
for compactness was high. It is a version ... which does best when it keeps
to surfaces and shallows; an opportunist version, cunning, prosaic and
vulgar.[16]

Many productions of *Richard III* like Olivier's and Pacino's mentioned
above, follow Shakespeare's text but also take their cues for cutting
from Cibber. It is perhaps difficult for audiences to realize how
deeply eighteenth-century changes – perhaps because they reflect
attitudes toward women that still exist – continue to intrude on,
shape, and gently distort the text.

Margaret's absence necessarily affects the total impact of the play;
her entrance, in Act I, scene iii, offers a welcome antidote to
Richard's swaggering triumph with Anne. Listening to Queen
Elizabeth and Richard arguing, Margaret, once again, as she did
so long ago in *1 Henry VI* speaks in asides. This time, however, her
asides are not the questions of a young virgin but the bitter comments
of an old woman. She listens to the conversation of those in power.
To Elizabeth's 'Small joy have I in being England's Queen' (109),
Margaret mutters to herself:

> And less'ned by that small, God I beseech him!
> Thy honour, state, and seat is due to me.
>
> (I.iii.110–11)

At once we are reminded that Margaret is a deposed queen. We
wonder at her presence in this court. Commenting on Richard's
words, but still speaking in aside, she exclaims:

> Hie thee to hell for shame, and leave this world,
> Thou cacodemon, there thy kingdom is.
>
> (142–43)

Only the audience hears her; nevertheless, her lines establish her
strange position. What is she doing at the court, this woman, so
unafraid of Richard who, in asides, tells us of the murder of Henry
in the tower and the killing of her son Edward? When she speaks
aloud, Margaret pierces the false veneer of Richard, but also reveals
antagonism for the woman who has made her a shadow, a nonbeing,
the woman who is Queen. Although Richard reminds Margaret that
she is 'banished on pain of death' (166), she dismisses the threat,

challenging him to enforce it. 'I do find more pain in banishment / Than death can yield me here by my abode' (167–8). He then pursues another direction. Always aware of his audience, the people around him on the stage, he attacks Margaret for the murders of York and Rutland. As a result the squabbling members of the court unite against her. Aware of Richard's technique, she taunts:

> What? were you snarling all before I came,
> . . . .
> And turn you all your hatred now on me?
>   (187–9)

She then curses each of them. Still wrestling with the patriarchal values she has absorbed, she first curses the Queen, her alter ego in this strange arrangement where kings are murdered to make way for kings but queens in number are permitted to survive. Listing the parallels between them, Margaret wishes the other woman a fate like her own:

> Though not by war, by surfeit die your king,
> As ours by murther, to make him a king!
> Edward thy son, that now is Prince of Wales,
> For Edward our son, that was Prince of Wales,
> Die in his youth by like untimely violence!
>   (i.iii.196–200)

She keeps returning to her role of mother.

> Long mayst thou live to wail thy children's death,
> And see another, as I see thee now,
> Deck'd in thy rights as thou art stall'd in mine!
>   (203–5)

Finally, she condemns Elizabeth to a fate too familiar to women.

> Long die thy happy days before thy death,
> And after many length'ned hours of grief,
> Die neither mother, wife, nor England's queen!
>   (206–8)

In this long passage, Margaret details her own life as queen. Unlike the curses one might choose for a man, those chosen for Elizabeth have a different emphasis – not death but life continued after joy has passed.

When the bitter woman fails to stop her cursing, Richard interrupts. In verbal battle, she responds, wishing him a fate more heinous than the others. Her curse concludes with 'Thou detested –.' Never one to refuse a challenge, Richard quickly interjects the word 'Margaret'. But she is not to be deflected from her purpose. Her sentence continues, ending with 'Richard!'. Elizabeth, although she bears no love for Richard, is still a victim of that minority status psychology that mandates she express her deepest contempt for another woman. 'Thus have you breath'd your curse against yourself' (239), she mocks. Her words are hardly worth including in this exchange except to remind us of the difference between the two women – the sibyl-like, intense, passionate Margaret, and the more pedestrian, rational Elizabeth.

Finally, Cassandra-like, Margaret warns the one person exempt from her vengeance to beware of Richard:

> Have not to do with him, beware of him;
> Sin, death, and hell have set their marks on him,
> And all their ministers attend on him.
>   (I.iii.291–93)

But Buckingham rejects her warning. Nevertheless, he shudders at her curses. Ironically, she is attacked as being a witch and a lunatic although her listeners recognize the core of truth in her words. During this scene Dorset, the new young lord who is Elizabeth's son, warns 'Dispute not with her, she is lunatic' (253). Buckingham expresses the impact of the curses for all of them, 'My hair doth stand an end to hear her curses' (303).

When her curses come true, she believes her mission is completed. But Shakespeare suggests that one possibility lies ahead – women extending their hands to each other in support – creating bonds with each other, rather than living in separate isolated worlds, connected only with the men whom they have wed. Entering in Act IV, scene iv, Margaret, in soliloquy, mutters 'So now prosperity begins to mellow' (IV.iv.1). Still bitter, overflowing with anger and hatred, she plans to go to France, hoping the lives of those who robbed her of son and husband will prove 'bitter, black, and tragical' (7). She is a figure from the revenge tragedy of the period, asking right for right and Plantagenet for Plantagenet. It is only after the Duchess of York exclaims

O Harry's wife, triumph not in my woes!
God witness with me, I have wept for thine
(iv.iv.59–60)

that Margaret explains herself to them: 'I am hungry for revenge' (61). She prays for Richard's end. Aware of her anomic position, Margaret returns to the theme of displacedness – 'Thou didst usurp my place' – and to the role of childlessness and widowhood. She cannot establish a bond with any woman – not lend support, or seek help, or accept friendship.

'Vain flourish of my fortune' (iv.iv.82), she had called Elizabeth. Detailing its meaning, the displaced Queen recognizes the role she played, 'One heav'd a-high, to be hurl'd down below' (86). She knows now that she was merely

> The flattering index of a direful pageant;
> . . . .
> . . . . a bubble;
> A queen in jest, only to fill the scene.
> (85–91)

She then enumerates the functions of a queen, listing the bending peers and thronging troops that followed her and Elizabeth when each was Queen. This speech, by the dramatist who later was to list the many roles of man as he progressed from infancy to old age, vibrates with the emptiness of a woman's roles. 'Vain flourish of my fortune', Margaret had repeated. It is a line that many older women might speak, watching young women seeking success in the world and misreading their husbands' glories for their own.

Although Margaret's words are full of venom, hatred, and disappointment, Elizabeth seeks to create some bond, some tenuous connection, with this other woman. The scene marks a shift in attitude and is the first in which these women finally speak to each other as equals. Frequently referred to as the scene of the wailing women, it is also the beginning of mutual supportiveness. 'My words are dull, O, quicken them with thine!' (124), Elizabeth begs, asking Margaret for instruction in cursing.

> Think that thy babes were sweeter than they were,
> And he that slew them fouler than he is.
> (iv.iv.120–1)

The older woman offers a basic premise that provides strength for Elizabeth's next encounter.

Clues to a sometimes ambiguous exchange between characters frequently appear in the sequential arrangement of Shakespeare's scenes. Moments after Margaret's advice to Elizabeth, Richard enters and asks for Elizabeth's daughter's hand in marriage. Uncle Richard, murderer of the young woman's brothers, now King, anticipates success. In the debate between them, Elizabeth has her first opportunity to apply her newly learned lesson. Questions rather than answers characterize most of her replies. 'Shall I be tempted of the devil thus?' (418), she asks. 'Ay, if the devil tempt you to do good' (419), Richard sanctimoniously replies. 'Shall I forget myself to be myself' (420), she continues. 'Ay, if yourself's remembrance wrong yourself' (421), he answers. When she seems to equivocate, Richard simply carries on as best he can, picking up what he thinks are hints of affirmation. Even Elizabeth's 'Yet thou didst kill my children' (422) fails to daunt him. He offers what he considers a perfectly logical response:

> But in your daughter's womb I bury them;
> Where in that nest of spicery they will breed
> Selves of themselves, to your recomforture.
>   (IV.iv.423–25)

This speech, so ugly in its lasciviousness, reflecting the character of the man who is speaking, must be answered without disgust by a mother. Again Elizabeth resorts to a question, rather than an answer. 'Shall I go win my daughter to thy will?' (426). Has she finally fooled Richard? Immediately after her departure, he gloats, 'Relenting fool, and shallow, changing woman' (431).

She should not fool us. We have heard her scene with Margaret. We have listened to her first words to Richard in this encounter – 'For my daughters, Richard,/They shall be praying nuns, not weeping queens' (201–2) – and we have seen her pity for Anne. The choice of a convent for her daughters grows not from religious conviction – we have not heard any deep expressions of religious faith from Elizabeth – but from the wish to give her daughters control over their own bodies. Elizabeth has expressed herself on this subject from the time of her first appearance in *3 Henry VI*.

When one compares Anne's response to Richard with Elizabeth's series of rhetorical questions topped by the instruction: 'Write to

me very shortly, / And you shall understand from me her mind'
(428–29), one realizes Shakespeare's artistry. Richard, thinking that
he is repeating an earlier wooing scene, assumes a repetition of that
success – this time with far less effort than in his encounter with
Anne. Because of his misogyny, he fails to hear the nuances that
separate the responses of the women. He forgets the differences
between them: one a young, unworldly heiress, the other a mature
woman who has lived a varied existence. Finally, he has figured
without understanding the impact of the death of one's child on a
parent. The superb manipulator of people, Richard fails to read a
woman accurately, because he fails to understand her feelings toward
herself and her children.

To an extent, then, Elizabeth has triumphed. She has begun to
understand the meaning of power and the necessity for choosing
one's language with care, for restraining one's words, refraining
from cursing. She has learned that she must function alone, leading,
not leaning. In this her first test after her encounter with Margaret
and her awareness of the role of queen as shadow, she has begun to
understand the limits of power for a woman. She succeeds in fooling
Richard, but had he not lost his life in battle, she probably would
have been powerless against him. Her daughter, instead of becoming
a nun, marries Richard's victorious adversary: Richmond, later
Henry VII. Thus, she too becomes a queen, wearing the borrowed
robes of power.

The women in these plays, queens and duchesses, wives of men
of political strength, seek to exert power but discover its elusiveness.
Margaret Fuller writes: 'A profound thinker has said "No married
woman can represent the female world, for she belongs to her
husband. The idea of Woman must be represented by a virgin."'
Perhaps the Queen in Shakespeare's audience believed this. The
women in these plays, however, demonstrate the powerlessness of
women whether virgins, wives, or widows. Fuller herself countered
the argument by blaming marriage and 'the present relation between
the sexes, that the woman *does* belong to the man, instead of forming
a whole with him'.[17]

This chapter opened with reference to power and to women's
powerlessness in a society where sexual politics is so pervasive that
women have internalized the message. Shakespeare illustrates this
by revealing the minority psychology of the women. They scorn
other women, attempt to imitate men, and tend to believe in their

own inferiority. The men too believe the women inferior to them, whether the women are self-confident and challenge male power, or whether they acquiesce, seeking to appease male anger. The stereotypes do not exist solely among the characters in the plays, but appear also in the world outside the plays – in the criticism and productions. We read of Margaret's unwomanly strength, and of Richard's womanly guile. A recent critic describes the character's histrionic talents and sensitivity to people and atmosphere: 'His awareness of other people has, in the best Hitlerian manner, an almost *feminine* subtlety. The list of roles he assumes is endless'[18] (italics mine). On the basis of evidence within the plays, one might have expected a different conclusion. For – as well as Richard – York, Edward, Buckingham, and Warwick have been the supreme manipulators, men of guile, organizing behind the scenes and plotting insurrection. Misogyny persists.

Optimistically, Fuller recommends that women not be influenced by men because they fail to see the entire picture. She instructs women to look within themselves to find their own 'peculiar secret.' This means rejecting the stereotypes and accepting their own strengths. Margaret, struggling with the concept that strength is 'masculine', is vulnerable to the attack of 'unwomanliness'. Elizabeth, perhaps discovering her own 'peculiar secret', tries to establish a bond of friendship or support with the woman she had scorned. But learning to curse is hardly a start on the path to understanding that the stereotypes (for 'maleness' strength, courage, and initiative; and for 'femaleness' docility, passivity, and weakness) must be denied if women are to gain power, not over the lives of others, but over their own lives. Shakespeare dramatizes the reality that women cannot do this alone. These plays reveal the limited world that exists as long as people believe that power belongs to men and powerlessness to women, refusing to recognize 'the benefits . . . the world would gain by ceasing to make sex a disqualification for privileges and a badge of subjection'.[19]

SOURCE: Extract from *Wooing, Wedding, and Power: Women in Shakespeare's Plays* (New York, 1981), pp. 155–157, 192–207.

NOTES

(Renumbered and adapted by Editors.)

1. Kate Millett, *Sexual Politics* (New York, 1970), p. 25.

2. *Ibid.*, p. 56.

3. Throughout this essay 'the women in the tetralogy' are taken to be only Margaret, Eleanor, Elizabeth and Anne.

4. Margaret Fuller, *Woman in the Nineteenth Century* (1845. Reprint, New York, 1971), p. 63.

5. G. Bullough, ed., *Narrative and Dramatic Sources of Shakespeare* (London, 1957–1975), vol. 3, pp. 206–7.

6. See, for example, Mark Eccles, ed., *Richard III* (New York, 1964), p. xxiv.

7. Donald R. Shupe, 'The Wooing of Lady Anne', *Shakespeare Quarterly* 29 (1978), pp. 28–36.

8. August W. von Schlegel, *Dramatic Art and Literature, Lectures*, tr. J. Black (London, 1815), p. 437.

9. William Richardson, *Essays on Shakespeare's Dramatic Characters* (London, 1797), p. 18.

10. Georg G. Gervinus, *Shakespeare Commentaries*, tr. Fanny Bunnett (London, 1963), vol. 1, p. 377.

11. Colly Cibber, *The Tragical History of King Richard the Third* (in *Plays Written by Mr. Cibber*, vol. 1, London, 1721).

12. David Wheeler, dir. *Richard III*, Cort Theatre, New York, 1979.

13. [Samuel Phelps, actor and manager], *Richard III* (1845; New York Public Library *NCP.164551).

14. American Shakespeare Festival, *Richard III* (1964, Stratford, Connecticut; New York Public Library *NCP+1964).

15. Laurence Olivier and Alan Dent, *Richard III* (London Films, 1956).

16. Arthur Colby Sprague, *Shakespeare's Histories: Plays for the Stage* (London, 1964), p. 124.

17. Fuller, *op. cit.*, p. 176.

18. A. L. French, 'The World of *Richard III*', *Shakespeare Studies* 4 (1969), p. 37.

19. John Stuart Mill, in John Stuart Mill and Harriet Taylor Mill, *Essays on Sex Equality* (ed. Alice S. Rossi, Chicago, 1970), p. 236.

Peter Reynolds (1987) Acting *Richard III*

Anthony Sher's book *Year of the King*[1] describes his preparation for the central role in the Royal Shakespeare Company's 1984 production of *Richard III*.[2] The part of Richard Crookback has always been a magnet for leading actors and performances of Shakespeare's *Richard III* are usually discussed, not in the light of the director's reading of the text, but in terms of the star's display of talent.[3] The 1984 *Richard III* was directed by Bill Alexander, one of the RSC's established and well-respected directorial team. What lives in the memory, though, is not Alexander's production, but Sher's virtuoso performance as Richard.

In an age which is inclined to elevate the art of the director over the craft of the actor, it is good to have at least one classic play in the repertoire which is generally celebrated as an actor's, rather than a director's, play. But if the part of Richard is made the almost exclusive source of dramatic interest, if it is played by a star actor and if that actor is encouraged to use it as an opportunity for displaying his own skill and wit and personality, the result may be entertaining theatre but the entertainment is bought at the expense of other elements in the play's potential meaning.

What has happened, in fact, is that a dominant reading of *Richard III* has emerged. The nature of this reading is reflected in the fact that, in his famous 1955 film version, Laurence Olivier added to the opening soliloquy ten lines from Act III scene ii of *Henry VI Part Three*, carefully listing Richard's physical deformities. Sher wore an elaborate rubber hump, which he describes in its

Brilliant anatomical detail – the skin bunched at the twisted hip, the vertebrae straining through the surface as if trapped. A magnificent shape . . . (p. 189)

As well as wearing this, and displaying it naked in the coronation scene, Sher used a pair of crutches to propel himself at lightning speed around the stage. Both Olivier and Sher assumed that Richard's behaviour is caused by the fact that he is rejected by other people; a rejection based on an unfortunate accident of birth which has scarred him mentally as well as physically. In such a reading of the play Richard is *explained*: he is deformed by society, and the moral responsibility for his actions is at least partially transferred on to others. He is an outsider, a social outcast deserving as much of pity as of fear.

Again like Olivier, Sher further distanced his audience from the question of individual morality by adopting a presentational style designed to generate laughter. He explains in his book how he approached his role by observing physically disabled people and reading about mass killers like Denis Neilson and the so-called Yorkshire Ripper, Peter Sutcliffe. But despite what sounds like appropriate preparation for the enactment of the role in the style of psychological naturalism, what emerged in his performance was much closer to a caricature psychopath caught up in a black comedy.

Olivier and Sher's approach to the role typifies the dominant reading of the play, a reading which resists moral judgment. Such a reading is not necessarily wrong. There is clearly no *right* reading of a Shakespeare text. But there are other readings available. There is, for example, Margaret's reading when she calls Richard a toad and suggests that his deformity is the outward sign of an inner corruption (i.iii.246).[5]

If we examine the stagecraft of the wooing scene (Act i scene ii) we are provided with a clear illustration of the limiting theatrical conventions which have grown up around the part of Richard. Usually the leading actor sees this as the first opportunity to display his character's charisma and virility, for he must seduce Lady Anne against apparently insurmountable odds. Sher confessed that he had 'never seen it work' (p. 18). Olivier believed that, as written, the scene could not work and therefore cut it in two, inserting the earlier episode in which Clarence is led off to the Tower to await execution.[6] Both actors spoke the famous soliloquy which concludes the scene as an invitation to the audience to share in Richard's triumphant victory: the misshapen outsider had dared to risk all and had succeeded against overwhelming odds in winning the physically-perfect object of male desire, Lady Anne. Sher spoke the first two lines with a smug air of self-satisfaction, adding an extrapolated 'hmm':

> Was ever woman in this humour woo'd?
> Was ever woman in this humour won? Hmm.

> (i.ii.232–3)

Of course it brought the house down. But with it came a smoke-
screen of laughter.

All this presupposes a difficulty in persuading the audience that
Richard's seduction of Anne is psychologically credible. (Olivier had
actually chosen to exacerbate the problem of belief by making the
corpse on stage not that of her father-in-law, Henry VI, but that of
her husband, who had been slain by Richard.)[7] But, if it is seen in
a dramatic context that encompasses the whole of the action on
stage and does not focus exclusively on Richard, what happens to
Lady Anne can be credited without much difficulty. A reading quite
different from the dominant reading can be created in the theatre of
the mind's eyes if one animates Shakespeare's stagecraft and
considers carefully such factors of casting, silent characters and the
use of properties.

Olivier cast Claire Bloom in the role of Lady Anne. Claire Bloom
was not only beautiful but exuded self-confidence and maturity.
However, the more impressive the physical presence of the actress
herself the greater will be the difficulty for the audience in finding
her character's seduction believable. Of course, Olivier was a highly
successful young actor and film star and what he patently wanted
to emphasise in his production was Richard's ability as a lover.[8]
But the scene shows events at a funeral and people at a funeral are
emotionally vulnerable. They may well be in need and seeking
consolation where they can find it. If the actress playing Anne were
really young – say, fifteen or sixteen – and physically slight and not
especially beautiful (we have only Richard's evidence to indicate
her physical appearance, and he is hardly a reliable source), she
might be able to display and emphasise that vulnerability.

There are other actors in the scene. The corpse is carried onto
the stage by pall-bearers and guarded. There are also two characters
named by Lady Anne: Tressel and Berkeley. If all these roles are
cast with tall, powerfully-built male actors, then the performance
presents a contrasting spectacle between them and the only woman,
who is very young, diminutive, isolated and vulnerable. It is *her*
difficulty that this casting emphasises, not Richard's difficulty in
wooing her.

In the Folio text, Act I scene ii opens with the following stage
direction:

Enter the Coarse of Henrie the sixt, *with Halberds to guard it.* Lady Anne *being
the Mourner.*

Now, the corpse of the dead King (played, presumably, by an actor and not by a dummy) cannot walk onto the stage, and it will therefore need to be carried by at least six actors. The directions specify that the corpse is guarded; it therefore seems reasonable to suppose that those who carry the body are in no position to guard it, and that we therefore require another group of actors to enact the guard. The reader has to decide how many guards would guard the funeral procession of a dead King. Shakespeare may have been thinking of the historical evidence contained in Edward Hall's *The Union of the Noble and Illustre Famelies of Lancastre and York* (1548). In Hall's account, the funeral of Henry VI is described as a poor affair:

without Prieste or Clarke, Torche or Taper, syngyng or saiyng . . . (*The prosperous reign of Kyng Edward the fourthe* (fol. ccxxiii[r].)

Given this, and the relatively small numbers of actors employed by an Elizabethan company, plus the fact that Lady Anne is the only person present of high social standing, there are probably few guards present. Even so, a minimum of six halberds might be expected to guard the corpse. At the same time (although the opening stage direction does not refer to them) Tressel and Berkeley's presence can be inferred from the spoken text (i.ii.225). There are therefore at least sixteen actors on-stage at the beginning of the scene: six pall-bearers, six halberds, Tressel, Berkeley, Lady Anne and the body of Henry VI. When the actor playing Richard enters the scene the stage is crowded.[9]

Let us suppose the funeral procession to be formal and solemn. There is no music to accompany the entrance, and the very silence creates an air of expectation and concentration on this strange sight. Lady Anne leads the procession followed by Tressel and Berkeley and the corpse, which is held shoulder high and closely guarded. It is important to make clear to the audience that control and responsibility for these events lies with Lady Anne. She commands and directs the progress of the funeral of a dead King.

The corpse appears to be heavy, and the progress across the stage is slow. This gives time for the audience both to note the solemnity of the occasion, and also to register that the only woman on stage (the slight figure of Anne) is ordering events: this impression is confirmed when Anne begins to articulate the first spoken text of the scene with a command: 'Set down, set down your honourable load' (I.ii.1). As the body is referred to by Anne throughout the scene, and as she uses it as her only defence against the onslaught of Richard's rhetoric, its position on-stage is important. The corpse ought to be physically, as it is metaphorically, central to the action of what follows. The actor playing the corpse is one of the silent characters, but throughout the scene he generates a text that reminds the audience of what Richard has done in the very recent past and the nature of the occasion on which he has chosen to do his wooing. Furthermore, his lonely bleeding body prefigures the slaughter still to come.

At Anne's command to set down the corpse, Tressel and Berkeley and the bearers and guards may seem to become passive spectators. They are not, however, dramatically passive. They become an on-stage audience to Anne's formal lamentation for 'virtuous Lancaster' (I.ii.4). The presence of the fifteen men gives this lament a public quality, and as a public act, a required performance, it imposes on Anne the added responsibility of appropriate behaviour.

Up to, and including this lament, Lady Anne has been controlling the progress of the ritual surrounding death. Immediately Richard enters the stage (I.ii.32), he destabilises the situation. Her tenuous grasp is loosened and then lost, never to be regained. He takes over management of events, directing and manipulating them according to his own design. Even before Richard enters we can see that Anne is uncertain and tentative. She undermines her own authority by giving an order to the procession to go on, only to countermand it seconds later:

> Come now towards Chertsey with your holy load,
> Taken from Paul's to be interred there;
> And still, as you are weary of this weight,
> Rest you, while I lament King Henry's corse.
>
> (I.ii.29–32)

Richard's entry is well-timed, catching the bearers with the heavy corpse on their shoulders, and the guards uncertain whether to go on or stay. The whole procession has yet to regain its impetus and momentum. Richard may well have been observing events (visible to the audience, perhaps?) and awaiting his opportunity.[10] When he does intervene, the bearers are not sure what to do. Anne has told them to take up their holy load again and, even as they are in the

act of so doing, orders them to rest. Richard's opening line, 'Stay
you that bear the corse, and set it down' (I.ii.33), is spoken with
authority, seemingly intervening on Anne's behalf. It is as if Richard
has immediately taken over responsibility for the continuance of the
ritual process. Once this has demonstrably happened, Anne's control
of events is critically weakened, just as her self-control will be
undermined by Richard's subsequent actions.

The formality of the funeral ritual, where all concerned know
what to do and what to expect, instantly disappears with the arrival
of Richard, and Anne is denied the relative security and comfort
which comes from her participating in a scenario that is known and
familiar. Those who, together with her, were a part of that ritual,
and had specific supporting roles to play (the fourteen men who
accompany the corpse) are equally suddenly denied their roles, and
their collective purpose is replaced by individual uncertainty about
how to act. Instead of participants, they become merely observers.
As such, their presence onstage during the action which follows
should remind the audience in the theatre that collectively they have
the physical power to intervene, but lack the necessary will to do
so.

Richard now controls events through fear of what he might do,
rather than through what he actually does. For Anne the events
become one of those nightmares in which a victim cries out for help,
and though help is all around, no help materialises into action. Her
seduction is witnessed by two equally helpless sets of spectators –
those on-stage and those in the auditorium watching the play. Only
two lines in the whole scene are spoken by anyone other than
Richard and Lady Anne. Yet the significance of what the principals
say can be understood only if recognition is given to the text being
made by the silent, but far from inconsequential, characters on-
stage with them.

Towards the end of their exchange, Richard apparently takes an
immense risk when he offers Anne

> . . . this sharp-pointed sword,
> Which if thou please to hide in this true breast,
> And let the soul forth that adoreth thee,
> I lay it naked to the deadly stroke,
> And humbly beg the death upon my knee.
>   (I.ii.178–182)

He then proceeds to admit his guilt in the murder of Anne's father-
in-law and husband. Why then does she not immediately kill him?
In Olivier's film it was clearly supposed to be because she had
already fallen under the irresistible charm and power of this
'superman'. For Anne to seize the opportunity for revenge in the
circumstances I have previously outlined (she is observed, young,
vulnerable, isolated and a woman) is extremely hard, but perhaps
not beyond the bounds of possibility. What might prevent her from
attempting to kill Richard is the sword itself.

The only description of the weapon comes from Richard. At 1.
182 the stage direction seems to indicate that it is a sword belonging
to him (*'he lays his breast open, she offers at [it] with his sword'*). But
there is nothing in the dialogue to suggest that it actually belongs
to Richard. If the actor playing him were to move quickly and take
a weapon from the hands of the silent on-stage characters (say, from
Tressel or Berkeley), then it could justifiably be a heavy, even a
two-handed sword. Obviously there is a great deal of difference
between offering a young and slight girl a dagger, and giving her a
sword almost half as tall as herself. I have seen an Anne striking at
Richard with a dagger and being restrained by his pinning her arm
against the coffin. But encumbering her with a massive and
unfamiliar weapon of war places her in a frustrating and humiliating
posture, emphasising her helplessness rather than Richard's bravery.

It is, I suppose, a fact of theatrical life that actors do not relish
playing unsympathetic roles. But if we allow the shadow cast by a
great performance to obscure the full dramatic context prepared for
it by Shakespeare (a context which includes such elements as casting,
silent characters and properties) then the myth will continue that
Richard III is really only a likeable monster. However, if a director
chooses to make clear in this early scene that there is no physical
risk involved for Richard, and that his 'victory' is hollow because
the combatants were never remotely equal to start with (he has
molested a child at a funeral), then their subsequent reaction may
move beyond admiration for performances like those of Olivier and
Sher towards moral judgments about the actions of the character
himself and their effect on others.

SOURCE: Essay written for, and first published in this Casebook.

NOTES

1. *Year of the King: An Actor's Diary and Sketchbook* (London, 1985).
2. The play opened at Stratford-upon-Avon on 19th June 1984.
3. There is perhaps one recent and notable exception to this. In 1983, as part of the BBC Television Shakespeare series, Jane Howell directed the history cycle from *Henry VI Part One* through to *Richard III*. She used the same cast in all four plays and there were no 'star' names in her company. The perspective gained for *Richard III* by presenting the genesis of the bloody events, together with the unselfish performance of Ron Cook in the title role, made a production of the play that could, for once, be discussed in its totality and not simply as one man's performance.
4. In fact, Sher was not happy with the hump which Chris Tucker had made for him: it was half the size that he wanted. *Year of the King*, p. 190.
5. All quotations from the play are from *The Arden Shakespeare* edition, edited by Antony Hammond (London, 1981).
6. 'On the stage his hideous wooing of Lady Anne works brilliantly, but if it's too sudden on the screen the unaccustomed audience would cry, "Hold. We don't believe this!" So I cut the scene in two, let time pass. . . .' Laurence Olivier, *On Acting* (London, 1986) p. 206.
7. Almost forty years on Olivier was still apparently convinced that the text was as he had wished to see it: '. . . to be able to woo Lady Anne from hatred to acceptance in a five-minute scene is pure magic. There she is, on her way to bury her husband, whom Richard has killed, and he steps coolly in with, of all things, a proposal. The audacity is wonderful.' *On Acting*, p. 77.
8. He speaks retrospectively about wanting to 'woo and charm the audience with my devilish villainy, using close-up and long shot to devastating effect'. *On Acting*, p. 204.
9. Antony Hammond argues in the 1981 Arden edition of the play that the total number of actors, including Lady Anne, might have been as low as nine (note to I.ii opening S.D., pp. 135–6). This seems too few to me, but Anne is still heavily outnumbered by men.
10. In the 1984 production Sher was already on-stage, part of a 'little crowd' when the procession carrying the corpse entered. *Year of the King*, p. 161.

TITUS ANDRONICUS

Albert H. Tricomi   The Aesthetics
of Mutilation   (1961)

When T. S. Eliot so flamboyantly denounced *Titus Andronicus* as 'one
of the stupidest and most uninspired plays ever written', he naturally
invited rebuttal.[1] But while an apology for *Titus* can certainly be
erected, the fact is that the imputed stupidities of the tragedy attract
far more interest than any of its mediocre achievements. Indeed, if
we would only persist in the study of those very 'stupidities' that
many critics would rather forget, we would discover that the ways
in which the figurative language imitates the literal events of
plot make *The Tragedy of Titus Andronicus* a significant dramatic
experiment. In the play's spectacularly self-conscious images that
keep pointing at the inventive horrors in the plotting, in its wittily-
obsessive allusions to dismembered hands and heads, and in the
prophetic literalness of its metaphors, *Titus* reveals its peculiar
literary importance.

The peculiar language of *Titus Andronicus* is particularly apparent
in the literalness of its central metaphors. In a play preeminently
concerned with the mutilation of the human body, *Titus* makes
nearly sixty references, figurative as well as literal, to the word
'hands' and eighteen more to the word 'head', or to one of its
derivative forms.[2] Far from being divorced from the action as many
critics claim,[3] the figurative language points continually toward the
lurid events that govern the tragedy. The figurative language, in
fact, imitates the gruesome circumstances of the plot, thus revealing
that Shakespeare subordinates everything in *Titus*, including
metaphor, to that single task of conveying forcefully the Senecan
and Ovidian horrors that he has committed himself to portraying.

Such a relationship between language and event is really quite
strange. Ordinarily metaphor is endowed with the capacity of
extending almost infinitely the imaginative compass of a play.
Through its embedded metaphors especially, a play usually trans-

tes its immediate events in images that reach far beyond the poor limitations of the stage. In *Titus Andronicus*, however, metaphor, for the most part, draws its images directly from the narrower events of plot. It becomes literalized. This is a very daring and even dangerous enterprise to undertake. Deliberately relinquishing its natural prerogatives, metaphor strives instead to unite language and action in an endeavour to render the events of the tragedy more real and painful. When Marcus offers Titus the throne, for example, he employs a peculiar metaphor, saying, 'And help to set a head on headless Rome' (1.i.186). Since Titus is being offered the throne of Imperial Rome, Marcus's statement seems to be a happy one. As such, the metaphor appears to be just that, an embellished phrase, a polished, if affected, mode of speech. But, as it happens, this mere metaphor, with all its ominous overtones, is later raised to factual reality when Saturninus, ironically made that 'head' of Rome through Titus's support, beheads two of Titus's sons. In a more specific sense as well, the figures employed direct our perceptions toward isolated parts of the human body. When in the first act Lavinia asks her father to bless her, she uses the rather precise phrase, 'with thy victorious hand' (1.i.163), and Bassianus does likewise when he explains how Titus, 'With his own hand' slew his youngest son (1.i.418). In both instances the figurative phrasing points ahead to the mutilations of future events, to the shearing off of Lavinia's hands, and then, to Titus's willing sacrifice of his own hand when bargaining for the lives of two of his sons.

But while the keen critic may discover a rather brutal principle of retribution in Titus's loss of a hand for having killed – with his own hand – one of his sons, I am more concerned here with the oddly alluring relationship between language and event. Constantly pointing toward and underlining the events that we witness upon the stage, metaphor in this tragedy strains to keep the excruciating images of mutilation ever before our imaginations even when the visual spectacle is no longer before us. The words 'hand' and 'head' appear copiously as figures of speech whose effect is to saturate every aspect of the play with remembered or foreshadowed horror. Following the scene of Lavinia's mutilation, Marcus presents his niece to Titus whose first words to her,

> Speak, Lavinia, what accursed hand
> Hath made thee handless in thy father's sight?
> (III.i.66–7)

recreate the horrible event in the imagination. Of course, the literate response is so artificial as to invite derision, and, no doubt, the whole idea of asking the dumb to speak is a questionable way of inviting pathos. But the pun on hands, which is equally self-conscious and full of artifice, is not without its redeeming features. Titus's paronomasia rests on two notably dissimilar kinds of usage. When he refers to 'the accursed hand', he employs a simple form of synecdoche, but when he speaks of Lavinia's handlessness, he alludes to nothing but the visual reality before him. Furthermore, the paronomasia draws our attention to the image of the rapist using his hand in the act of shearing off Lavinia's own, effectively underlining, Hamlet-like, the 'unkindness' and unnaturalness of the act. So while we may argue that Titus's self-conscious word-play largely replaces genuine personal response, we must acknowledge that the bitter contrast between the mere metaphor and the experienced reality of Lavinia's handlessness is powerfully conceived.

This remark of Titus's illustrates one of the play's basic concerns – exploring the gulf between metaphoric descriptions of events and the irrefutable realities they purport to communicate. Shakespeare's interest in these matters, so abstract in its way, appears grounded, however, in the dramatist's involvement in the relative merits of words as contrasted with dramatic events. So concerned is the play with the deceptive powers of poetic description that it offers several instructive lessons contrasting the vacuous rhetoric of rape and the palpable reality of Lavinia's ravishment, hands lopped off, mouth bleeding. As the play opens, Saturninus, who has just announced his betrothal to Lavinia, finds that Bassianus has already married her and berates him in an exaggerated rhetorical outburst, saying, 'Thou and thy faction shall regret this rape' (i.i.404). Bassianus, sensitive to the proper signification of words, rejoins hotly,

> Rape call you it, my lord, to seize my own,
> My true-betrothed love. . . ?
>
> (i.i.405–6)

In this way the play continually investigates the chasm between the spoken word and the actual fact, an investigation, incidentally, whose meaning is fully experienced only when Lavinia appears before us raped and bleeding in fact. Similarly, this ironic denigration of metaphor occurs again when Lucius, hearing the villainous Aaron explain how,

> They cut thy sister's tongue and ravish'd her,
> And cut her hands and trimm'd her as thou sawest.
>
> (v.i.93)

seizes on the disgustingly prettified figure and retorts, 'O detestable
villain! call'st thou that trimming?' (v.i.93). Far from being used
inadvertently then, the language self-consciously focuses upon itself
so as to demonstrate the manner in which figurative speech can
diminish and even transform the actual horror of events. But since
the purpose of the tragedy is not to dilute but to highlight the
nightmare that befalls the Andronici, the play deliberately 'exposes'
the euphemisms of metaphor by measuring their falseness against
the irrefutable realities of dramatized events. On these occasions,
the play turns its back on metaphor, rejecting it as a device that
tends to dissipate the unremitting terrors of the tragedy. Only in
the literalization of its metaphors, it appears, does the tragedy seem
to be at ease with itself.

II

Such a self-consciously didactic use of metaphor is really quite
distinctive in Elizabethan drama, to say nothing of Elizabethan
tragedy, but far more strange is the deliberate constriction of the
figurative language as it binds itself to the gory plot. So firmly does
the figurative language yoke itself to the action of *Titus* that mere
rhetorical flourishes tend, prophetically, to realize themselves in
actual events. In the scene where Titus first bears witness to his
daughter's mutilation, for example, he expresses his grief, not
unexpectedly, in hyperbolic outburst,

> My grief was at the height before thou cam'st,
> . . . .
> Give me a sword, I'll chop off my hands too,
> For they have fought for Rome, and all in vain
>
> (iii.i.70–3)

To be sure, the unusual nature of the event goes far to justify the
strained pitch of the rhetoric, but the speech fully realizes its tragic
possibilities only in subsequent events. For while Titus begins by
speaking an exaggerated language of sorrow, Shakespeare forces his

hero to live up to the terrible potential of his hyperbolic outburst. Shylock-like, the dramatist takes Titus's speech out of the realm of mere rant and exacts of him the pound of flesh he promises. That is to say, the exaggeration of Titus's rhetorical figure is, through an act of the dramatist's imagination, realized in terms of a hyperbole of plot, which acts as if it were a figure of speech brought to monstrous birth. Thus, in a vain effort to save his two imprisoned sons, Titus renders up his hand to the ravenous Emperor of Rome. The words he speaks at the time explain precisely the bizarre relationship between language and events that typifies the method of the play. 'Come hither, Aaron. . . .' he says, 'Lend me thy hand, and I will give thee mine' (III.i. 186–7).

Since *The Tragedy of Titus Andronicus* is predicated on the notion that the most excruciating horrors pertain to the experienced reality of events, the metaphoric impact of the tragedy can only be realized by forcing the metaphors to take on dramatic life. Accordingly, hands become powerful dramatic symbols, not simply because they are mentioned sixty times in the text, but because they become *images in action* whose significance we experience visually and not merely verbally, in abstraction. Stated metaphorically, the most profound impulse in *Titus* is to make the word become flesh. That the literary symbolism of hands indeed becomes flesh is obvious, not only in Titus's hand-lopping scene, but also in the scene in which Titus's son Quintus offers to assist his brother Martius after the latter has fallen into a pit that the cunning Aaron has prepared. Trapped inside, Martius implores Quintus's aid, crying, 'O brother, help me with thy fainting hand' (II.iii.233), and Quintus in turn replies, 'Reach me thy hand, that I may help thee out' (II.iii.237). After his first effort fails, Quintus again underscores the dramatic significance of hands, saying,

> Thy hand once more; I will not loose again,
> Till thou art here aloft, or I below.
> Thou canst not come to me – I come to thee.
> [*Falls in.*]
>
> (II.iii.243–5)

Here the hands of Titus's kin, vainly stretched to help one another, epitomize a central tragic movement in the play. Symbols of Rome's defence, civic pride, and filial love, the hands of the Andronici are, in the aftermath of the Gothic war, rendered useless, not metaphorically, but literally.

Moreover, even while Quintus's allusion to hands attunes us to future events, his specific remark about 'loos[ing]' hands becomes, by virtue of the hand mutilations that are to follow, a visual, theatrical device for dramatizing the helplessness of the Andronici. Like Titus's witticism on Aaron's lending him a hand and like his imaginative question to Lavinia, 'What hand hath made thee handless. . . ,' Quintus's remark reveals again Shakespeare's unstinting exploration of the gap between a metaphoric use of language and a referential use of language anchored in the afflictions of actual events. Indeed, considering the contrast that exists between Quintus's fear of 'losing' his brother's outstretched hand and the actual lopping off of Lavinia's hands, which immediately follows this first event, we must admit that Shakespeare confers upon the ghoulish notion of losing hands, not one, but several literal meanings!

III

This unrelieved and, in truth, witty exploration of the relationship between language and event marks a notably disinterested, even detached, involvement in the values of language with respect to dramatic events. This cool distance between the playwright and his materials helps to explain one of the distinguishing features of *Titus Andronicus* – the odd way that this tragedy leaps with an inextinguishable wittiness toward the multiple perceptions that ordinarily belong to the world of intellectual comedy. From incidents like the one in which Titus asks his mute daughter to speak or like the one in which he wonders whether the Andronici should

> bite our tongues, and in dumb shows
> Pass the remainder of our hateful days
> (iii.i.131–2)

it becomes obvious that these gruesomely ironic perceptions are rooted in an irrepressible wittiness. This witty impulse expresses itself further in a hideously satanic atmosphere that permeates the unbelievable events of the tragedy, and the personification of this atmosphere is Aaron, whose satanic drollery is not unworthy of his spiritual brother, Richard Crookback. When the fiendish blackamoor instructs Tamora's oafish sons to ravish Lavinia in the woods, he

employs an evocatively poetic language that lasciviously focuses
upon the image of physical violation:

> The woods are ruthless, dreadful, deaf, and dull.
> There speak, and strike, brave boys, and take your turns;
> There serve your lust, shadowed from heaven's eye,
> And revel in Lavinia's treasury.
>
>   (ii.i.128–31)

The source of Aaron's wittiness, we find, emerges from the
deliberate exposure of the literal meanings that underlie our figurative use of language. The poetic decorum of the clause, 'And revel
in Lavinia's treasury' is savage in that it simultaneously creates, in
prurient delight, a literally-imagined picture of Lavinia's ravished
chastity at the moment of violation. Enveloped as it is in a dark
language of hushed expectancy, the picture creates an ugly beauty.
Like Iago and Richard III, Aaron relishes poetic language because
he can force it to serve the baser appetites, which is to say that
Aaron appropriates the beauties of language for foul purposes, rapes
it as it were, so that it may serve the literalness of his own coarse
imaginings.

This deliberate transformation of the beauties of lyrical poetry
into a house of horrible imaginings is, however, not just Aaron's,
but Shakespeare's, for in *Titus Andronicus* brutality, which is always
conceived with the utmost literalness of imagination, continually
parades in the parodic disguise of metaphoric loveliness. In the
scene where Titus rouses the court and bids them to join him in the
sport of hunting a proud panther, Demetrius declines the invitation,
saying to his brother,

> Chiron, we hunt not, we, with horse nor hound,
> But hope to pluck a dainty doe to ground
>   (ii.ii.25–6)

Expecting to use his time to rape Lavinia in the forest, Demetrius
riddles shallowly on the instrument with which he and his brother
will 'hunt' Lavinia. But the couplet is more than indecent; it is
brutal and obscene. The venereal suggestiveness of the hunt itself,
combined with the image of the 'pluck[ed]' doe being brought to
the ground, focuses with salacious relish on the anticipated act of
violation. Here again, the poetry, which seems at first to offer only
a metaphoric suggestion of Lavinia's rape, is in reality shackled –
through the salacious wit – to the literal ugliness of the rape itself.

Whatever we may think about the success of this use of figurative language, there is no escaping the fact that *Titus Andronicus* is, in the broadest sense of the term, a very witty play. It is, in fact, as witty in the circumstances of its plotting as it is in its exploitation of metaphor and in its evocation of atmosphere. The two outstanding cases in point occur in the hand-lopping scene in the third act and in the special technique Lavinia uses to reveal her assailants in Act IV. The former instance comes about when Aaron convinces Titus to cut off his right hand as ransom for his two sons imprisoned by the Emperor. Throughout the scene Aaron displays an odd kind of detached artistry, a lunatic humor. After Aaron chops off Titus's hand, he commends the old warrior, saying,

> for thy hand
> Look by and by to have thy sons with thee
> [*Aside.*]   Their heads, I mean.
>   (III.i.201–3)

A crude joke indeed. In a play filled with the devices of metonymy and synecdoche, especially on the subject of the human body, Aaron employs the same device with respect to the action. Metaphorically speaking, Aaron does engineer the return of Titus's sons in that he returns the part for the whole. Like a literary artist Aaron has created an act of synecdoche. For the two sons he has returned a metaphor!

This irrepressible wit of plotting is, however, only partly explicable as an expression of Aaron's personality, which in some important measure derives from the ingenious vice figures of the medieval moralities. The wit of plot is, finally, much larger than Aaron's; it is Shakespeare's, and it is worth noting that the scene most universally scorned for its ludicrous flight of lyric poetry, the one in II, iv, where Marcus first spies the ravished Lavinia wandering in the woods, keeps pointing to its own achievements in rendering Ovid's pathetic tale of Tereus's rape of Philomel even more pathetic:

> *Marcus:* Fair Philomel, why, she but lost her tongue,
>   And in a tedious sampler sew'd her mind;
>   But, lovely niece, that mean is cut from thee.
>   A craftier Tereus, cousin, hast thou met,
>   And he hath cut those pretty fingers off
>   That could have better sew'd than Philomel.
>   (II.iv.38–43)

The explicit allusions to Ovid's tale invite comparison. That 'craftier Tereus' Marcus speaks of is really Will Shakespeare laying claim to having out-witted the Roman poet in the telling of a tale. In *Titus* the young playwright even invites the audience to ponder how Lavinia, his heroine, unable to 'sew her mind' as Ovid's Philomel did, will be able to reveal her ravisher's identity. Lavinia's rapists, unschooled as they are, make quite a bit of the problem they have raised:

> *Chiron:* [to Lavinia] Write down thy mind, bewray thy meaning so,
> And if thy stumps will let thee play the scribe.
> *Demetrius:*   See how with signs and tokens she can scrowl.
>   (II.iv.3–5)

But if the shearing off of Lavinia's hands raises a kind of suspense because we are uncertain how she will be able to expose her assailants, the solution to this puzzle is that much more unexpected and original than Ovid's. In having Lavinia scrawl out the names of her ravishers by holding a pole between her stumps and grasping the pole's end inside her mouth, Shakespeare effects a most witty poetic justice. Lavinia's lips do speak; her handless hands, indeed, do write![4]

IV

In this witty competition with Ovid and Seneca, Shakespeare is just what Greene said he was, 'an upstart Crow' striving to overreach his masters in their own vein.[5] In *Titus* the especial competition with Ovid fully insinuates itself into Shakespeare's poetic statement and is one of the basic reasons why the tragedy sometimes runs aground on the shoals of Ovidian lyricism. As Eugene Waith points out, the play apparently fails to transpose a narrative tale of horror into a convincing dramatic story.[6] The characters, he observes, respond to events with poetic declamations that lack psychological appropriateness or verisimilitude. Yet, the problem is not one of dramatic ineptitude, pure and simple. The scenes derived from Ovid's story are confidently aware of their transposed existence in the added dimension of drama.[7] When Titus first beholds his ravished daughter, he laments,

> Had I but seen thy picture in this plight
> It would have madded me; what shall I do
> Now I behold thy lively body so?
>
> (III.i.103–5)

So too, when Marcus first spies the mutilated Lavinia wandering in
the woods, his monologue effectively underlines the dramatic mode
of Shakespeare's story:

> *Marcus:* Cousin, a word;
> . . . .
> Speak, gentle niece. . . .
> Why dost not speak to me?
> . . . .
> Shall I speak for thee? Shall I say 'tis so?
>
> (II.iv.12–33)

That the anticipated dialogue is denied Marcus only emphasizes
how effectively Shakespeare has exploited the visual resources of
drama. Moreover, inasmuch as dialogue is necessarily impossible
in this episode, Shakespeare casts the greater focus upon the visual
spectacle of the mutilated Lavinia. Through Marcus who acts as
commentator on the event, Shakespeare forces us to see, detail by
descriptive detail, the spectacle that we are already beholding:

> Speak, gentle niece, what stern ungentle hands
> Hath lopp'd and hew'd and made thy body bare
> Of her two branches. . . ?
> . . . .
> Alas, a crimson river of warm blood,
> Like to a bubbling fountain stirr'd with wind,
> Doth rise and fall between thy rosed lips,
> Coming and going with thy honey breath.
> But, sure, some Tereus hath deflow'red thee,
> And, lest thou should'st detect him, cut thy tongue.
> Ah, now thou turn'st away thy face for shame!
> And, notwithstanding all this loss of blood. . . .
>
> (II.iv.16–29)

Clearly enough, the visual image is intended to be so powerfully
immediate that the characters themselves believe the image of
Lavinia must be imaginary. Among Marcus's first words in the
above speech are, 'If I do dream, would all my wealth would wake
me' (II.iv.13). Later, Titus complains, 'When will this fearful slumber
have an end?' (III.i.252). The fact that the characters often react to

the play's events as if they had been transported into another realm altogether demonstrates Shakespeare's endeavor to reach the utmost verge of realizable horror. By utilizing Ovid's already affecting narrative in a theatrical context that exploits Lavinia's presence upon the stage, Shakespeare reaches to outdo the Roman poet for pathos, and Seneca as well for horror.

But despite the resourcefulness of this theater of horrors, there are unavoidable limits in *Titus Andronicus* to dramatic spectacle. For all the severed heads, for all the poignance of Lavinia's mutilated beauty, the one horror the dramatist could not depict upon the stage was the fact of Lavinia's violated chastity, which loss was to Titus the worst violation of all,

> that more dear
> Than hands or tongue, her spotless chastity
> (v.ii.176–7)

In overcoming this necessary limitation, however, Shakespeare chooses to identify Lavinia's violation with the violation of Rome and of all civilized value. It is upon this enlarged conception of violation – Lavinia's and Rome's – that Shakespeare docs confer visual life by introducing the enduring the theatrical symbol of the middle acts, the pit. As Tamora's premonitory speech indicates –

> And when they show'd me this abhorred pit,
> They told me, here, at dead time of the night,
> A thousand fiends, a thousand hissing snakes,
> Ten thousand swelling toads, as many urchins,
> Would make such fearful and confused cries,
> As any mortal body hearing it
> Should straight fall mad, or else die suddenly
> (ii.iii.98–104)

– the pit symbolizes an inferno of evil and is directly associated, as Professor Hamilton has shown, with the classical underworld.[8] The demonic portentousness of the pit is further highlighted by Lavinia's own ironic protestations, made before her captors. Fearing rape, she begs of Tamora,

> one thing more
> That womanhood denies my tongue to tell:
> O, keep me from their worse than killing lust,
> And tumble me into some loathsome pit.
> (ii.iii.173–6)

Speaking a language of chaste circumlocution, Lavinia asks to die rather than to be sexually defiled, but her inadvertent pun upon the word 'tumble', meaning, as Eric Partridge records, 'To copulate with (girl or woman), to cause to *fall backward*,'[9] ironically prophesies the circumstances of her later violation. Just ten lines later Lavinia is dragged off the stage to her rape, and the pit, just alluded to, becomes the central image upon the stage.

In the passage immediately following, Bassianus's bloody corpse is heaved into the pit and Lavinia's brothers, Martius and Quintus, deceived by the cunning Aaron, become entrapped within it. Already depicted vividly by Tamora as an abyss in which a world of evil spawns, the pit is now described as a womb, malignant and devouring.[10] Pictured by Quintus and Martius as 'this unhallow'd and blood-stained hole' (II.iii.210), then as a

> fell, devouring receptacle,
> As hateful as Cocytus' misty mouth
> (II.iii.235–6)

and, finally, as

> the swallowing womb
> Of this deep pit
> (II.iii.239–40)

the pit reveals the dark recesses of evil and also carries at least a suggestive reminder of the rape of Lavinia that is simultaneously transpiring off-stage. Moreover, with Bassianus's blood upon it, his body within, and the two entrapped Andronici accused of his murder trapped inside, the pit – that is, the trap door at the front of the Elizabethan stage – becomes not only a symbol of the demonic power, but a theatrical embodiment of it. Grotesque then as the image appears, the pit creates, by virtue of its visibility and concreteness as a device of theater, a powerful and synthesizing poetic image of the horrible fecundity of evil.

This éclat in exploiting the resources of the stage is just what we should expect from a wit-enchanted and ambitious poet who has lately discovered the wider world of theater. Just as the young Shakespeare endeavors to out-plot Plautus in *The Comedy of Errors* by doubling the number of identical twins, and just as he tries to out-marvel Marlowe by creating in *Richard III* a villain more joyous in the performance of evil than Barabas, so in *Titus Andronicus*

Shakespeare seeks to outdo both Seneca and Ovid by utilizing his living stage in the telling of a tale more horrifying and pathetic than that of either of his models.[11] Small wonder that the characters in this earliest of Shakespeare's tragedies appear to participate actively in the dramatist's own ambitious search for ever more fabulous events:

> *Titus:* . . . shall we cut away our hands like thine?
> Or shall we bite our tongues, and in dumb shows
> Pass the remainder of our hateful days?
> What shall we do? let us that have our tongues
> Plot some device of further misery,
> To make us wonder'd at in time to come.
>
> (iii.i.130–5)

Whatever our final aesthetic judgment concerning the merits of *Titus Andronicus*, we must understand that we are dealing, not with a paucity of imagination, but with an excess of dramatic witness, with a talent untamed. However flawed the tragedy may be in other respects, we must grant that the playwright has exploited the language of the stage with inventive brilliance and has taxed the resources of drama in making death and mutilation vivid to us.

If we wish, we can, of course, treat this tragedy with orthodox sobriety in order to demonstrate its thematic integrity, but the real vitality and interest of *Titus Andronicus* lies, it seems to me, in just those parts that are in some ways speculative, or even impossible dramatically. By shackling the metaphoric imagination to the literal reality of the play's events, the tragedy strives for an unrelieved concentration of horrific effect. Through its prophetic allusions to physical dismemberment, its incurably literalized figures of speech, and its ambitious use of the stage as a dramatic metaphor, *Titus Andronicus* strives to exhaust the language as well as the events of tragedy. We do not all have to like the tragedy, but we ought to recognize that *Titus* is a uniquely important experiment in drama, for in it Shakespeare is exploring the resources inherent in a referential use of metaphor and is trying to integrate the power of the poetic language with the immeasurable potential of dramatic action itself.

SOURCE: 'The Aesthetics of Mutilation in *Titus Andronicus*', *Shakespeare Survey 27* (Cambridge, 1974), pp. 11–19.

NOTES

1. *Selected Essays: 1917–1932* (London, 1932), p. 82. Effective rebuttal has occurred with relative infrequency.

2. Laura Jepsen, 'A Footnote on "Hands" in Shakespeare's *Titus Andronicus*', *Florida State Univ. Studies*, xix (1955), 7–10; *Oxford Shakespeare Concordance: Titus Andronicus* (Oxford, 1972), pp. 95–6, 99.

3. The works of Muriel Bradbrook, *Themes and Conventions of Elizabethan Tragedy* (Cambridge, Eng., 1935), pp. 98–9, and *Shakespeare and Elizabethan Poetry* (New York, 1952), pp. 104–10; J. Dover Wilson (ed.), *Titus Andronicus* (Cambridge, Eng., 1948), pp. ix–xii; and Wolfgang Clemen, *The Development of Shakespeare's Imagery* (New York, 1951), pp. 22–7, have provided deservedly influential insights into the discontinuity between image and occasion in *Titus Androniucs*, but the sense in which the figurative language embodies the events in *Titus* has never been analysed. An explanation of the decorous tone of the poetry in *Titus* can, however, be found in Eugene Waith's essay, 'Metamorphosis of Violence in *Titus Andronicus*', *Shakespeare Survey 10* (Cambridge, 1957), pp. 39, 49.

4. Although Shakespeare courts comparison with Ovid, he makes no effort to disclose his own native sources. The story of Lavinia's scribbling the names of her assailants by the use of her two stumps occurs in a prose narrative, which in all probability Shakespeare knew. The convincing evidence is set forth by Ralph M. Sargent, 'The Source of *Titus Andronicus*', *Studies in Philology*, xlvi (1949), 167–84. The prose narrative itself is reprinted by Sylvan Barnet (ed.), *The Tragedy of Titus Andronicus* (New York, 1963), pp. 135–48. See also, Geoffrey Bullough (ed.), *Narrative and Dramatic Sources of Shakespeare* (New York, 1966), vi.7–13. The witty justice that emerges from Lavinia's using her stumps *and her mouth* to reveal her rapists is, however, Shakespeare's own invention.

5. G. B. Harrison (ed.). *Robert Greene, M.A.: Groats-Worth of Witte* (1592; New York, 1966), p. 45. Although the context in which the phrase appears shows that Greene was thinking of Shakespeare as actor as well as playwright, the colourful phrase aptly captures the ambitiousness that is evident in the writing of *Titus Andronicus*.

6. 'Metamorphosis of Violence', pp. 47–8.

7. A. C. Hamilton, *The Early Shakespeare* (San Marino, 1967), pp. 68–9.

8. *Ibid.*, pp. 69–72.

9. *Shakespeare's Bawdy* (1947; rpt., London, 1961), p. 210.

10. This association is characteristically Shakespearian. Most strikingly, it appears again in *King Lear* (Kenneth Muir (ed.), London, 1959), where Lear imagines the female sexual organs as the pit of hell:

> Down from the waist they are Centaurs,
> Though women all above:
> But to the girdle do the Gods inherit,
> Beneath is all the fiend's: there's hell, there's darkness,
> There is the sulphurous pit – burning, scalding,
> Stench, consumption, fie, fie, fie! pah, pah!
>
> (iv.vi.123–8)

11. For a close analysis of the influence of these models, see Bullough (ed.), *Narrative and Dramatic Sources*, VI.23–33.

G. K. Hunter   Shakespeare's Earliest Tragedies: *Titus Andronicus* and *Romeo and Juliet*   (1974)

It is a clear critical fact that these plays are not normally considered together, or even apart, in a description of Shakespearean Tragedy. Shakespeare, it is implied, had to throw away this dispersed prentice work, set it against experience rather than achievement, when he began to compose the sequence of truly 'Shakespearean' tragedies beginning with *Julius Ceasar* and growing out of the political interests of the English history plays.

These pre-judgements bear more heavily against *Titus Andronicus* than *Romeo and Juliet*, for *Romeo* has, whatever its generic implication, the refuge of being a 'well-loved' play, where *Titus* can only be called 'much disliked'. I begin, however, by assuming an equality of interest and importance, taking it that in both plays Shakespeare was writing as well as he knew how. The subsequent reputations of the plays may be thought to tell us more securely about audience preferences in the period between Shakespeare and the present than about the author's intention. My concern in this paper is not with differences of valuation but with the formal similarities and relationships that can be established between the two tragedies.

In making this point I am not, of course, forgetting that *Titus* is the most horrific of Shakespeare's tragedies. To some minds this implies that it is exceptional and that its evidence about Shakespeare's tragic mode is out of court. The idea that true tragedy is essentially about the mental suffering of noble natures, and therefore unbloody, is, however, probably a delusion, based on the social assumptions of a post-Enlightenment society which has shown itself incapable of writing tragedy. The Victorian sub-genre, 'the tragedy of blood', invented to deal with plays like *Titus Andronicus*, offers us, in fact, only a pointless tautology: the *Oedipus Rex*, *The Bacchae*, *King*

Lear, *The Duchess of Malfi*, are all blood-spattered and horrific; but who would be so bold as to confine such plays to a sub-genre?

That Shakespeare when he wrote *Titus* was under the influence of classical examplars must also be allowed; but this does not mean that his mind can be cleared of responsibility for it. Shakespeare was no doubt like other artists, and achieved his own voice by working through aesthetic enthusiasms and derivative exercises, and in this *Titus* is no different from other early plays. Like *Lucrece* and its comic counterpart, *Venus and Adonis*, *Titus Andronicus* is deeply indebted to Ovid's sense of human mutability, the frailty of man's happiness and of his capacity for reason. In a similar way *The Comedy of Errors* is indebted to Plautus, *The Taming of the Shrew* to Italianate comedy, *Romeo and Juliet* to the atmosphere and conventions of the Italian novella. The real difference between *Titus Andronicus* and *Romeo and Juliet* seems to emerge not from the derivativeness of the one and the originality of the other, but from the different implications of the genres used. If *Titus* is exceptional among Shakespeare's tragedies in its devotion to a hysterically bleak view of human potential, *Romeo* is exceptional also, in its general sunniness, its closeness to comedy. It is, of course, particularly close to the kind of comedy that Shakespeare was writing in these years, 'Italian', courtly, exploring the romantic sensibilities of well-bred youth. It goes without saying that we are the better able to understand *Romeo and Juliet* because we know these cognate comedies.

The distinction I have so far made between the two plays suggests that Shakespeare's first move in tragedy was to seek to delimit the space within which he could operate, marking out the extreme polarities of his tragic range. He was never again to pursue the image of man's bestiality with the single-mindedness he showed in *Titus*. And likewise he was never, after *Romeo*, to write another tragedy which was so clearly a diversion by malign fate of materials that would normally form the basis of comedy. From time to time hereafter he will, of course, come close to one pole or the other, but always in a manner which invokes the presence of its opposite. *King Lear*, for example, can be regarded as in some ways a reworking of themes from *Titus Andronicus*. We have the same grieved and deprived father, hounded from dignity into madness by a malignant group whose authority comes from his gift, and rescued in the end by a foreign invasion led by his loyal child. We have the same pervading image of man as a beast of prey, the same contrast between extremes of female rapacity and female innocence, the same overlapping of lust and political ambition. But the role of the family in society is very different in the two plays. In both, the good and evil quickly sort themselves out as opposing forces. In *Titus* the social gap between the two groups is what is emphasised: on the one hand we have the barbarian outsiders, on the other the Andronici, the pious Roman family. In *Lear*, however, the opposition of good and bad emerges from the matrix of a single family. Among the sufferings of Titus the fact that Saturninus betrayed the favour he received does not bulk large; but for Lear the ingratitude of the daughters is the central agony. Thus the social rituals through which the conflict is expressed in *Titus* (feasting, family reading, the birth of a child, etc.) must give way in *Lear* to more unstructured domestic confrontations, and in these the side of Shakespeare's tragic vision represented by *Romeo* re-emerges. Something of Old Capulet's irascible absurdity survives into the very different world of Lear and his daughters.

Not only in *Lear* but throughout Shakespeare's mature tragedies the ritual of *Titus* is complemented by the domesticity of *Romeo*, the hieratic flanked by the familiar. Shakespeare achieves his later tragic centrality not only by diluting the unreality of *Titus* but also by making more remote and overpowering the cosinesses of Verona. Among the later tragedies *Antony and Cleopatra* is probably the one that most closely resembles *Romeo and Juliet*: in both plays the poetic power is centrally involved in projecting the love emotions of a socially significant couple, whose relationship defies the prevailing political and ethical assumptions of their society. Both are plays whose minor characters (Nurse, Mercutio, Enobarbus, Charmian, Alexis) are much given to comic routines. The lovers are finally united by quasi-sacrificial deaths; their deaths open the way to a unification of their society; and they are memorialised by joint tombs of exemplary splendour. But *Antony and Cleopatra*, in spite of its high comedy, does not in any sense give us a comic world wrenched by fate to a tragic conclusion. The characters are not like us; they are colossuses, and their laughter shakes the world. Here there is no private sphere into which lovers can escape from the pressures of other men's expectations. The love gestures of Antony and Cleopatra, all made in the world's eye, have to have the ritual quality of great public occasions. Their quarrels mirror the clash of alternative moral systems, Roman severity and barbarian self-indulgence. And in these respects the play may be seen to be closer to *Titus Andronicus*, or at least to the pole of tragedy it represents, than to *Romeo and Juliet*.

I have been arguing for a relationship between *Titus Andronicus* and *Romeo and Juliet* and between these two and the rest of Shakespeare's tragedies in terms of the polar characteristics of tragedy they exhibit. But *Titus Andronicus* and *Romeo and Juliet* are not related only as opposites. As one might expect with a playwright finding his way into his craft, similar structural skeletons serve for both plays, though the flesh hung on top of them is very different. We may note how the two plays open:

Flourish. Enter the Tribunes and Senators aloft; and then enter below Saturninus and his followers at one door, and Bassianus and his followers at the other, with drums and trumpets.

The scene that follows fleshes out the diagram thus established: first Saturninus (the elder) speaks, claiming his right to the crown, derived from primogeniture; then Bassianus (the younger) repeats the speech claiming the crown as his right, derived from election. Then

Enter Marcus Andronicus aloft, with the crown.

Marcus tells us that the *populus Romanus* has chosen Titus Andronicus as its representative to take to himself the issue being contested. The contenders then leave the stage to allow Titus to enter in his *triumphus*.

The opening diagram of the forces in *Romeo and Juliet* is extraordinarily similar:

Enter [at one door] Sampson and Gregory, of the house of Capulet . . . Enter [at the other door] two other Servingmen, Abraham and Balthazar [of the house of Montague] . . . Enter [at one door] Benvolio [a nobleman of the house of Capulet] . . . Enter Tybalt [a nobleman of the house of Montague] . . . [they fight] . . . Enter an Officer and three or four citizens . . . Enter [at one door] Old Capulet . . . and his wife . . . Enter [at the other door] Old Montague and his wife . . . Enter [? above] Prince Escalus with his Train.

In both plays the opening movement establishes discord against rule. The formalised stage-pictures set one competitor for power against another, the greater social range of the representatives of faction in *Romeo and Juliet* measuring the variety of social experience that play will draw on, the more concentrated concern with political power in *Titus Andronicus* marking that play's range of significant action. In both cases power is denied to the competitors. A central justice in the possession of power is demonstrated, and the establishment of this central authority over the brawling factions leads to their departure from the stage at the end of this dramatic phrase or movement.

In both tragedies, however, the remedy for discord which this opening diagram displays is a matter for display rather than acceptance. The failures to accept are, of course, very different. In *Romeo and Juliet* the Prince remains throughout the action an objective and unsubverted guarantor of order. The discord that persists is, in political terms, a hole-and-corner affair, dealt with by easy penalties. In *Titus Andronicus*, however, the supreme authorities of the opening, Marcus and Titus Andronicus, the representatives of the citizens and of the army, quickly lose their central position *aloft*. Titus is soon self-subverted and then hounded into grotesque subservience and madness. Astraea leaves the country; justice and order cease to have a political dimension. The movement by which moral order vanishes from Rome is, of course, without parallel in *Romeo and Juliet*. But the process by which Titus, in his wrong-headed and high-principled choice of Saturninus, his abject surrender of all rights to the new Emperor, falls from arbiter to suppliant does not end by breaking the parallel with *Romeo*. It ends, in fact, by re-forming the opening diagram of strife into a more stable and more exactly parallel shape.

The central conflict of *Titus Andronicus* stabilises itself as the story of two family groupings, whose conflict destroys (or threatens to destroy) the civilisation represented by the city. The opening chorus of *Romeo and Juliet* can easily be adapted to fit the other play:

> Two households, both alike in dignity,
> In Rome's fair city, where we lay our scene,
> From early grudge break to new mutiny,
> Where civil blood makes civil hands unclean.

It must be confessed, of course, that the 'two households' of *Titus* are less obvious than those of *Romeo*. By the middle of Act II, however, it is clear that the action is going to hinge on the conflict between the Andronicus family and that alternative 'household' of Saturninus/Tamora/Aaron with Tamora's assorted children, Chiron

and Demetrius (later joined by the black baby). That this latter
grouping can only be called a 'family' by a radically deformed
definition does not reduce the significance of the parallel; indeed it
strengthens it. The family ties of the Andronici suggest the strength
of the family unit as the basis of all social order, and particularly
that of Rome, demonstrating loyalty, mutual support and above all
pietas, drawing on the dutifulness of the past to secure the dutifulness
of the future. The household of husband, lover and assorted children
that clusters round Tamora suggests the opposite: a dreadful
burgeoning of uncontrolled nature into a rank and unweeded plot,
where parental love cannot compensate for the various disorders
and mismatings that result. Within a short time we are shown the
wife over-ruling the husband, the mismating of Emperor and enemy,
of Empress and slave, of white and black, the mother encouraging
the sons to rape and murder, the brothers ready to kill one another
until reduced to 'order' by the black lover (acting as surrogate
father). Finally we have the black baby itself 'as loathsome as a
toad', the complete image of instinctual wickedness.

   In the two plays the conflicts of the households are handled, of
course, in very different terms. In *Romeo and Juliet* the conflict between
Montagues and Capulets has little political reality. It exists to
maintain a certain pressure on what the play presents as more real –
the personal emotions of the two lovers. In *Romeo and Juliet* evil exists
only in so far as the traditional conflict exists. It is not presented as
a facet of the normal human will (even in the case of Tybalt);
stability and concord are always possible, as a result of spontaneous
human action, and we are always aware that peace is only a hand's
breadth away. The narrow distance between tragedy and comedy
is of course one of the principal effects of the play. But in *Titus* the
political conflict remains central and cannot possibly be evaded. It
arises from the fact of being human, from the need to resist
destruction, the imposition of chaos, the reduction of civilisation to
appetite and man to beast, all of which here grows out of a personal
will to evil, deeply implanted in human nature, and requiring for
its neutralization every energy and every resource available in the
play. Here no aspect of life can be thought of as merely personal
and private, and so exempted from the struggle. The loves of Aaron
and Tamora, the rape of Lavinia, are political as well as moral
offences. There is no Duke to intervene; the conflict is not simply a
relic of past bitternesses, but a monstrous burgeoning of manic

energies; death or flight are the only alternatives to absorption into the system.

And in the end, flight is not possible either. The world of the play demands a return to the scene of the struggle. This is equally true of both tragedies: the two plays are (uniquely among Shakespeare's tragedies) tales whose significance is expressed in terms of single cities, though *Rome* has, of course, a very different civic resonance from *Verona*. Verona suggests to us when we hear that it is in 'fair Verona, where we lay our scene' the anticipation of Italian passions, Italian family honour, the hot blood stirring in the sun, balconies, friars, domestic luxury and homely social display, a cosy familiarity of masters and servants, a world poised between the bourgeois and the aristocratic; though we must try to beware of finding in the play an 'Italianism' which entered English literature through *Romeo and Juliet*. Rome on the other hand suggests *ab initio* a military civilisation, severity, self-conscious masculinity, stoical self-denial, the inexorable rule of law – the collection of ethical icons that long dominated the European sense of culture: Horatius defending the bridge, Mutius Scevola burning off his right hand, Regulus returning to Carthage, Lucretia preferring death to dishonour, Manlius Torquatus killing his son for disobedience, etc., etc.

It appears in consequence that the two cities are well chosen by Shakespeare as points of focus, for a love story on the one hand, and on the other hand for a story of civilisation and its enemies, concerned with fortitude and brutality. In both plays the city walls measure the limit of the ordered world.

> There is no world without Verona walls

says Romeo with what might seem merely adolescent exaggeration; but the exaggeration is in fact quite close to truth. Meaning does not exist for the play outside Verona; the only non-Veronese of whom we hear is the Apothecary, who is death's emissary:

> Famine is in thy cheeks,
> Need and oppression starveth in thy eyes,
> Contempt and beggary hangs upon thy back,
> The world is not thy friend, nor the world's law . . .
> (v.i.69–72)

The balance of love and hate, of personal life and public reputation, the context within which meaning exists – this can be found only in Verona.

In *Titus*, very similarly, the play's meaning can only be brought to focus inside the walls of its city. Of course the focus is very different, the city being so different. We are here concerned with self-sacrifice and self-indulgence, rule and disobedience, with suffering and cruelty, with the destructive will to chaos, set against personal commitment to justice as the only meaningful basis for society. Only in Rome, it is implied, can the victory of cosmos or chaos be fully significant; Rome is seen as the hub of things, where final decisions are made and known to be final. That is why at the end of the play:

> As for that ravenous tiger, Tamora,
> No funeral rite, nor man in mourning weed,
> No mournful bell shall ring her burial;
> But throw her forth to beasts and birds to prey.
> (v. iii. 195–8)

Rome is here finally returned to the status appropriate to it, a status it has seemed to lose in the course of the action, when the city came to seem no different from the barbarism outside. When, as Titus tells us,

> Rome is but a wilderness of tigers,

when Lucius has to flee to the Goths to raise an army 'to be revenged on Rome and Saturnine', Rome clearly has forgotten how to be Rome. It takes a political convulsion and a blood-bath to re-establish the city as different from the wilderness of tigers. In the meantime Titus is required to carry the role of Rome's speaking conscience, when Rome cannot speak for herself. Where is Astraea gone? Why do the gods not answer, or not listen? Such questions keep continuously before our minds a sense of meaning in the city which is elsewhere out of sight. Meaning cannot be given to the world again, it is implied, till the mind of Rome and the mind of Titus are at one, when Moors and Goths know their place outside the walls and Roman *severitas* rules all within.

The only locale established in *Titus Andronicus* outside the walls of Rome is the forest of Act II where the major crimes are committed.

It is to be noticed that those who are at home and effective here are
Aaron and Tamora, Chiron and Demetrius. For Tamora everything
in the forest 'doth make a gleeful boast':

> The snakes lie rolled in the cheerful sun;
> The green leaves quiver with the cooling wind
> And make a chequer'd shadow on the ground;
> Under their sweet shade, Aaron, let us sit . . .
> (II. iii. 13–16)

For Lavinia, however, the forest scene is, like Aaron, dark and evil:

> let her joy her raven-coloured love;
> This valley fits the purpose passing well.
> (II. iii. 83–4)

Aaron is skilful in the use of forest pits and stratagems; his energy
sprouts at the thought of them. The young Andronici, however,
grow uncertain and dim of sight:

> *Quintus:* My sight is very dull, whate'er it bodes.
> *Martius:* And mine, I promise you; were it not for shame,
> Well could I leave our sport to sleep awhile.
>
> . . .
>
> *Quintus:* I am surprised with an uncouth fear;
> A chilling sweat o'er-runs my trembling joints;
> My heart suspects more than mine eye can see.
> (II. iii. 195–7, 211–13)

Within the dim light of the forest meanings change at the whim of
the observer; this is no place for the hard clear minds of the
Andronici. It is, however, a natural context for Tamora's Gothic
deceptions and shifts of role. At one point the forest is for her, as
noted above, a place of love and repose. It is also Tamora, however,
who expresses most eloquently the idea of the forest as a place of
horror – without even the excuse that it is 'another part of the
forest':

> A barren detested vale you see it is:
> The trees, though summer, yet forlorn and lean,
> Overcome with moss and baleful mistletoe;
> Here never shines the sun; here nothing breeds,
> Unless the nightly owl or fatal raven.
> (II. iii. 93–7)

This description, like the previous one designed to encourage Aaron
to acts of love, is, of course, not organised as a scientific account of
a place actually there, but presents a rhetorical backdrop, appropriate in this case to murder, rape and mutilation. When Titus asks
for 'proof' that his sons performed the murder he brings a Roman
attachment to the rules of evidence to a Gothic dream of total
personal fulfilment, where the world becomes what the dreamer
desires it to be. At the end of Act II when the night-world of the
forest is giving way again to the daylight clarities of Rome, Marcus
Andronicus sees the nightmare figure of his niece; he remarks:

> If I do dream, would all my wealth would wake me!
> If I do wake, some planet strike me down,
> That I may slumber an eternal sleep!
>
> (II. iv. 13–15)

Henceforth in the play, however, such nightmare shadows have to
be allowed as part of the daylight population of Rome. The ghosts
are only laid, the shadows of the forest dispelled, when nightmare
and truth have faced one another in Tamora's last disguise – as
Revenge, the mother of Rapine and Murder ('A pair of cursed hell-
hounds and their dam' as Titus puts it) – so that mutilators and
mutilated can perish together in a shared universe of absurdity and
Rome be restored to rule and the daylight processes of justice.[1]

At the centre of the city, as its soul you may say, stands the family
of the Andronici, and at the centre of the Andronici's sense of
themselves stands one essential object, which the stage-picture
should surely highlight – the tomb. The structural use of the family
vault or tomb provides another point of correspondence between
Titus and *Romeo*. We are shown the tomb of the Andronici very early
in the play: when Titus first enters in his Roman Triumph, bearing
the Gothic family into Rome among his prisoners, the first action
he undertakes is the burial of the dead in the family vault:

> Romans, of five and twenty valiant sons . . .
> Behold the poor remains, alive and dead!
> These that survive let Rome reward with love;
> These that I bring unto their latest home,
> With burial amongst their ancestors . . .
> Make way to lay them by their brethren.
> There greet in silence, as the dead are wont,
> And sleep in peace, slain in your country's wars.

> O sacred receptacle of my joys,
> Sweet cell of virtue and nobility,
> How many sons hast thou of mine in store
> That thou wilt never render to me more!
>
> (I. i. 79–95)

And it is the tomb that stimulates the first statement of the conflict that will dominate the play. Lucius demands, in what is clearly part of a controlled ritual:

> Give us the proudest prisoner of the Goths,
> That we may hew his limbs, and on a pile
> Ad manes fratrum sacrifice his flesh
> Before this earthy prison of their bones,
> That so the shadows be not unappeas'd,
> Nor we disturb'd with prodigies on earth.
>
> (I. i. 96–101)

Shakespeare seems here to be dramatising a clear conception of the religious bias of the Roman way of life; there is no suggestion that he is criticising the system. The dead citizen-warriors claim the right to be returned to their family place within the city. There they will rest in peace, provided the appropriate honour is paid to them; and the appropriate honour is that the living should hear their claim for the propitiatory sacrifice of 'the proudest prisoner of the Goths', and be absolutely obliged to fulfil this claim.

Against this Roman ritual Shakespeare sets the personal plea of Tamora:

> Victorious Titus, rue the tears I shed,
> A mother's tears in passion for her son.
>
> (I. i. 105–6)

Modern readers naturally feel more sympathy for the more personal position taken up by Tamora and argued by her with eloquence and passion. But the play hardly supports the view that these Roman rituals are in themselves barbarous, or that Tamora is in some sense 'justified' in taking up revenge against the Andronici. The stern suppression of self in the interest of family, community or state is certainly presented in an extreme form, but it is the extreme form of a value-system consistently preferred in the play before subjective passion or individual emotionalism. The military dead are represented as an essential part of the living family and of the national destiny; they cannot be fobbed off with something less than their right. As in other military civilisations, the valiancy of the living is preserved by the promise that they, too, in their turn will have the right to enter the family tomb, to join the honoured bones of their ancestors and be rewarded with reverence and with sacrificial victims. This is why the tomb becomes the primary focus again at the end of the play. The new conqueror and paterfamilias, Lucius Andronicus, throws out the tiger Tamora for birds to peck at; Aaron is treated very similarly – half buried in the earth and left to the mercies of a Nature that 'swallows her own increase'. Both are replaced in the extra-mural world of unhallowed appetite. But

> My father and Lavinia shall forthwith
> Be closed in our household's monument.
>   (v. iii. 193–4)

Interment in the tomb validates the efforts of the life preceding, and ensures the continuity of past, present and future under the same standards of civilisation.

The parallel importance of the tomb in *Romeo and Juliet* suggests that the Andronicus 'household's monument' reflects more than Shakespeare's study of Roman antiquities. It implies that Shakespeare found the tomb property a convenient expression of his sense of the tragic importance of family and social continuities. The Capulet family monument is not, of course, a military symbol. But the choice of it as the most appropriate final setting for the tragedy brings out the structure of significances this play shares with *Titus Andronicus*. It is entirely appropriate that the 'public' wedding-bed of Romeo and Juliet (as against their previous private bedding) should be placed in the Capulet tomb, for it is there that Romeo may be most effectively seen to have joined his wife's clan, there where their corporate identity is most unequivocally established:

> Where all the kindred of the Capulets lie,
>   (iv. i. 112)

> Where for this many hundred years the bones
> Of all my buried ancestors are pack'd.
>   (iv. iii. 40–1)

The rash and personal passion of Romeo and Juliet can hardly claim a truly tragic significance if it cannot be caught up in the corporate and continuing life of Verona. Here, as in *Titus Andronicus*, the presence of tomb assures us that the extreme acts of tragic individuals

contribute to the past and future as well as to the brilliant present
of personal assertion, here where they join the confluence of acts
that make up social continuity.

In both plays a woman as well as a man is placed in the tomb at
the end of the action. One might have expected the Andronicus
tomb to exclude women; but Lavinia is clearly said to be Titus's
companion in death. I do not think, however, that this implies any
weakening of the military significance of the family monument.
Lavinia, too, has like a soldier triumphed over her enemy. The
battle has, of course, been a strange and even a grotesque one. The
code of military ethics does not provide much guidance for dealing
with a wilderness of tigers; and the cunning ploys of the mad Titus
are only marginally 'Roman'. But it is worth noticing that the appeal
to Roman precedent and tradition returns at the moment of Lavinia's
death:

> Was it well done of rash Virginius
> To slay his daughter with his own right hand,
> (v. iii. 36–7)

asks Titus, and, being told by the Emperor, 'It was, Andronicus',
he stabs and kills her. This is often seen as yet another senseless
butchery; but in the light of the precedent explicitly established one
may prefer to see it as the restoration of truly Roman or meaningful
death. To have killed Lavinia earlier would have been an act of
despair, for the standards by which such an act might be justified
seemed to have vanished. To have enclosed her in the tomb then
would have devalued the generations of soldiers already inhearsed.
Now, with the mutilators mutilated, and with Tamora and Saturninus securely within the grasp of punishment, the practical possibility
of justice reappears, the tomb can reopen and receive the honourable
dead. Their presence there can now give meaning to the continuing
efforts of the living. The persistent *Romanitas* of the family is spelt
out in Marcus's submission of the 'poor remainder of Andronici' to
the will of the Roman people:

> Now have you heard the truth: what say you, Romans?
> Have we done aught amiss, show us wherein,
> And, from the place where you behold us pleading,
> The poor remainder of Andronici
> Will hand in hand all headlong hurl ourselves,
> And on the ragged stones beat forth our souls,
> And make a mutual closure of our house.
> (v. iii. 128–34)

On the contrary, of course, the people exalt the family and the family, in its turn, must exalt the dead. It is in this context that Lavinia, like another Lucrece, comes to represent something like a Roman tutelary deity, raped, mutilated, rendered incapable of crying out against these invasive barbarisms, but, by virtue of family *pietas* and unflinching self-sacrifice, enabled to take up her niche in the household monument and to represent to later ages a mode of tragic experience appropriate to a meaningfully 'Roman' world.

SOURCE: 'Shakespeare's Earliest Tragedies: *Titus Andronicus* and *Romeo and Juliet*', *Shakespeare Survey 27* (Cambridge, 1974), pp. 1–9.

NOTE

1. In these terms *Titus* looks like a tragic version of the city–forest–city pattern found in *A Midsummer Night's Dream* – a play which also has close affinities with *Romeo and Juliet*.

Michael Hattaway   Strange Images
of Death   (1982)

This play . . . must be considered not simply in dramatic terms but as an artefact for the theatre. Its structure, as Jacques Petit noted without appreciating, is visual rather than literary, and although it may have the relentless consistency of a dream or nightmare, it is not just a bloodbath of classical horrors but does make a political statement – as a pageant, however, and not in conventional literary-dramatic terms. It is very different, therefore, from the other plays Shakespeare was writing at this time. In the early histories Shakespeare was fostering his skills in dramatic narrative and developing concepts of monarchy and state. In *Romeo and Juliet* he went to a tragic narrative of a simple kind and developed the psychological dimensions of the central characters to make it significant. In *Titus Andronicus*, however, he seems to have turned his attention to the creation of dramatic images, explored kinds of spectacle that produce a compulsive response from the audience, and, like Kyd, tried to work towards a dramatic rhythm based on word, gesture, and music in which concord is invaded by discord. The effect is to lay bare the piece of work that is man and, specifically, to remind the audience of the irrational and violent elements in classical culture. Perhaps the play's popularity was due to the strident claims it makes against the elitist Apollonian plays of the court, 'English Seneca read by candlelight', as Nashe archly described them. It hints also that the neo-classical ideal of consistency of character is not true to experience as it traces the awesome metamorphosis of a choleric soldier into a crazed revenger – like Kyd, Shakespeare knew the dramatic power of a figure seized by monomania. It portrays Goths on stage and arguably is the first 'Gothic' work in the language. In this respect it is shocking because it violates not social norms but the sense of self (the rape scene is accordingly central); it tears aside not Burckhardt's veil of faith but Dostoevsky's veil of familiarity. It is a reminder to popular audiences of what they already know of the precarious foundations of society where hatred is as common as love, faction as familiar as league, quaintness as widespread as normality. It resembles the underworld literature of the period where reality and fancy are indistinguishable, where characters 'from life' people a looking-glass world where morality and order are strangely displaced. Those who were familiar with the picturesque roles attributed to rogues in, say, Harman's *Caveat for Common Cursetors* (1567) would have no trouble in seeing Tamora play her part as Revenge.

The overall pattern is simple: the play begins and ends with the election of a Roman Emperor: the middle is occupied by a grim vision of the wild justice of revenge. Within that pattern Shakespeare worked in an experimental but methodical and schematic way to explore the theatrical effects at his disposal. He tried out, for example, using the gallery aloft, putting characters above others and also by using a pit on the stage – in a 'Roman' play from which the traditional Christian associations of the gallery with grace or moral superiority and the pit with evil and hell have been conspicuously banished. His characters, like those of Marlowe, are icons, realist in the sense that they are created with some degree of individuality and that they violate the moral ideals of a world modelled on law or restraint, but unreal in the sense that they are, as Roy

Strong wrote of the portraits of the time, 'isolated, strange, and
exotic'.[1] There is no sense of families in this play, only of powers –
Tamora's pleading for her sons, Aaron's defence of his child, the
gathering of family remnants at Marcus' banquet are political rather
than domestic affairs. And Shakespeare was seeing what happens
when a thing, a human hand, for example, is thrust repeatedly
before the audience's consciousness. The word occurs forty-six times
in the play, and as if that were not enough, a hand, Titus' severed
hand, is carried off by the handless Lavinia who holds it between
her teeth. Shakespeare is deliberately getting us to look at it purely
as an object, quite displaced from its usual position in the world
and therefore strange and frightening. In the next scene when
Marcus remonstrates with his brother not to teach his daughter to
'lay such violent hands upon her tender life', Titus rejoins in manic
compulsion:

> How now! has sorrow made thee dote already?
> Why, Marcus, no man should be mad but I.
> What violent hands can she lay on her life?
> Ah, therefore dost thou urge the name of hands,
> To bid Aeneas tell the tale twice o'er,
> How Troy was burnt and he made miserable?
> O, handle not the theme, to talk of hands,
> Lest we remember still that we have none.
> Fie, fie, how franticly I square my talk,
> As if we should forget we had no hands,
> If Marcus did not name the word of hands!
> (III.ii.23–33)

In fact severed hands were a common motif in Renaissance emblems
of justice,[2] but that haunting phrase, 'name the word of hands',
suggests that Shakespeare was displacing the figure from the moral
to the psychological domain, exploring a world so terrifying that all
action is meaningless because the words used to describe it have
been raped of their metaphorical significance. We may compare the
repetition of words like 'shadow' and 'face' in *Richard II*, but whereas
in the latter play these words become symbols in that they accrete
meanings that can be arranged into statements about the action of
the play, the hands of Titus and Lavinia remain remorselessly
hands. The word designates only its accustomed object and moves
towards neither metaphor nor metonym, the thing moves no distance
towards emblem. We have therefore an index of the play's peculiar

kind of realism. It is not based on exactness to life but on the creation of a series of images, academic 'figures' and popular fancies, that by iteration etch themselves on our imagination.

Tragedy at this time was modelled on Seneca, and Senecan tragedies had strong stories and were built about a fairly consistent moral philosophy, although they did present in narrative, if not in spectacle, scenes of horrific violence. *Titus Andronicus*, however, is as Ovidian as it is Senecan.[3] Shakespeare's theatrical imagination has been siezed by the images of the poet.

Overall the play creates dramatic images out of Ovid's vision (*Metamorphoses*, trs. Golding, I. 154–70) of an Iron Age – ironically the home of *Titus Andronicus* under Saturninus is shown during its most un-Saturnine reign. Saturn had presided over the Gold Age of plenty and justice. Aaron, whose malignity lies at the centre of the play, is specifically identified as Saturnine in temperament (II.iii.31), and his blackness is the appropriate colour for that humour; the passionate Tamora is governed by Venus, whose colour was yellow, appropriate for a fair-haired Goth. Titus is obviously Martian and choleric – a red costume could have suited his temper late in the play. Motivation therefore is created by their generic and psychological characteristics not by singular traits of personality. These mythic resonances as well as the play's mode of characterization are what prevents the work being merely sensational, a parade of obscene violence.

Although Shakespeare may have felt that tragedy, until then mainly academic tragedy, had excluded direct experience of horror and suffering, he was as concerned to demonstrate how we perceive violence as well as the violence itself. Marcus, confronted with the mutilated figure of his niece, anaesthetizes himself by attempting to see her as an emblem:

> Fair Philomel, why, she but lost her tongue,
> And in a tedious sample sewed her mind:
> But, lovely niece, that mean is cut from thee;
> A craftier Tereus, cousin, hast thou met,
> And he hath cut those pretty fingers off,
> That could have better sewed than Philomel.
>
> (II.iv.38–43)

Because of the play's concern with perception, naturalism of presentation is quite inappropriate: members of the audience fainted at

Peter Brook's 1955 production at Stratford not because Lavinia was really bleeding but because of the suggestiveness of the image. Richard David describes it thus:[4]

> Who could forget the return of the ravishers with Lavinia? They bring her through the leafy arch that was the central pillar and leave her standing there, right arm outstretched and head drooping away from it, left arm crooked with the wrist at the mouth. Her hair falls in disorder over face and shoulders, and from wrist and wrist-and-mouth trail scarlet streamers, symbols of her mutilation. The two assassins retreat from her, step by step, looking back at her, on either side of the stage. Their taunts fall softly lingeringly, as if they themselves were in a daze of horror of their deed; and the air tingles and reverberates with the slow plucking of harp strings.

Seventeen years later Trevor Nunn presented this scene in another way:

> Where Brook presented the violence symbolically, Mr. Nunn gives it rapid materialistic weight and stress: the raped, tongueless Lavinia, for instance here becomes a pitiable, hunched grotesque, crawling out of the darkness like a wounded animal and even moments like Titus' severance of his own hand are deprived of their crude sensationalism by the stress on the sheer physical difficulty of the action.

> (*Guardian*, 13 October 1972)

These then are the principles of the dramaturgy of *Titus Andronicus*. The play accordingly is related to the last plays in which Shakespeare was also working by juxtaposing great images or ceremonies and fusing them into a whole that cannot be explained from the shape of the narrative or by development of character. Significantly the play focuses narrowly on an oligarchy – the populace do not appear here as they do in *Coriolanus* and the spectacles of violence are images of corruption in this decadent class. No dialectic is possible. As Gareth Lloyd Evans wrote: 'Like Seneca, the play is concerned exclusively with the affairs of the highborn in which political and social life is conditioned entirely by lust, greed, cruelty, ambition, and revenge.'[5] Fantastic though the verse may be, like *Edward II* the play has a documentary quality to it and sometimes demands the kind of naturalistic playing the *Guardian* reviewer described where players are, as it were, called upon to work on the stage.

Like *Coriolanus*, on the other hand, and so many popular plays, *Titus Andronicus* demands more than the usual amount of music. Shakespeare's frequent calls for flourishes and trumpets are not a tacit admission that non-verbal devices are required to flesh out the text nor do they serve merely to create a martial atmosphere. Rather, as we have seen, music serves for perspective, for symbols of concord and discord, political league and political chaos, the harmony of love and the broken chords of passion. A musical metaphor is used in connection with the state in II.i. where Aaron quiets the 'braving' of Tamora's sons Chiron and Demetrius who are rivals for the possession of Lavinia:

> What, is Lavinia then become so loose,
> Or Bassianus so degenerate,
> That for her love such quarrels may be broached
> Without controlment, justice, or revenge?
> Young lords, beware; and should the empress know
> This discord's ground, the music would not please.
>
> (II.i.65–70)

Two scenes later Tamora woos Aaron using commonplace conceits of the hunt where the harmony of echoes, hounds, and horns ironically symbolizes a legitimate and decorous love. The sexual images (snake, horns, etc.) lead towards images not only of storm and disruption but of children and generation (babbling, and the nurse's song):

> My lovely Aaron, wherefore look'st thou sad
> When everything doth make a gleeful boast?
> The birds chant melody on every bush,
> The snake lies rollèd in the cheerful sun,
> The green leaves quiver with the cooling wind,
> And make a chequered shadow on the ground;
> Under their sweet shade, Aaron, let us sit,
> And, whilst the babbling echo mocks the hounds,
> Replying shrilly to the well-tuned horns,
> As if a double hunt were heard at once,
> Let us sit down and mark their yellowing noise;
> And – after conflict, such as was supposed
> The wandering prince and Dido once enjoyed,
> When with a happy storm they were surprised,
> And curtained with a counsel-keeping cave –
> We may, each wreathèd in the other's arms,
> Our pastimes done, possess a golden slumber,
> Whiles hounds and horns and sweet melodious birds
> Be unto us as is a nurse's song
> Of lullaby to bring her babe asleep.
>
> (II.iii.10–29)

The verse is of notable complexity, again a pointer to how far the play is from Kyd or from naturalism, yet able as well to suggest not only a moral frame for this tableau and to forecast its outcome – the conception of the bastard child – but also Tamora's wistfulness and capacity for self-deception. The association of hounds with the passions derives from moralizations of the Actaeon myth – Chapman's *The Shadow of Night* (1594) provides an example. In *Twelfth Night* Orsino laments that the sight of Olivia made him an Actaeon:

> O, when mine eyes did see Olivia first,
> Methought she purged the air of pestilence;
> The instant was I turned into a hart,
> And my desires, like fell and cruel hounds,
> E'er since pursue me.
>
> (i.i.18–22)

Shakespeare developed the conceit in the hunting scene of *A Midsummer Night's Dream* where he combined images of the hunt with the Ovidian paradox of the *discors concordia*, that discordant harmony that from the fusion of opposites creates generation (*discors concordia fetibus apta est – Metamorphoses*, i.433). In that play, after the trials of the night, the lovers are prepared for marriage and Theseus has learnt that the state cannot be ruled simply by applying the strictness of the recorded law. In *Titus Andronicus*, however, the play is resolved only by deaths, and there is no sense that the state has been renewed or that the characters have attained maturity through adversity. It is therefore significant that the final lines of the play, Lucius' instructions for the disposing of the bodies of the Emperor and Tamora, explicitly forbid the sounding of ritual funeral music:

> Some loving friends convey the Emperor hence,
> And give him burial in his father's grave.
> My father and Lavinia shall forthwith
> Be closèd in our household's monument.
> As for that ravenous tiger, Tamora,
> No funeral rite, no man in mourning weed,
> No mournful bell shall ring her burial;
> But throw her forth to beasts and birds to prey.
> Her life was beastly and devoid of pity;
> And being dead, let birds on her take pity.
>
> (v.iii.191–200)

Modern productions have been notable for their use of music. Richard David describes how Peter Brook matched spectacle to sound:[6]

The compulsive and incantatory nature of the production (which sent some spectators off into faints before ever a throat was cut) was reinforced by the musical effects, all of a marvellous directness. The overture was a roll of drum and cymbal, the dirge for the slain Andronici, so strange and powerful, no more than the first two bars of *Three Blind Mice*, in the minor and endlessly repeated. A slow seesaw of two bass notes, a semitone apart, wrought the tension of the final scene to an unbearable pitch, and ceased abruptly, with breath-taking effect, as the first morsel of son-pie passed Tamora's lips.

Later Trevor Nunn began his production with groans that turned to exclamations, while in the first scene dirges alternated with shouts of agony. As B. A. Young reported, his Titus (Colin Blakely)

delivers his lines in a kind of Schoenbergian speech-song, prolonged vowels as if to music; his gestures, mostly made with both arms together as long as both his arms are complete to make them with, are bold and artificial but expressive.

(*Financial Times*, 13 October 1972)

The play opens with a flourish and a stately entrance of tribunes and senators on the gallery above the black-draped stage. They represent justice and the constituted power of Rome and have gathered to hear pleas for the crown from Bassianus and Saturninus, sons of the late Emperor and rivals for power. The latter enter from opposite doors with their own drums and trumpets: perhaps their music was a challenge to the established order like the musical battle at the opening to *Mucedorus*, anticipating the anarchy that is to prevail throughout the play. There is a preliminary touch of comedy as Marcus reveals in a formal speech that both their pleas are vain as the crown will be awarded out of the family, to Titus Andronicus who has recently saved Rome from the Goths.[7] He is successful, but Saturninus' suave Marlovian rejoinder, 'How fair the tribune speaks to calm my thoughts', and Bassianus' immediate proclamation of love for Titus' daughter Lavinia suggest they both have an eye for the main chance. It is like the political scenes of *The Jew of Malta*: the cynicism of the potentates adds a dimension of savage farce, feeds the fancies of the audience concerning the realities of power at court. Saturninus formally dismisses his followers and then bluntly demands, 'Open the gates and let me in' (1.i.62), as he turns to the stage doors to mount with his brother to the gallery, the fountainhead of power. From there they witness the next procession, the arrival of Titus with Tamora captive. The stage direction is probably authorial:

Sound drums and trumpets, and then enter two of Titus' sons, and then two men bearing a coffin covered with black; then two other sons; then Titus Andronicus; and then Tamora, the Queen of Goths, and her sons Alarbus, Chiron, and Demetrius, with Aaron the Moor, and others as many as can be; then set down the coffin, and Titus speaks.

The establishing of powers above witnessing a procession of powers below resembles the opening gest of *The Spanish Tragedy*. The succession of 'thens' suggests a prolonged entrance to music through one of the doors or, effectively, as with the procession of captives early in *The Spanish Tragedy*, through one of the yard entrances. The two parties, captors and captives, take up positions on opposite sides of the stage. For once we have a drawing that may depict an early staging of part of this scene. It comes from a manuscript attributed to Henry Peacham but it is impossible to tell whether it was sketched at a performance or done afterwards from memory. Some of the lines accompanying the sketch begin at line 105. It is interesting that Titus wears something approaching Roman costume – a toga-like garment, sandals, and a crown of oak-leaves – while his attendants are obviously Elizabethans with halberds, although one carries an exotic-looking sword.[8] Aaron is black, has negroid hair and features, and may be helpfully pointing out which of the hand-bound sons is Alarbus doomed to sacrifice. (The third son, other characters, and the coffin do not appear in the drawing.) There is no indication in the text that he does this, but it may be in character for this humorous opportunist villain, even if he is later to become Tamora's lover. The fact that he bears a sword suggests that Shakespeare may not have thought of him as a Roman captive as the stage directions imply. The conventions of the costuming remind us of the play as myth, the double awareness of the audience that what they are watching is of the past and of the present.

Another gest is created as the coffin of one of Titus' sons is laid to rest in the tomb. Lucius' demand that the son of Tamora be sacrificed 'Before this earthly prison of their bones' (1.i.99, reading *F*'s 'earthly' rather than *Q*'s 'earthy') suggests that the discovery space would have been used rather than the stage trap. So the first procession and action created an emblem of vaulting ambition, the second a figure of death – the architecture of the tiring-house was such that these images of senate house and tomb were placed, significantly, one below the other – and the two leading ideas of the play have been thus economically established. This double visual image resembles the structuring of emblems on the arches erected for civic shows and royal progresses. It creates a significant frame for the ensuing action when the funerary ceremonies are interrupted by the savage spectacle of Alarbus being led off to vengeful execution.

It is significant that the Tribunes, joined by Saturninus and Bassianus, re-enter aloft. This is indicated by *F*'s later stage direction after line 233, '*A long flourish till they come down.*' The effect is to leave the Andronici vulnerable on the stage below. There they stay during the manoeuvring that leads to Saturninus' acceptance of the crown from Titus. Like the Ghost and Revenge in *The Spanish Tragedy*, their presence creates a speaking picture, or visual irony: Titus' gift of the crown takes place under their shadow, or as if, like the planets, their 'virtue' influences those below. It is also notable that Aaron has remained on stage (with Tamora?) during this sequence. He remains silent throughout the Act, a black and ominous presence.

The interest now moves from politics to passion. Saturninus, having like Tamburlaine invested himself with the costume of office (here the white toga of the candidate), comes down to announce his betrothal to Lavinia, even as he hints broadly to the Venerian Tamora that she can expect 'princely usage'. The white robe scarce conceals his 'black' nature. Formalities are yet again invaded when Bassianus with the apparent connivance of Titus' brother and two sons, seizes Lavinia. Titus impetuously slays Martius, his son, and during the fray Saturninus and Tamora ascend to the gallery together. These two supremes and stars of love have played their coup. They vaunt their passion and leave Titus to a debate that is obviously now irrelevant to the realities of power: whether or not his son should be buried in the family tomb. The Act ends with a return to a kind of equilibrium as the Emperor and Tamora, Bassianus and Lavinia enter symmetrically at opposite doors to stage a reconciliation and plan 'to hunt the panther and the hart' (1.i.493) – by now the symbolism is all too obvious.

The Act has been like a dance in which partners and patterns have been changed in marching and counter-marching, ascents and descents. Titus has been elbowed aside and his personality has been established by his extremes of stoic resignation and fits of fury. The use of stage levels and the emblematic rhythm and its consequent ironies enable us to feel that the scene is firmly planned and give us a weapon with which to meet Kenneth Muir's blunt challenge: 'in the early part of the play . . . characters portrayed with little skill orate at considerable length in undifferentiated verse.'[9] Certainly the characterization is schematic. To my description of Titus we can add Irving Wardle's account of the 1972 Saturninus:

John Wood's marvellous performance of the Emperor Saturninus. From his murderously hysterical first speech, Mr. Wood presents a man governed by whims; and it is characteristic of him to drop Lavinia because she is momentarily unavailable and marry the Queen of the Goths instead.

His performance is spell-binding to watch: endlessly mobile and unpredictable as it drops into the chatty cadences of modern English or rises into spitty fury: linking blood-drenched inhumanity with domestic realism. Mr. Wood arrives for the morning hunt bleary-eyed after his first night with Tamora; and at the news of the Goths' invasion, he raises a finger to his lips warning the messenger not to wake the baby. The performance is a wonderful blend of deadly vigilance, petty rancour, and buffoonery.

(*The Times*, 13 October 1972)

Likewise, we shall see the player of Tamora called upon to swing from pained impotence to cool calculating triumph.

Act I established the patterns of politics in Rome. Act II will reveal the natures, the characters in action, of those we have been introduced to in the exposition of the play. After his political manoeuvring and spurts of action, Titus has, it seems in this Act, settled into acceptance of the new political order. When he appears at the opening of scene ii there is no indication that he resents the settlement, although the opening words may well be ironical:

> The hunt is up, the morn is bright and grey,
> The fields are fragrant and the woods are green.
> Uncouple here and let us make a bay,
> And wake the Emperor and his lovely bride,
> And rouse the Prince, and ring a hunter's peal,
> That all the court may echo with the noise.
>   (II.ii.1–6)

The revenge of the Goths and the Moor therefore is the more outrageous in that it befalls him suddenly and is revealed as being personal and not political in motivation.

The act is symmetrical in that it begins and ends with soliloquies: Aaron's plans to vault to power with his mistress and Marcus' lament for the violation of his niece. Between these we have a pattern in which the Goths appear, and in their dialogues or soliloquies unfold the chaos and violence which they then proceed to wreak when the innocent appear. The effect is of a cancer working fearful change on the body politic. Evil has moved inside the city and innocent and active alike succumb. This movement from public to private action is symbolized by Aaron's appearance in this scene on the level of the main stage, the world of political action. His presence below counterpoints the metaphors he uses to describe Tamora's rise: his power is such that it need not be impressed on others from above:

> Now climbeth Tamora Olympus' top,
> Safe out of Fortune's shot, and sits aloft,
> Secure of thunder's crack or lightning flash,
> Advanced above pale envy's threat'ning reach.
> As when the golden sun salutes the morn,
> And, having gilt the ocean with his beams,
> Gallops the zodiac in his glistering coach,
> And overlooks the highest-peering hills;
> So Tamora.
>
> (ii.i.1–9)

The speech is obviously Marlovian, and in ll. 16–17:

> Away with slavish weeds and servile thoughts!
> I will be bright, and shine in pearl and gold

Shakespeare quotes the famous moments in which Tamburlaine divests himself of shepherd's weeds and dons the armour of a warrior. There is no indication in the text, however, that Aaron should actually change his costume on the stage at this moment. His power comes from his personality and his sexual vitality; with Tamburlaine there is little sense of sexual vigour (although we note his power of words over Zenocrate) and we feel that his power derives from his success-breeding success, his robes of office. The difference between them is like the difference between the heroic figures of Verrocchio and Bernini: Marlowe's hero gains his effect by filling the stage space others create for him, Shakespeare's player must be fuelled by energy within. Aaron, like Gaveston having announced his intentions, demonstrates his sway immediately when

Chiron and Demetrius enter 'braving'. He converts their rival lusts for Lavinia to a plan to rape her together in the forest while she is hunting. They had insulted each other by mocking each other's potency:

> Why, boy, although our mother, unadvised,
> Gave you a dancing-rapier by your side,
> Are you so desperate grown to threat your friends?
> Go to; have you lath glued within your sheath
> Till you know better how to handle it.
>
> (II.i.38–42)

Aaron controls them cunningly by inviting them to join him in an exchange of bawdy:

> *Aaron:* Why, then, it seems some certain snatch or so
>   Would serve your turns.
> *Chiron:*   Ay, so the turn were served.
> *Demetrius:* Aaron, thou hast hit it.
> *Aaron:*   Would you had hit it too!
>   Then should not we be tired with this ado.
>
> (II.i.95–8)

The scene ends with two great verse emblems. First we hear described the forest, a fine Arcadian place until it is invaded by Aaron's naming of 'rape and villainy':

> My lords, a solemn hunting is in hand;
> There will the lovely Roman ladies troop:
> The forest walks are wide and spacious,
> And many unfrequented plots there are
> Fitted by kind for rape and villainy.
> Single you thither then this dainty doe,
> And strike her home by force, if not by words.
>
> (II.i.112–18)

Second, a vision of the House of Fame, drawn either from Chaucer's poem or Ovid (*Metamorphoses*, XII.42ff. in the Golding version):

> The emperor's court is like a house of Fame,
> The palace full of tongues, of eyes, and ears:
> The woods are ruthless, dreadful, deaf and dull:
> There speak, and strike, brave boys, and take your turns;
> There serve your lust, shadowed from heaven's eyes,
>   And revel in Lavinia's treasury.
>
> (II.i.126–31)

Such a dramatic technique, of course, is completely unsuited to any illusionistic stage. Here it serves to remind us that in Elizabethan playhouses the concept of place existed only so far as it was perceived by the characters or, to put it more briefly, place is a stage of mind (remember Mephostophilis' 'Why this is hell, nor am I out of it'). Palace and wood are imposed on one another: the Court may seem a moral wilderness, nature may be corrupted by the ubiquity of man's evil. The juxtaposition of these two images is an emblem of the metamorphosis of the characters in the play, a change that is imposed by the pattern of the action as much as it originates from their personalities. This is demonstrated in another way when Demetrius concludes the scene with some words in Latin:

> *Sit fas aut nefas*, till I find the stream
> To cool this heat, a charm to calm these fits,
> *Per Stygia, per manes vehor.*
>
> (ii.i.133–5)

Some editors have translated the last line as 'I am ready for anything' (it derives from Seneca's *Phaedra*, 1180, where Phaedra proclaims she will follow Hippolytus over Styx and the fiery rivers) but it makes more sense to interpret it as 'I am carried through the Stygian regions of the underworld, i.e. I am in hell'. The Latin quotation, like those used in *The Spanish Tragedy*, turns the scene to emblem, transforms the character from individual to archetype. Personality dissolves and hence the possibility of audience 'identification' with a particular character. Rather the play assumes the quality of a phantasmagoria where legitimacy is challenged by evil in a realm that is nowhere and everywhere.

The same technique is repeated in the next two sequences. Titus greets the newly married Emperor and Empress with a cry of hounds and a peal of horns, a musical confusion of ceremonial love and anarchic passion like that we saw in our examination of analogous emblems in *A Midsummer Night's Dream*. The musical emblem is accompanied by a pastoral description of the woods. This composite emblem serves as an ironic accompaniment to the adulterous love-making of Aaron and Tamora – the familiar device of thrusting Elysium into hell that Nashe saw in *The Spanish Tragedy*.

The rest of the Act contains one of the principal sequences of violence in the play. In it we witness the death of Bassianus, see

Lavinia led off to rape and mutilation, the fall into Bassianus' grave
of Quintus and Martius and their false accusation of the murder of
the Emperor's brother, and finally Marcus' discovery of the ravaged
Lavinia. The whole sequence has been master-minded by Aaron. It
seems that Shakespeare has gone again to Marlowe for the mode of
this part of the play, to the quaint devices of Barabas. He indulges
popular fancies of destruction – Hamlet's *Mousetrap* provides another
example. Like Barabas, Aaron displays a grim humour (that
provokes audience laughter in modern productions) as he cynically
plants the gold and then leads Titus' son to fall into the stage
trapdoor, 'A very excellent piece of villainy' (II.iii.7). But this
sequence is far more disturbing than analogous scenes in *The Jew of
Malta*. Marlowe's characters remain consistent, mere silhouettes in
a sort of shadow play. The audience's lack of involvement with the
savage farce is a corollary of their awareness that the subject of that
play is not the fates of those individuals but the degenerate natures
of all the inhabitants of Malta – Christians, Jews, and infidels. But
there never was a God for pagan Rome, and there is no comforting
moral generality to shield us from the violence of the action. It is
not even a morality play or a melodrama that has run out of control,
for Lavinia is no helpless piece of fair virtue set against the swart
villainy of the Moor. Instead we hear her vilely taunting Tamora
with what Nicholas Brooke calls 'the beastliness of conscious
virtue':[10]

> Under your patience, gentle Empress,
> 'Tis thought you have a goodly gift in horning,
> And to be doubted that your Moor and you
> Are singled forth to try thy experiments.
> Jove shield your husband from his hounds today!
> 'Tis pity they should take him for a stag.
>
> (II.iii.66–71)

This makes her later prolonged plea for mercy to Tamora the more
disturbing: she has our sympathies for her general predicament, but
we are equally aware that she has precipitated her catastrophe.

Shakespeare refuses to let the comedy he had established inform
the next episode of the scene, that in which Martius and Quintus
successively fall into the pit. (It is significant that the Arden editor,
J. C. Maxwell, does not even supply the necessary stage directions
for this sequence.) The tone at first seems to be that of farce.

> *Quintus:* . . . I have no strength to pluck thee to the brink.
> *Martius:* Nor I no strength to climb without thy help.
> *Quintus:* Thy hand once more; I will not loose again,
>   Till thou are here aloft, or I below.
>   Thou canst not come to me – I come to thee. [*Falls in.*]
>   (II.iii.241–5)

But in the pit they find the body of Bassianus, 'a fearful sight of blood and death' (II.iii.216). The savage spectacle is described with a mixture of imaginative realism:

> Lord Bassianus lies berayed in blood,
> All on a heap, like to a slaughtered lamb,
> In this detested, dark, blood-drinking pit
>   (II.iii.222–4)

and baroque formality in which the perceived reality is turned into something akin to a sculptured funerary icon:

> Upon his bloody finger he doth wear
> A precious ring, that lightens all this hole,
> Which, like a taper in some monument,
> Doth shine upon the dead man's earthy cheeks,
> And shows the ragged entrails of this pit.
>   (II.iii.226–30)

Like the fancy of destruction this is the fancy of the graveyard: the images are like those in modern fairground ghost trains or the chamber of horrors at Madame Tussaud's. But Shakespeare extends the conceit to the utmost – and to horrific seriousness in the famous speech in which Marcus describes the violated Lavinia who is standing before him:

> Speak, gentle niece, what stern ungentle hands
> Hath lopped and hewed and made thy body bare
> Of her two branches, those sweet ornaments,
> Whose circling shadows kings have sought to sleep in,
> And might not gain so great a happiness
> As half thy love? Why dost not speak to me?
> Alas, a crimson river of warm blood,
> Like to a bubbling fountain stirred with wind,
> Doth rise and fall between thy rosed lips,
> Coming and going with thy honey breath.
> But, sure, some Tereus hath deflowered thee,
> And, lest thou should'st detect him, cut thy tongue.

> Ah, now thou turn'st away thy face for shame!
> And, notwithstanding all this loss of blood –
> As from a conduit with three issuing spouts –
> Yet do thy cheeks look red as Titan's face
> Blushing to be encountered with a cloud.
>
> (ii.iv.16–32)

Dover Wilson thought that this was a burlesque of similar moments in the works of Shakespeare's lesser contemporaries,[11] but I think that Shakespeare's mind was captured by the idea of translating to the playhouse images of violence he had found in the prototype of this story, Ovid's telling of the rape of Philomel in *Metamorphoses*, vi.702–15:

> . . . drawing out his naked sword that at his girdle hung,
> He took her rudely by the hair, and wrung her hands behind her,
> Compelling her to hold them there while he himself did bind her.
> When Philomela saw the sword, she hoped she should have died,
> And for the same her naked throat she gladly did provide.
> But as she yearned and callèd aye upon her father's name,
> And strivèd to have spoken still, the cruel tyrant came
> And with pair of pinsons fast did catch her by the tongue,
> And with his sword did cut it off. The stump whereon it hung
> Did patter still. The tip fell down and quivering on the ground
> As though that it had murmured it made a certain sound.
> And as an adder's tail cut off doth skip a while: even so
> The tip of Philomela's tongue did wriggle to and fro,
> And nearer to her mistress-ward in dying still did go.

The rape and the wriggling tongue could not be portrayed on the stage, but Shakespeare seems insistent on exposing to the audience what Marlowe had flinched from. Its necessary stylization may serve in fact a kind of psychological realism: as H. T. Price pointed out, Marcus enters 'in that mood of hearty cheerfulness which is always produced by a day's hunting in the forest' to find Lavinia in her sorry plight. His attempt to emblematize the sight, turn her into a kind of Marlovian figure not unlike the portrait of Hero [in *Hero* and *Leander*], is a kind of shield from the awfulness of the sight, an imposition of fancy on reality. Yet again, Shakespeare is concentrating on violence not for itself but as it is perceived. It is an experiment, not wholly successful, as the playwright relentlessly uncovers what emblems conceal, reveals the savagery that underlines comedy.[12]

In Act III Shakespeare returns to the city. Grotesqueries and violence continue and for the first time Titus becomes an object of pity as he enters before the Tribunes' procession and, presumably walking backwards until he prostrates himself before them, begs in vain for the life of his son. They pass by, and like Richard II on his return from Ireland, Titus grovels on the ground in childlike petulance:

> . . . I tell my sorrows to the stones,
> Who, though they cannot answer my distress,
> Yet in some sort they are better than the Tribunes,
> For that they will not intercept my tale.
> When I do weep, they humbly at my feet
> Receive my tears, and seem to weep with me;
> And were they but attirèd in grave weeds,
> Rome could afford no tribunes like to these.
>
> (III.i.37–44)

(Does 'stones', however, mean 'statues' here?) Here is incipient madness, but Titus' anguish is cauterized by the appearance of Lavinia. From the strong simplicity of

> *Marcus:* This was thy daughter.
> *Titus:*   Why, Marcus, so she is.
>
> (III.i.63)

he embarks on one of the play's most memorable speeches:

> For now I stand as one upon a rock,
> Environed with a wilderness of sea,
> Who marks the waxing tide grow wave by wave,
> Expecting ever when some envious surge
> Will in his brinish bowels swallow him.
> This way to death my wretched sons are gone;
> Here stands my other son, a banishèd man,
> And here my brother, weeping at my woes;
> But that which gives my soul the greatest spurn
> Is dear Lavinia, dearer than my soul.
>
> (III.i.93–102)

The lines remind us of some of the final gnomic utterances of Timon of Athens, but whereas Timon was attempting to draw his life to a significant close, Titus is, like Marcus, protecting himself by this heroic self-dramatization. For his agony is not done and Shakespeare again drives the rest of the scene through fancy into nightmare. In

his torrent of passion before the silent Lavinia he had made a
rhetorical offer to sever his own hands:

> Give me a sword, I'll chop off my hands too;
> For they have fought for Rome, and all in vain;
> And they have nursed this woe, in feeding life;
> In bootless prayer have they been held up,
> And they have served me to effectless use.
>   (III.i.72–6)

By employing a species of irony that we might claim to encounter
in life but which few authors would dare use in fiction, Aaron comes
in with an offer that Titus cannot refuse: his sons will be spared by
the Emperor in return for a hand severed from one of the Andronici.
The announcement confirms our suspicion that the impassivity of
the Tribunes was a symptom of the complete corruption of the new
regime and begins an absurd comedy in which the men vie with
one another for the privilege of losing a hand until Aaron intervenes
with lines that might have come out of *Alice in Wonderland*:

> Nay, come, agree whose hand shall go along,
> For fear they die before their pardon come.
>   (III.i.174–5)

After the fearsome clarity of this and the abrupt shock of seeing
Aaron quickly cut off Titus' hand on stage, Titus' lament is
magnificently emblematic and histrionic:

> If there were reasons for these miseries,
> Then into limits could I bind my woes:
> When heaven doth weep, doth not the earth o'erflow?
> If the winds rage, doth not the sea wax mad,
> Threatening the welkin with his big-swol'n face?
> And wilt thou have a reason for this coil?
> I am the sea. Hark how her sighs doth blow;
> She is the weeping welkin, I the earth:
> Then must my sea be movèd with her sighs;
> Then must my earth with her continual tears
> Become a deluge, overflowed and drowned;
> For why my bowels cannot hide her woes,
> But like a drunkard must I vomit them.
>   (III.i.219–31)

In a way that neither Kyd nor Marlowe was able to do, Shakespeare
is making Titus' consciousness the centre of the stage as his state of

mind creates the place. Later in *Lear* he would use the technique in a more modulated form. The speech serves, however, only as a prelude to a further shock, the appearance of the Messenger bearing two heads and Titus' hand. Marcus and Lucius compete in insensitive exclamations, Lavinia in silent reproach to them kisses her father, but Titus' silence, a contrast with the fury of his tirade, is broken only by his line (cried or whispered?), 'When will this fearful slumber have an end?' (iii.i.252), until, without warning, he laughs. This, rather than the speeches that came before, is Titus' recognition, a moment when, to quote Timon of Athens, language has ended, a recognition that what is horrible is defined not theologically by the absence of good but by a vision of a cosmos geared only to the survival of the fittest. The moment must have impressed contemporaries: Marston may have been parodying it when he has Pandulpho laugh at the catastrophes of i.ii. of *Antonio's Revenge*. Shakespeare uses the device to mark the moment when Titus realizes that his compulsive energies must be harnessed to revenge. Now the thrustful energies he revealed as a warrior will be harnessed to the half-crazed half-witty contrivances of the revenger.

It is possible, moreover, that Aaron's confession in Act v describes a piece of stage action in this scene:

> I played the cheater for thy father's hand,
> And, when I had it, drew myself apart,
> And almost broke my heart with extreme laughter.
> I pryed me through the crevice of a wall
> When, for his hand, he had his two sons' heads;
> Beheld his tears, and laughed so heartily
> That both mine eyes were rainy like to his.
>
> (v.i.111–17)

Aaron might have concealed himself in the discovery space and there would be a grim and ironic counterpoint if Titus were to thus unwittingly join him in a gale of laughter.

Shakespeare confirms this impression of Titus' monomania in the 'situational' scene (that appears only in the Folio) that follows. It demands a banquet, thus prefiguring the final Thyestean banquet and, as Nicholas Brooke suggests, it resembles the Painter scene in *The Spanish Tragedy*,[13] being an emblem of Titus' derangement. In it Titus' persistive laments give way to a sentimental plea for the kindred of the fly that Marcus stabs as the family sits at table. When Marcus remonstrates that the fly was as black as Aaron, Titus takes his knife to it himself in unremitting savagery. The scene works, concentrating the audience on the effects rather than the sensational spectacles of violence, so that Harold Hobson could write of the 1972 production: 'Mr. Nunn has decided not to do [the horror scenes] wholeheartedly. The most excessive horror to which he lends himself is Titus' savage stabbing of a fly' (*The Sunday Times*, 15 October 1972).

In Act iv the succession of violent spectacles abates in intensity for a while in preparation no doubt for the enormities of the play's conclusion. The Act opens with a scene where Lucius' son runs on stage fleeing from Lavinia. Her purpose is to obtain his copy of the *Metamorphoses* and to indicate that she like Philomel had been rudely forced. In an agonising sequence she writes out the names of her attackers in the sand with a stick held in her mouth and then quotes in Latin an anguished plea to the gods from Seneca's *Phaedra*. The moment is symmetrical with that when Demetrius, one of her violators, quoted from the same play (ii.i.135), and like the use of divers languages in *The Spanish Tragedy*, gives the scene an archetypal significance. Although the scene is too obviously emblematic, there is also a more immediate awareness for the audience: that horror does not cease when the physical violence has abated, that to a child the innocent Lavinia is as terrible as the villainous Aaron. After his instinctive terror at this moment, the boy is converted to revenge by his grandfather and great uncle:

> I say, my lord, that if I were a man
> Their mother's bedchamber should not be safe
> For these base bondmen to the yoke of Rome.
>   (iv.i.108–10)

We might remember the pathetic moment when Lady Macduff's son boasts that he could be a warrior, but this is a horrible moment as the child puts on the antic and monstrous disposition of the revenger.

In the next scene another encounter with innocence is played out. We meet the steely Aaron who realizes that Chiron and Demetrius have not the wit to see that the weapons wound with mottoes sent them by Titus are a signal that they have been found out. He does not disclose the danger that they are in, thinking that he might leap to even higher power, but his mood is changed when the nurse brings him his bastard blackamoor child by Tamora. He is not

moved to tenderness: on the contrary he coldly and cruelly dispatches
the nurse:

> 'Wheak, wheak!'
> So cries a pig preparèd to the spit.
> (iv.ii.146–7)

The sight of his child inspires him to a vitality and confidence of
character that is shared by no one else in the play:

> I tell you, younglings, not Enceladus,
> With all his threat'ning band of Typhon's brood,
> Nor great Alcides, nor the god of war,
> Shall seize this prey out of his father's hands.
> What, what, ye sanguine, shallow-hearted boys!
> Ye white-limed walls! ye alehouse painted signs!
> Coal-black is better than another hue,
> In that it scorns to bear another hue;
> For all the water in the ocean
> Can never turn the swan's black legs to white,
> Although she lave them hourly in the flood,
> Tell the Empress from me, I am of age
> To keep mine own – excuse it how she can.
> (iv.ii.93–105)

This borders on rant, but its lurching movement displays a nascent
self-sufficiency and a celebration of natural values that is in its way
attractive. As a politician too Aaron stands in contrast to the
blundering of the Saturnines and the impotence of the Andronici
who under the direction of the distracted Titus now shoot arrows to
the gods and send a petition to the court to be carried by the
unwitting Clown, with his pigeons on his way to the Tribunes over
a threepenny brawl. There are elements of allegory here too: Titus
proclaims that Astraea has left the earth and Lucius is said to have
reached the constellation Virgo with his arrow. Frances Yates
argues that this has to do with the Astraea cult that was built up
around Elizabeth the Virgin Queen, and that the final enthronement
of Lucius heralds the return to the golden age and is therefore an
oblique compliment to the monarch.[14] But like the preceding Lavinia
scene which also tended towards allegory or archetype it has a more
immediate dramatic effect. In its mixture of grotesquerie created by
the sight of arrows being fired into the playhouse gallery while the
archers announce they are being sent to the heavens, pathos as we
hear the rantings of Titus, cheerful obscenity when he remarks that

Lucius has hit the virgin in the lap, and bathos when the Clown emerges to be the messenger, it serves as an emblem of the confusion in Titus' mind. It is a play within a play, like the trial scene in *Lear*, and the deliberate violation of decorum that occurs when a grand anagogic concept – communicating with the gods – is literally enacted on the stage is parallel to the indecorum of having Gloucester make an ungainly leap at his moment of spiritual enlightenment. In both cases Shakespeare seems to be deliberately disowning the significance of these climaxes in the dramatic action. It also serves to illustrate a point that Shakespeare was to raise repeatedly in his history plays, that the search for a final cause or providential pattern is fruitless. As Machiavelli had demonstrated and a popular audience would suspect, history is made by the actions of men, and we know that the fate of Rome will depend more on Aaron's conspiracy with the Goths than on any divine intervention. The casual execution of the Clown, ordered by Tamora with as little concern as Aaron had shown over the death of the nurse, is scarcely noticed as we hear that at last the Andronici are on the march, having made a firmer alliance with the Goths than that Aaron boasted of.

With the Thyestean banquet, the final horror of the sons baked in a pie and served to their mother and the swift successions of stabbings, Act v offers a culmination to the nightmare of violence in the play. But it also contains a rising movement that is as strong as any in Shakespearean tragedy. It is not a question of good supplanting evil – the Thyestean banquet will strip Titus of any sympathy – but of a victory by main force of those who respect the state over those whose respect is only for themselves. There is an uncomfortable pause when it looks as though Lucius will hang Aaron's baby on the stage, but mercy prevails and the scene is resolved with a long confession of dastardly deeds from the captured Aaron. Among others, the speech describes one incident like that actually performed by Marlowe's Barabas when he set two dead men 'upright at their dear friend's door' (v.i.136). Here Shakespeare, however, cauterizes any humour. But the speech is at the centre of the first of two scenes in which Shakespeare, perhaps rather desperately, crystallizes themes out of the play's action, having, if my interpretation is correct, tried to eschew significance in some of the preceding sequences. As Muriel Bradbrook describes Aaron he is 'half-symbol, half stage formula'[15] and we may go further and say that he becomes the evil which Lucius must purge from the body

politic. Or we may regard the speech as the equivalent to that at
the end of *Richard III* in which Richard realizes that he has become
the part he had created to play before others ('I am I'). Aaron has
become what the Goths needed in order to legitimize their invasion,
a black devil, a stage villain.

In the second scene Shakespeare resorts to actual allegory as
Tamora invests herself in the costume of Revenge. We are reminded
of Death the Mower in *Edward II*, the Old Man in *Faustus*. The
dividing line between realism and allegory was obviously less
perceptible to the Elizabethans than to us. Tarquin moves towards
the sleeping Lucrece through a landscape of the mind, Macbeth
sees himself as 'withered Murder' (II.i.52), and we think of the way
characters in Spenser easily become what they represent. In the
visual arts, we might think of the allegorical portraits of the time
such as the famous Eworth painting of Sir John Luttrell (1550) in
the Courtauld Institute in which we see what is presumably a good
likeness of the subject wading heroically as a bringer of peace
through seas of wreck and turmoil. So Tamora enters as Revenge
with her two sons. She may have been as Ripa describes her in the
Iconologia, clad in red, bearing a naked dagger and biting a finger to
express anguish,[16] or bearing a whip and sounding a drum as she
appeared in Act II of an Admiral's play, Peele's *The Battle of Alcazar*,
or dressed in imitation of the well-known figure from *The Spanish
Tragedy*. Titus, in his madness, recognizes her immediately and
begins the grim stage game that will end only with the deaths of
them both. He names her sons Rape and Murder and invites her to
'Stab them, or tear them on thy chariot-wheels' (v.ii.47). This and
the related lines describing a chariot may simply be a figment of
Titus' festering imagination: they may, however, indicate that
Tamora entered in a chariot, like Tamburlaine's drawn by her
princely sons, a familiar figure of the Triumph of Revenge. If that
is the case the entrance may have been into the playhouse yard to
summon Titus out on to the stage for his final conflict. Alternatively
the Goths might come out on to the stage (a chariot enters '*through
the curtains*' in Act II of *The Battle of Alcazar*) and knock at one
doors, for Titus to appear aloft in response to their knock. Strangely
the Arden editor and Richard Hosley assert but without argument
or evidence that the gallery was not in fact used.[17] Tamora's repeated
bids to Titus to come down (ll.33–43) and her covering aside while
he descends, presumably down the stair within the tiring-house,

seem sufficient evidence to me. Shakespeare may in fact have used the gallery as an ironic reminder of the action in Act I. There Tamora appeared aloft while her power was in the ascendant, here Titus has seen through to her true nature and is in a position to have her seized and brought to summary justice. The cruel Lavinia whom we have heard taunting Tamora reappears with a basin between her wrists to catch the blood of the sons, her violators, as her father slits their throats.

It must have been difficult to avoid excess. Shakespeare avoids it by invoking yet again a mythic archetype for the climax of the play, the Thyestean banquet, a suitable final image of the action. Familiar from *The Battle of Alcazar* (1588–9), *A Warning for Fair Women* (after 1585), and later to be used in *Antonio's Revenge* (1599), *The Golden Age* (1610), and *The Bloody Banquet* (1639), it was presumably less sensational for Renaissance audiences than it is now. Shakespeare also lightens the sequence by bringing on Titus as a cook to serve up the cannibal's pie. The tone of nineteenth-century pantomime is heard here:

> Let me go grind their bones to powder small,
> And with this hateful liquor temper it;
> And in that paste let their vile heads be baked.
>   (v.ii.198–200)

And yet this is not farce for children, but the kitchen humour of a distracted man. Its naïveté, however, serves a serious and humane purpose as the audience is delighted by the spectacle of politicians punished for their corruption. Once the spectacle is established the action moves very quickly as the pie is brought in, Lavinia is slain in imitation of the legend of Virginius' slaughter of his daughter, and Tamora, Titus himself, and Saturninus are despatched. The death of Lavinia may have quoted visually the scene in which she first appeared: there she knelt as Titus raised his hand to bless her, here she kneels as Titus raises his hand to kill her. A modern director might want to attempt the sequence in a kind of nightmarish slow motion, although a swift fury of slaughter might be equally effective, to contrast with the formalized pathos as the Andronici lament their dead and the ceremony of acclamation as Lucius is made Emperor. Peter Brook cut ruthlessly to avoid laughs and played the whole scene formally: 'in the glare of the torches the victims topple forward in succession across the dinner table like a row of ninepins skittled from behind. It was as if the actors were engaged in a ritual at once fluent from habitual performance and yet still practised with concentrated attention.[18] Rather, the scene has the combination of grotesquerie, savagery, and fundamentalist detachment from what is inhuman and inhumane that we find in *Alice in Wonderland*. Shakespeare, in other words, has taken what is naïve in folk culture and turned it into a sophisticated and serious kind of theatre. He marks this by turning from surrealist and fanciful nightmare to customary theatrical ceremony: the play must have ended with a double funeral procession, probably, as I noted, without music: the noble borne out shoulder high with due honour, the base drawn out ignominiously by their feet.

SOURCE: Extract from *Elizabethan Popular Theatre* (London, 1982), pp. 186–207

NOTES

(Renumbered by editors.)

1. Roy Strong, *The English Icon* (London, 1969) p. 3.

2. See Ann Haaker, '*Non Sine Causa*: the Use of Emblematic Method and Iconology in the Thematic Structure of *Titus Andronicus*', *Research Opportunities in Renaissance Drama*, XIII–XIV, 1970–1, pp. 143–68.

3. See Eugene M. Waith, 'The Metamorphosis of Violence in *Titus Andronicus*', *Shakespeare Survey 10*, 1957, pp. 39–49.

4. Richard David, 'Drama of Eale', *Shakespeare Survey 9*, 1956, pp. 126–34.

5. Gareth Lloyd Evans, *Shakespeare*, 1, Edinburgh, 1969, p. 73.

6. See David, op. cit.

7. See Haaker, op. cit.

8. See W. M. Merchant, 'Classical Costume in Shakespearian Production', *Shakespeare Survey 10*, 1957, pp. 71–6; the fullest discussion of the drawing is to be found in R. A. Foakes, *London Theatres Illustrated* (forthcoming).

9. Kenneth Muir, *Shakespeare's Tragic Sequence* (London, 1972) p. 24.

10. Nicholas Brooke, *Shakespeare's Early Tragedies* (London, 1968) pp. 33–4.

11. J. Dover Wilson, ed., *Titus Andronicus* (Cambridge, 1948) pp. li–lii.

12. See Waith, op. cit.; one might argue that like many men he is suppressing the hatred of women that has its end in rape.

13. Brooke, *Shakespeare's Early Tragedies*, p. 40.

14. Frances Yates, *Astraea* (London, 1975) p. 75. Cf. Haaker, op. cit.

15. Muriel Bradbrook, *Shakespeare and Elizabethan Poetry* (London, 1961) p. 107.

16. C. Ripa, *Iconologia* (Padua, 1611).

17. See v.ii.69n., and Hosley, 'Shakespeare's Use of a Gallery over the Stage', *Shakespeare Survey 10*, 1957, p. 86, n. 4.

18. David, op. cit.

ROMEO AND JULIET

M. M. Mahood   Wordplay in
Romeo and Juliet   (1957)

Romeo and Juliet is one of Shakespeare's most punning plays;
even a really conservative count yields a hundred and seventy-
five quibbles. Critics who find this levity unseemly excuse it by
murmuring, with the Bad Quarto Capulet, that 'youth's a jolly
thing' even in a tragedy. Yet Shakespeare was over thirty, with a
good deal of dramatic writing already to his credit, when *Romeo and
Juliet* was first performed. He knew what he was about in his
wordplay, which is as functional here as in any of his later tragedies.
It holds together the play's imagery in a rich pattern and gives an
outlet to the tumultuous feelings of the central characters. By its
proleptic second and third meanings it serves to sharpen the play's
dramatic irony. Above all, it clarifies the conflict of incompatible
truths and helps to establish their final equipoise.

Shakespeare's sonnet-prologue offers us a tale of star-crossed
lovers and 'The *fearfull passage* of their *death-markt* loue'.[1] *Death-marked*
can mean 'marked out for (or by) death; fore-doomed'. If, however,
we take *passage* in the sense of a voyage (and this sub-meaning
prompts *trafficque* in the twelfth line) as well as a course of events,
death-marked recalls the 'euer fixed marke' of Sonnet 116 and the sea-
mark of Othello's utmost sail, and suggests the meaning 'With death
as their objective'. The two meanings of *fearful* increase the line's
oscillation; the meaning 'frightened' makes the lovers helpless, but
they are not necessarily so if the word means 'fearsome' and so
suggests that we, the audience, are awe-struck by their undertaking.
These ambiguities pose the play's fundamental question at the
outset: is its ending frustration or fulfilment? Does Death choose the
lovers or do they elect to die? This question emerges from the
language of the play itself and thus differs from the conventional,
superimposed problem: is *Romeo and Juliet* a tragedy of Character or
of Fate? which can be answered only by a neglect or distortion of

the play as a dramatic experience. To blame or excuse the lovers'
impetuosity and the connivance of others is to return to Arthur
Brooke's[2] disapproval of unhonest desire, stolen contracts, drunken
gossips and auricular confession. Recent critics have, I believe, come
nearer to defining the play's experience when they have stressed the
Liebestod of the ending and suggested that the love of Romeo and
Juliet is the tragic passion that seeks its own destruction. Certainly
nearly all the elements of the *amour-passion* myth as it has been
defined by Denis de Rougemont[3] are present in the play. The love
of Romeo and Juliet is immediate, violent and final. In the voyage
imagery of the play[4] they abandon themselves to a rudderless course
that must end in shipwreck:

> Thou desperate Pilot, now at once run on
> The dashing Rocks, thy seasick weary barke:
> Heeres to my Loue.
>
> (v. iii. 117–19)

The obstacle which is a feature of the *amour-passion* legend is partly
external, the family feud; but it is partly a sword of the lovers' own
tempering since, unlike earlier tellers of the story, Shakespeare leaves
us with no explanation of why Romeo did not put Juliet on his horse
and make for Mantua. A *leitmotiv* of the play is Death as Juliet's
bridegroom; it first appears when Juliet sends to find Romeo's name:
'if he be married, / My graue is like to be my wedding bed'. At the
news of Romeo's banishment Juliet cries 'And death not Romeo,
take my maiden head', and she begs her mother, rather than compel
her to marry Paris, to 'make the Bridall bed / In that dim Monument
where Tibalt lies'. The theme grows too persistent to be mere
dramatic irony:

> O sonne, the night before thy wedding day
> Hath death laine with thy wife, there she lies,
> Flower as she was, deflowred by him,
> Death is my sonne in law, death is my heire.
> My daughter he hath wedded.
>
> (IV. v. 35–9)

Romeo, gazing at the supposedly dead Juliet, could well believe

> that vnsubstantiall death is amorous,
> And that the leane abhorred monster keepes
> Thee here in darke to be his parramour.
>
> (v. iii. 103–5)

Most significant of all, there is Juliet's final cry:

> O *happy* dagger
> This is thy sheath, there rust and let me *dye*.
> (v. iii. 169–70)

where *happy* implies not only 'fortunate to me in being ready to my hand' but also 'successful, fortunate in itself' and so suggests a further quibble on *die*. Death has long been Romeo's rival and enjoys Juliet at the last.

In all these aspects *Romeo and Juliet* appears the classic literary statement of the *Liebestod* myth in which (we are told) we seek the satisfaction of our forbidden desires; forbidden, according to Freud, because *amour-passion* is inimical to the Race, according to de Rougemont because it is contrary to the Faith. Shakespeare's story conflicts, however, with the traditional myth at several points. Tragic love is always adulterous. Romeo and Juliet marry, and Juliet's agony of mind at the prospect of being married to Paris is in part a concern for her marriage vow: 'My husband is on earth, my faith in heauen'. Again, Romeo faces capture and death, Juliet the horror of being entombed alive, not because they want to die but because they want to live together. These woes are to serve them for sweet discourses in their time to come. In contrast to this, the wish-fulfilment of the *Liebestod* is accomplished only by the story of a suicide pact. Drama has furnished many such plots since the middle of the last century. Deirdre and her lover deliberately return to Ireland and the wrath of Conchubar[5] because it is 'a better thing to be following on to a near death, than to be bending the head down, and dragging with the feet, and seeing one day a blight showing upon love where it is sweet and tender'. What makes Synge's play a tragedy is that the blight does show before the lovers are killed. By itself, the suicide pact offers the audience wish-fulfilment and not *katharsis*. The good cry we enjoy over the worn reels of *Meyerling*[6] bears only a remote relationship to the tragic experience of *Romeo and Juliet*.

The real objection to reading *Romeo and Juliet* as the *Liebestod* myth in dramatic form is that it is anachronistic to align the play with pure myths like that of Orpheus and Eurydice or with the modern restatement of such myths by Anouilh and Cocteau.[7] Shakespeare's intention in writing the play was not that of the post-Freud playwright who finds in a high tale of love and death the objective

correlative to his own emotions and those of his audience. We may
guess that the story afforded Shakespeare an excited pleasure of
recognition because it made explicit a psychological experience; but
he did not, on the strength of that recognition, decide to write a
play about the death wish. Like Girolamo de la Corte, whose *History
of Venise* appeared about the time *Romeo and Juliet* was first acted,
Shakespeare believed his lovers to be historical people. He read and
retold their adventures with the detached judgment we accord
history as well as with the implicated excitement we feel for myth.
The story is both near and remote; it goes on all the time in
ourselves, but its events belong also to distant Verona in the dog
days when the mad blood is stirred to passion and violence. The
resultant friction between history and myth, between the story and
the fable, kindles the play into great drama. When we explore the
language of *Romeo and Juliet* we find that both its wordplay and its
imagery abound in those concepts of love as a war, a religion, a
malady, which de Rougemont has suggested as the essence of
amour-passion. If the play were pure myth, the fictionalising of a
psychological event, all these elements would combine in a single
statement of our desire for a tragic love. But because the play is also
an exciting story about people whose objective existence we accept
during the two hours' traffic of the stage, these images and quibbles
are dramatically 'placed'; to ascertain Shakespeare's intentions in
using them we need to see which characters are made to speak them
and how they are distributed over the course of the action.

2

Act I begins with some heavy-witted punning from Sampson and
Gregory – a kind of verbal tuning-up which quickens our ear for
the great music to come. The jests soon broaden. This is one of
Shakespeare's most bawdy plays, but the bawdy has always a
dramatic function. Here its purpose is to make explicit, at the
beginning of this love tragedy, one possible relationship between
man and woman: a brutal male dominance expressed in sadistic
quibbles. After the brawl has been quelled, the mood of the scene
alters 'like a change from wood wind, brass and tympani to an
andante on the strings'[8] in Benvolio's tale of Romeo's melancholia;
and Romeo himself appears and expresses, in the numbers that

Petrarch flowed in, the contrary relationship of the sexes: man's
courtly subjection to women's tyranny. Rosaline is a saint, and by
his quibbles upon theological terms Romeo shows himself a devotee
of the Religion of Love:

> She is too faire, too wise, wisely too faire,
> To merit blisse by making me *dispaire*.
>
> (227–8)

Love is a sickness as well as a cult, and Romeo twists Benvolio's
request to tell in sadness (that is, seriously) whom he loves, to an
expression of *amour-maladie:*

> A sicke man in *sadnesse* makes his will:
> A word ill vrgd to one that is so ill.
>
> (208–9)

It is characteristic of this love learnt by rote from the sonnet writers
that Romeo should combine images and puns which suggest this
slave-like devotion to his mistress with others that imply a masterful
attack on her chastity.[9] Love is a man of war in such phrases as 'th'
incounter of assailing eies' which, added to the aggressive wordplay
of Sampson and Gregory and to the paradox of 'ô brawling loue, ô
louing hate', reinforce the theme of ambivalence, the *odi-et-amo*
duality of passion.

All the Petrarchan and anti-Petrarchan conventions are thus
presented to us in this first scene: love as malady, as worship, as
war, as conquest. They are presented, however, with an exaggeration
that suggests Romeo is already aware of his own absurdity and is
'posing at posing'. 'Where shall we dine?' is a most unlover-like
question which gives the show away; and Benvolio's use of 'in
sadnesse' implies that he knows Romeo's infatuation to be nine parts
show. Romeo is in fact ready to be weaned from Rosaline, and the
scene ends with a proleptic pun that threatens the overthrow of this
textbook language of love. 'Examine other bewties' Benvolio urges,
but for Romeo, 'Tis the way to call hers (exquisit) in question more'.
By *question* he means, with a play upon the etymology of *exquisite*,
'consideration and conversation'; but we guess, if we do not know,
that Rosaline's charms will be called into question in another sense
when set beside the beauty of Juliet.

Love in Verona may be a cult, a quest or a madness. Marriage is a business arrangement. Old Capulet's insistence to Paris, in the next scene, that Juliet must make her own choice, is belied by later events. Juliet is an heiress, and her father does not intend to enrich any but a husband of his own choosing:

> *Earth* hath swallowed all my hopes but she,
> Shees the hopefull Lady of my *earth*.
> (I. ii. 14–15)

This quibbling distinction between *earth* as the grave and *earth* as lands (. . . *fille de terre* means an heiress) is confounded when Juliet's hopes of happiness end in the Capulets' tomb. We recall the dramatic irony of this pun when Old Capulet speaks his last, moving quibble:

> O brother Montague, giue me thy hand,
> This is my daughters *ioynture*, for no more
> Can I demaund.
> (v. iii. 296–8)

The ball scene at Capulet's house is prologued by a revealing punning-match between Romeo and Mercutio. Romeo's lumbering puns are the wordplay of courtly love: the other masquers have nimble soles, he has a soul of lead: he is too bound to earth to bound, too sore from Cupid's darts to soar in the dance. Mercutio's levity, on the other hand, is heightened by his bawdy quibbles. Mercutio appears in early versions of the tale as what is significantly known as a ladykiller, and his dramatic purpose at this moment of the play is to oppose a cynical and aggressive idea of sex to Romeo's love-idolatry and so sharpen the contrast already made in the opening scene. Yet just as Romeo's touch of self-parody then showed him to be ready for a more adult love, so Mercutio's Queen Mab speech implies that his cynicism does not express the whole of his temperament. The falsity of both cynicism and idolatry, already felt to be inadequate by those who hold these concepts, is to be exposed by the love between Romeo and Juliet. Like Chaucer two centuries previously, Shakespeare weighed the ideas of the masterful man and the tyrannical mistress and wisely concluded that 'Love wol nat be constreyned by maistrie'.

For the ball scene, Shakespeare deploys his resources of stagecraft and poetry in a passage of brilliant dramatic counterpoint. Our attention is divided, during the dance, between the reminiscences of the two old Capulets (sketches for Silence and Shallow) and the rapt figure of Romeo who is watching Juliet. Nothing is lost by this, since the talk of the two pantaloons is mere inanity. We are only aware that it has to do with the passage of years too uneventful to be numbered, so that twenty-five is confused with thirty; simultaneously we share with Romeo a timeless minute that cannot be reckoned by the clock. Yet the old men's presence is a threat as well as a dramatic contrast. They have masqued and loved in their day, but "'tis gone, 'tis gone, 'tis gone'.

Romeo's first appraisal of Juliet's beauty is rich not only in its unforgettable images but also in the subtlety of its wordplay. Hers is a 'Bewtie too rich for vse, for earth too deare'. When we recall that *use* means 'employment', 'interest' and 'wear and tear', that *earth* means both 'mortal life' and 'the grave', that *dear* can be either 'cherished' or 'costly' and that there is possibly a play upon *beauty* and *booty* (as there is in *Henry IV* part 1, I.ii.28), the line's range of meanings becomes very wide indeed. Over and above the contrast between her family's valuation of her as sound stock in the marriage market and Romeo's estimate that she is beyond all price, the words contain a self-contradictory dramatic irony. Juliet's beauty is too rich for use in the sense that it will be laid in the tomb after a brief enjoyment; but for that very reason it will never be faded and worn. And if she is *not* too dear for earth since Romeo's love is powerless to keep her out of the tomb, it is true that she is too rare a creature for mortal life. Not all these meanings are consciously present to the audience, but beneath the conscious level they connect with later images and quibbles and are thus brought into play before the tragedy is over.

The counterpoint of the scene is sustained as Romeo moves towards his new love against the discordant hate and rage of her cousin. Tybalt rushes from the room, threatening to convert seeming sweet to bitter gall, at the moment Romeo touches Juliet's hand. The lovers meet and salute each other in a sonnet full of conceits and quibbles on the Religion of Love – 'palme to palme is holy Palmers kis'; 'grant thou least faith turne to dispaire'; 'Saints do not moue' – for the place is public and they must disguise their feelings beneath a social persiflage. The real strength of those feelings erupts in Romeo's pun – 'O *deare* account!' – and in Juliet's paradox – 'My onely loue sprung from my onely hate' – when each learns the other's identity, and the elements of youth and experience, love and hate, which have been kept apart throughout the scene, are abruptly juxtaposed. Then the torches are extinguished and the scene ends with a phrase of exquisite irony, when the Nurse speaks to Juliet as to a tired child after a party: 'Come lets away, the strangers all are gone'. Romeo is no longer a stranger and Juliet no longer a child.

A quibbling sonnet on love between enemies and some of Mercutio's ribald jests separate this scene from that in Capulet's orchard.[10] It is as if we must be reminded of the social and sexual strife before we hear Romeo and Juliet declare the perfect harmony of their feelings for each other. At first Romeo seems still to speak the language of idolatry, but the 'winged messenger of heauen' belongs to a different order of imagination from the faded conceits of his devotion to Rosaline. The worn commonplaces of courtship are swept aside by Juliet's frankness. One of the few quibbles in the scene is on *frank* in the meanings of 'generous' and 'candid, open', and it introduces Juliet's boldest and most beautiful avowal of her feelings:

> *Rom:* O wilt thou leaue me so vnsatisfied?
> *Iul:* What satisfaction canst thou haue to night?
> *Rom:* Th'exchange of thy loues faithful vow for mine.
> *Iul:* I gaue thee mine before thou didst request it:
> And yet I would it were to giue againe.
> *Rom:* Woldst thou withdraw it, for what purpose loue?
> *Iul:* But to be franke and giue it thee againe,
> And yet I wish but for the thing I haue,
> My bountie is as boundlesse as the sea,
> My loue as deepe, the more I giue to thee
> The more I haue, for both are infinite.
>
> (II.ii.125–35)

Thus the distribution of wordplay upon the concepts of love-war, love-idolatry, love-sickness, serves to show that the feelings of Romeo and Juliet for each other are something quite different from the *amour-passion* in which de Rougemont finds all these disorders. For Romeo doting upon Rosaline, love was a malady and a religion; for Mercutio it is sheer lunacy ('a great naturall that runs lolling vp and downe') or a brutal conquest with no quarter given. All these notions are incomplete and immature compared to the reality. When Romeo meets Mercutio the next morning a second quibbling-match ensues in which the bawdy expressive of love-war and love-madness is all Mercutio's. Romeo's puns, if silly, are gay and spontaneous in comparison with his laboured conceits on the previous evening. Then, as he explained to Benvolio, he was not himself, not Romeo.

Now Mercutio cries: 'now art thou sociable, now art thou Romeo'. In fact Romeo and Juliet have experienced a self-discovery. Like Donne's happy lovers, they 'possess one world, each hath one and is one'; a world poles apart from the Nirvana quested by romantic love. The play is a tragedy, not because the love of Romeo for Juliet is in its nature tragic, but because the ending achieves the equilibrium of great tragedy. The final victory of time and society over the lovers is counterpoised by the knowledge that it is, in a sense, *their* victory; a victory not only over time and society which would have made them old and worldly in the end (whereas their deaths heal the social wound), but over the most insidious enemy of love, the inner hostility that 'builds a Hell in Heaven's despite' and which threatens in the broad jests of Mercutio. For we believe in the uniqueness of Romeo's and Juliet's experience at the same time as we know it to be, like other sublunary things, neither perfect nor permanent. If our distress and satisfaction are caught up in the fine balance of great tragedy at the end of the play, it is because, throughout, the wordplay and imagery, the conduct of the action and the grouping of characters contribute to that balance. The lovers' confidence is both heightened and menaced by a worldly wisdom, cynicism and resignation which, for the reason that candle-holders see more of the game, we are not able to repudiate as easily as they can do.

3

The play's central paradox of love's strength and fragility is most clearly expressed in the short marriage scene (II. vi). On the one hand there is Romeo's triumphant boast:

> come what sorrow can,
> It cannot counteruaile the exchange of ioy
> That one short minute giues me in her sight:
> Do thou but close our hands with holy words,
> Then loue deuouring death do what he dare,
> It is inough I may but call her mine.
>
> (3–8)

On the other hand there are the forebodings of Friar Laurence:

> These violent delights haue violent endes,
> And in their triumph die like fier and powder:
> Which as they kisse *consume*,
>
> (9–11)

where *consume* means both 'reach a consummation' (*N.E.D.* v.[2]) and 'burn away, be destroyed'. These conflicting themes of satisfaction and frustration coalesce in the Friar's words on Juliet's entry:

> Here comes the Lady, Oh so *light* a foote
> Will *nere weare out* the euerlasting flint.
> (16–17)

An ambiguity of pronunciation between 'near' and 'ne'er' and another of meaning in *wear out*[11] enable us to distinguish four possible readings here before, with cormorant delight, we swallow the lot. Juliet's foot is so light that

(i)   it will never wear away the everlasting flint;
(ii) it will never last it out;
(iii) it will nearly outlast it;
(iv) it will nearly wear it away.

The first of these is the obvious meaning, platitudinously suited to the speaker. The second anticipates our fear that the lovers are too beset with enemies on the hard road of life to be able to last the course, whereas the third contradicts this by saying that Juliet's love and beauty, because time will not have the chance to wear them away, will last in their fame nearly as long as the rocks of earth. And this contradiction is heightened by (iv) in which *light* has a suggestion of Juliet's luminous beauty,[12] and the flint is that of a flintlock; so that the line is connected with the sequence of paradoxical light images running through the play. Love is spoken of as a sudden spark or a flash of lightning. Juliet's forebodings in the balcony scene –

> I haue no ioy of this contract to night,
> It is too rash, too vnaduisd, too sudden,
> Too like the lightning which doth cease to bee,
> Ere one can say, it lightens
> (II.ii.117–20)

– are deepened here by the Friar's talk of fire and powder and again in the next act by his reproaches to Romeo:

> Thy wit, that ornament, to shape and loue,
> Mishapen in the conduct of them both:
> Like powder in a skillesse souldiers flaske,
> Is set a fier by thine owne ignorance.
> (III.iii.129–32)

In sum, love is as easily extinguishable as it appears to Lysander in
A Midsummer Night's Dream:

> Briefe as the lightning in the collied night,
> That (in a spleene) vnfolds both heauen and earth;
> And ere a man hath power to say, behold,
> The iawes of darknesse do deuoure it vp:
> So quicke bright things come to confusion.
>
> (i.i.145–9)

Yet Romeo, when he experiences 'a *lightning* before death', uses the
pun not only to imply that he has enjoyed a lightning brief happiness
before being

> dischargd of breath,
> As violently, as hastie powder fierd
> Doth hurry from the fatall Canons wombe,
>
> (v.i.63–5)

but also to sustain the image of Juliet's luminous beauty which
makes 'This Vault a feasting presence full of light'. For alongside
the images of sparks, torches, lightning, are others which associate
Romeo and Juliet with the unquenchable heavenly lights. Mercutio's
'We waste our lights in vaine, light lights by day' is ironically
apposite to Romeo's love of Rosaline, who is a mere candle before
the sun that breaks from Juliet's window. Two passages which have
been slighted as conceits are an essential part of this theme:

> Two of the fairest starres in all the heauen,
> Hauing some busines do[13] entreate her eyes,
> To twinckle in their spheres till they returne.
> What if her eyes were there, they in her head,
> The brightnesse of her cheek wold shame those stars,
> As day-light doth a lampe, her eye in heauen,
> Would through the ayrie region streame so bright,
> That birds would sing, and thinke it were not night.
>
> (ii.ii.15–22)

> Giue me my Romeo, and when I shall die,
> Take him and cut him out in little starres,
> And he will make the face of heauen so fine;
> That all the world will be in loue with night,
> And pay no worship to the garish Sun.
>
> (iii.ii.21–5)

Romeo and Juliet stellify each other, the love which appears to be
quenched as easily as a spark is extinguished is, in fact, made as
permanent as the sun and stars when it is set out of the range of
time.

The same paradox is sustained by the flower images which are
closely associated with those of light. The 'gather the rose' theme
was of course inevitable in a love tragedy of the High Renaissance.
Shakespeare's rose imagery, however, is more than rhetorical, and
serves to stress the central themes of the play.[14] The rose was
dramatically appropriate as a love symbol because it was so often a
prey to the invisible worm: 'Loathesome canker liues in sweetest
bud'. Romeo is devoured by his infatuation for Rosaline 'as is the
bud bit with an enuious worme' and the Friar, gathering herbs,
moralises over the adulteration of the good in a life by its evil until
'the Canker death eates vp that Plant'. Romeo and Juliet are spared
this. Death lies on Juliet just as its earlier semblance had done.

> like an vntimely frost,
> Vpon the sweetest flower of all the field.
> (IV.v.28–9)

This early frost forestalls the heat of the sun as well as the blight in
the bud, since a further fitness of the image consists in the speed
with which both roses and 'fresh female buds'[15] bloom and wither
in the south. Although Lady Capulet seems never to have been
young she tells Juliet

> I was your mother, much vpon these yeares
> That you are now a maide,
> (I.iii.72–3)

and the cruelty of Verona's summer is implicit in Old Capulet's
words:

> Let two more Sommers wither in their pride,
> Ere we may thinke her ripe to be a bride.
> (I.ii.10–11)

The marriage scene, after its strong statement of love as the victor-
victim of time, closes with a quibbling passage in which Romeo and
Juliet defy time's most powerful allies. Romeo, in an image of music,
challenges the notion that passion is discordant by nature, Juliet
rejects the prudence of social considerations in her declaration of
love's richness – 'I cannot sum vp sum of halfe my wealth'. This
last image is a foretaste of *Antony and Cleopatra*, and it would be

interesting to compare the success of love's three enemies in Shakespeare's three double-titled tragedies. In *Troilus and Cressida* they win hands down. Society, in the shape of the Trojan War, again compels secrecy and again separates the lovers; the inner corruption of love itself makes Cressida unfaithful; and the burden of the play is that 'Loue, friendship, charity, are subjects all / To enuious and calumniating time'. By contrast, *Antony and Cleopatra* is a clear victory for the lovers. Society, seen as the pomp of Rome, is a world well lost; the dismal drunken party we witness on Pompey's barge contrasts poorly with the revels of Antony and Cleopatra – which are left to our imagination. The lovers are old and wise enough to be reconciled to the ambivalence of their feelings, which is implicit in the play's imagery. Finally, time cannot harm them when they have eternity in their lips and eyes; at the end of the play Cleopatra is again for Cydnus to meet Mark Antony.

In *Romeo and Juliet* love's enemies have a Pyrrhic victory which begins with the slaying of Mercutio at the beginning of Act III. Like many of Shakespeare's characters, Mercutio dies with a quibble that asserts his vitality in the teeth of death. He jests as long as he has breath; only if we ask for him *tomorrow* shall we find him a grave man. But it is a grim joke, to accompany a dying curse. The Elizabethans, who believed in the power of curses, would have seen in the play's subsequent events the working-out of Mercutio's cynical knowledge that love is inseparably commingled with hate in human affairs. Romeo kills Tybalt, the cousin whose name he now tenders as dearly as his own. Juliet responds to the news with an outburst – 'O serpent heart hid with a flowring face . . .' which, by recalling the loving hate of Romeo's infatuation with Rosaline, threatens the harmony and permanence of the love between Romeo and Juliet. She recovers her balance, but we have felt the tremor and know that even these lovers cannot sustain many such shocks.

Some of the most notorious puns in Shakespeare occur in this scene between Juliet and her Nurse, when the Nurse's confusion misleads Juliet into thinking Romeo has killed himself:

> Hath Romeo slaine himselfe? say thou but *I*,
> And that bare vowell *I* shall poyson more
> Then the death darting[16] *eye* of Cockatrice,
> *I* am not *I*, if there be such an *I*.
> Or those *eyes* shut,[16] that makes thee answere *I*:
> If he be slaine say *I*, or if not, no.
>
> (III.ii.45–50)

Excuses might be made for this. It does achieve a remarkable sound-effect by setting Juliet's high-pitched keening of 'I' against the Nurse's moans of 'O Romeo, Romeo'. It also sustains the eye imagery of Juliet's great speech at the opening of this scene: the runaways' eyes, the blindness of love, Juliet hooded like a hawk, Romeo as the eye of heaven. But excuses are scarcely needed since this is one of Shakespeare's first attempts to reveal a profound disturbance of mind by the use of quibbles.[17] Romeo's puns in the next scene at Friar Laurence's cell are of the same kind: flies may kiss Juliet, but he must fly from her; the Friar, though a friend *professed*, will offer him no sudden mean of death, though ne'er so mean; he longs to know what his concealed lady says to their cancelled love. This is technically crude, and perhaps we do well to omit it in modern productions; but it represents a psychological discovery that Shakespeare was to put to masterly use in later plays. Against this feverish language of Romeo's, Shakespeare sets the Friar's sober knowledge that lovers have suffered and survived these calamities since the beginning of time. For the Friar, 'the world is broad and wide', for Romeo, 'there is no world without Verona wall'. When the Friar tries to dispute with him of his 'estate', the generalised, prayer-bookish word suggests that Romeo's distress is the common human lot, and we believe as much even while we join with Romeo in his protest: 'Thou canst not speak of that thou dost not feele.' Tragedy continually restates the paradox that 'all cases are unique and very similar to others'.

The lovers' parting at dawn sustains this contradiction. Lovers' hours may be full eternity, but the sun must still rise. Their happiness has placed them out of the reach of fate; but from now on, an accelerating series of misfortunes is to confound their triumph in disaster without making it any less of a triumph. With Lady Capulet's arrival to announce the match with Paris, love's enemies begin to close in. Juliet meets her mother with equivocations which suggest that Romeo's 'snowie Doue' has grown wise as serpents since the story began, and which prepare us for her resolution in feigning death to remain loyal to Romeo:

> Indeed I neuer shall be satisfied
> With Romeo, till I behold him. Dead
> Is my poore heart so for a kinsman vext.
> (III.v.94–6)

This is a triple ambiguity, with one meaning for Juliet, another for her mother and a third for us, the audience: Juliet will never in fact see Romeo again until she wakes and finds him dead beside her.

A pun which has escaped most editors is made by Paris at the beginning of Act iv. He tells the Friar he has talked little of love with Juliet because 'Venus smiles not in a house of teares'. Here *house of tears* means, beside the bereaved Capulet household an inauspicious section of the heavens – perhaps the eighth house or 'house of death'. Spenser's line 'When oblique Saturne sate in the house of agonyes'[18] shows that the image was familiar to the Elizabethans, and here it adds its weight to the lovers' yoke of inauspicious stars. But this is one of very few quibbles in the last two acts. The wordplay which, in the first part of the play, served to point up the meaning of the action is no longer required. What quibbles there are in the final scenes have, however, extraordinary force. Those spoken by Romeo after he has drunk the poison reaffirm the paradox of the play's experience at its most dramatic moment:

> O *true* Appothecary:
> Thy drugs are *quicke*. Thus with a kisse I die.
> (v.iii.119–20)

Like the Friar's herbs, the apothecary's poison both heals and destroys. He is *true* not only because he has spoken the truth to Romeo in describing the poison's potency, but because he has been true to his calling in finding the salve for Romeo's ills. His drugs are not only speedy, but also *quick* in the sense of 'life-giving'. Romeo and Juliet 'cease to die, by dying'.

It is the prerogative of poetry to give effect and value to incompatible meanings. In *Romeo and Juliet*, several poetic means contribute to this end: the paradox, the recurrent image, the juxtaposition of old and young in such a way that we are both absorbed by and aloof from the lovers' feelings, and the sparkling wordplay. By such means Shakespeare ensures that our final emotion is neither the satisfaction we should feel in the lovers' death if the play were a simple expression of the *Liebestod* theme, nor the dismay of seeing two lives thwarted and destroyed by vicious fates, but a tragic equilibrium which includes and transcends both these feelings.

SOURCE: Extract from *Shakespeare's Wordplay* (London, 1957), pp. 56–72.

NOTES

(Reorganised and renumbered and added to by Editors.)

1. Line 9. The prologue is not given in the Folio, but is found in the second, third and fourth Quartos. Quotations are all from the Second Quarto.

2. Arthur Brooke (died 1563) wrote *The Tragicall Historye of Romeus and Juliet* (1562), the main source of Shakespeare's play. The Preface to this long poem is highly moralistic. [Eds]

3. *L'Amour et l'Occident* (Paris, 1939).

4. See Kenneth Muir and Sean O'Loughlin, *The Voyage to Illyria* (London, 1937), p. 72.

5. Characters in an unfinished play by John Synge (1871–1909), *Deirdre of the Sorrows.* [Eds]

6. A French film made in 1936, directed by Anatole Litvak. It tells of the tragic love affair between Archduke Rudolph and Marie Vetsera. [Eds]

7. Jean Anouilh's *Eurydice* (1942) and Jean Cocteau's *Orphée* (1926). [Eds]

8. Harley Granville-Barker, *Prefaces to Shakespeare, Second Series* (London, 1930), p. 6.

9. See G. E. Matthews, 'Sex and the Sonnet', *Essays in Criticism* II (1952), pp. 119–37.

10. Mercutio's 'This field-bed is too cold for me to sleepe' seems to be an echo the the Nurse's words to the lovers in Brooke's poem: 'Loe here a fielde, (she shewd a fieldbed ready dight) / Where you may, if you list, in armes, revenge your selfe by fight.' As often with Shakespeare, a piece of rhetorical decoration in the source has become an integral part of the play's imagery, by prompting its quibbles on love as war.

11. As in the shoe polish advertisement: 'They're well-worn but they've worn well.' For discussion of the *Romeo and Juliet* passage see the correspondence in the *Times Literary Supplement* for April 3, 17, and 24 and May 1, 1943.

12. There are previous puns on *light*: 'Away from light steales home my heauie sonne' (1.i.42); 'Being but heauie I will beare the light' (1.4.12); 'And not impute this yeelding to light loue, / Which the darke night hath so discouered' (2.ii.105–6).

13. For the Second Quarto's *to.*

14. As the author of *2 Henry VI*, Shakespeare must almost unconsciously have connected rose images with the rivalry of two great houses. For the light-flowers cluster see 1.i.139–45 and 156–8; 1.ii.24–30; 2.ii.117–22.

15. I borrow the phrase from the Bad Quarto. The accepted texts have 'fresh fennell buds'.

16. For the Second Quarto's *arting* and *shot.*

17. He had already done so in *Two Gentlemen of Verona* but the device is less startling in a comedy.

18. *The Faerie Queene*, 2.9.52.

Susan Snyder   The Comic Matrix of
Romeo and Juliet   (1979)

The movement of *Romeo and Juliet* is unlike that of any other
Shakespearean tragedy. It becomes, rather than is, tragic. Other
tragedies have reversals, but here the reversal is so complete as to
constitute a change of genre. Action and characters begin in the
familiar comic mold and are then transformed, or discarded, to
compose the shape of tragedy.[1] In this discussion I shall have to
disregard much of the play's richness, especially of language and
characterization, in order to isolate that shaping movement. But
isolating it can reveal a good deal about *Romeo*, and may suggest
why this early experimental tragedy has seemed to many to fall
short of full tragic effect.

It was H. B. Charlton, concurring in this judgment, who classed
the play as 'experimental'. According to Charlton, Shakespeare in
his early history-based tragic plays failed to find a pattern of event
and character that would make the dramatic outcome feel inevitable;
in *Romeo* he took a whole new direction, that of the modern fiction-
based tragedy advocated by the Italian critic Giraldi Cinthio.[2]
Certainly dramatic thrust and necessity are unsolved problems in
Titus Andronicus and *Richard III*, and perhaps in *Richard II* too. But
one need not turn to Italian critical theory to explain the new
direction of *Romeo*. Given the novella-source, full of marriageable
young people and domestic concerns, it seems natural enough that
Shakespeare would think of turning his own successful work in
romantic comedy to account in his apprenticeship as a tragedian.

We have seen that comedy is based on a principle of 'evitability'.
It endorses opportunistic shifts and realistic accommodations as
means to new social health. It renders impotent the imperatives of
time and law, either stretching them to suit the favored characters'
needs or simply brushing them aside. In the tragic world, which is
governed by inevitability and which finds its highest value in personal
integrity, these imperatives have full force. Unlike the extrinsic,
alterable laws of comedy, law in tragedy is inherent – in the
protagonist's own nature and in the larger patterns, divine, natural,
and social, with which that personal nature brings him into conflict.

Tragic law cannot be altered, and tragic time cannot be suspended. The events of tragedy acquire urgency in their uniqueness and irrevocability: they will never happen again, and one by one they move the hero closer to the end of his own personal time.

Comedy is organized like a game. The ascendancy goes to the clever ones who can take advantage of sudden openings, contrive strategies, and adapt flexibly to an unexpected move from the other side. But luck and instinct win games as well as skill, and I have discussed in the preceding chapter the natural law of comedy that crowns lovers, whether clever or not, with final success. Romeo and Juliet, young and in love and defiant of obstacles, are attuned to the basic movement of the comic game toward marriage and social regeneration. But they do not win: the game turns into a sacrifice, and the favored lovers become victims of time and law. We can better understand this shift by looking at the two distinct worlds of the play and at some secondary characters who help to define them.

If we divide the play at Mercutio's death, the death that generates all those that follow, it becomes apparent that the play's movement up to this point is essentially comic. With the usual intrigues and go-betweens, the lovers overcome obstacles and unite in marriage. Their personal action is set in a broader social context, so that the marriage promises not only private satisfaction but renewed social unity:

> For this alliance may so happy prove
> To turn your households' rancour to pure love.
>   (II.iii.91–92)

The households' rancor is set out in the play's first scene. This Verona of the Montague-Capulet feud is exactly the typical starting point of a comedy described by Frye — 'a society controlled by habit, ritual bondage, arbitrary law and the older characters'.[3] The scene's formal balletic structure, a series of matched representatives of the warring families entering neatly on cue, conveys the inflexibility of this society, the arbitrary barriers that limit freedom of action.

The feud itself seems more a matter of mechanical reflex than of deeply felt hatred. Charlton noted the comic tone of its presentation in this part of the play.[4] The 'parents' rage' that sounded so ominous in the prologue becomes in representation an irascible humour: two old men claw at each other, only to be dragged back by their wives

and scolded by their prince. Charlton found the play flawed by this
failure to plant the seeds of tragedy; but the treatment of the feud
makes good sense if Shakespeare is playing on *comic* expectations.
At this point, the feud functions in *Romeo* very much as the various
legal restraints do in Shakespearean comedy. Imposed from outside
on the youthful lovers, who feel themselves no part of it, the feud is
a barrier placed arbitrarily between them, like the Athenian law
giving fathers the disposition of their daughters which stands between
Lysander and Hermia in *A Midsummer Night's Dream* – something
set up in order to be broken down.

Other aspects of this initial world of *Romeo* suggest comedy as
well. Its characters are the gentry and servants familiar in romantic
comedies, and they are preoccupied, not with wars and the fate of
kingdoms, but with arranging marriages and managing the kitchen.
More important, it is a world of possibilities, with Capulet's feast
represented to more than one young man as a field of choice. 'Hear
all, all see,' says Capulet to Paris, 'And like her most whose merit
most shall be'(i.ii.30–31). 'Go thither,' Benvolio tells Romeo, who
is disconsolate over Rosaline, 'and with unattainted eye / Compare
her face with some that I shall show' (85–86) and she will be
forgotten for some more approachable lady. Romeo rejects the
words, of course, but in action he soon displays a classic comic
adaptability, switching from the impossible love to the possible.

Violence and disaster are not totally absent from this milieu, but
they are unrealized threats. The feast again provides a kind of comic
emblem, when Tybalt's proposed violence is rendered harmless by
Capulet's festive accommodation.

> Therefore be patient, take no note of him;
> It is my will; the which if thou respect,
> Show a fair presence and put off these frowns,
> An ill-beseeming semblance for a feast.
>   (i.v.69–72)

This overruling of Tybalt is significant because Tybalt in his
inflexibility is a potentially tragic character, indeed the only one in
the first part of the play. If we recognise in him an irascible humour
type, an *alazon*, we should also recognise that the tragic hero is an
alazon transposed.[5] Tybalt alone takes the feud really seriously. It
is his *inner* law, the propeller of his fiery nature. His natural frame
of reference is the heroic one of honour and death:

> What, dares the slave
> Come hither, cover'd with an antic face,
> To fleer and scorn at our solemnity?
> Now, by the stock and honour of my kin,
> To strike him dead I hold it not a sin.
>   (I.v.53–57)

Tybalt's single set of absolutes cuts him off from a whole range of speech and action available to the other young men of the play: lyric love, witty fooling, friendly conversation. Ironically, his imperatives come to dominate the play's world only when he himself departs from it. While he is alive, Tybalt is an alien.

In a similar way, the passing fears of calamity voiced at times by Romeo, Juliet, and Friar Laurence are not allowed to dominate the atmosphere of the early acts. The love of Romeo and Juliet is already imaged as a flash of light swallowed by darkness, an image invoking inexorable natural law; but it is also expressed as a sea venture, which suggests luck and skill set against natural hazards and chance seized joyously as an opportunity for action. 'Direct my sail', says Romeo to his captain Fortune. Soon he feels himself in command:

> I am no pilot; yet, wert thou as far
> As that vast shore wash'd with the farthest sea,
> I should adventure for such merchandise.[6]

The spirit is Bassanio's as he adventures for Portia, a Jason voyaging in quest of the Golden Fleece (*Merchant of Venice* I.i.167–172). Romeo is ready for difficulties with a traditional lovers' stratagem, one which Shakespeare had used before in *Two Gentlemen*: a rope ladder, 'cords made like a tackled stair; / Which to the high top-gallant of my joy / Must be my convoy in the secret night' (II.iv.183–185).

But before Romeo can mount his tackled stair, Mercutio's death intervenes to cut off this world of exhilarating venture. Shakespeare developed this character, who in the source is little more than a name and a cold hand, into the very incarnation of comic atmosphere. Mercutio is the clown of romantic comedy, recast in more elegant mold but equally ready to take off from the plot in verbal play and to challenge idealistic love with his own brand of comic earthiness.

> Nay, I'll conjure too.
> Romeo! humours! madman! passion! lover!
> Appear thou in the likeness of a sigh;
> Speak but one rhyme and I am satisfied;
> Cry but 'Ay me!' pronounce but 'love' and 'dove';

. . . .
I conjure thee by Rosaline's bright eyes,
By her high forehead and her scarlet lip,
By her fine foot, straight leg, and quivering thigh,
And the demesnes that there adjacent lie.

(II.i.6–20)

He is the best of game-players, endlessly inventive and full of quick moves and countermoves. Speech for him is a constant exercise in multiple possibilities: puns abound, roles are taken up at whim (that of conjuror, for instance, in the passage just quoted), and his Queen Mab brings dreams not only to lovers like Romeo but to courtiers, lawyers, parsons, soldiers, maids. These have nothing to do with the case at hand, which is Romeo's premonition of trouble, but Mercutio is not bound by events. They serve him merely as convenient launching pads for his flights of wit. When all this vitality, which has till now ignored all urgencies, is cut off abruptly by Tybalt's sword, it must come as a shock to a spectator unfamiliar with the play. In Mercutio's sudden, violent end, Shakespeare makes the birth of tragedy coincide exactly with the symbolic death of comedy. The alternative view, the element of freedom and play, dies with Mercutio. Where many courses were open before, now there seems only one. Romeo sees at once that an irreversible process has begun:

This day's black fate on moe days doth depend [hang over];
This but begins the woe others must end.

(III.i.116–117)

It is the first sign in the play's dialogue pointing unambiguously to tragic necessity. Romeo's future is now determined: he *must* kill Tybalt, he *must* run away, he is Fortune's fool.

This helplessness is the most striking feature of the second, tragic world of *Romeo*. The temper of this new world is largely a function of onrushing events. Under pressure of events, the feud turns from farce to fate; tit for tat becomes blood for blood. Lawless as it seems to Prince Escalus, the feud is dramatically 'the law' in *Romeo*. Before, it was external and avoidable. Now it moves inside Romeo to be his personal law. This is why he takes over Tybalt's rhetoric of honor and death:

Alive in triumph and Mercutio slain!
Away to heaven respective lenity,
And fire-ey'd fury be my conduct now!
Now, Tybalt, take the 'villain' back again
That late thou gav'st me.

(III.i.119–123)

Even outside the main chain of vengeance, the world is suddenly full of imperatives. Others besides Romeo feel helpless. Against his will Friar John is detained at the monastery; against his will the Apothecary sells poison to Romeo. Urgency becomes the norm. Nights run into mornings, and the characters seem never to sleep. The new world finds its emblem not in the aborted attack but in the aborted feast. As Tybalt's violence was out of tune with the Capulet festivities in Act II, so in the changed world of Acts III and IV the projected wedding of Juliet and Paris is made grotesque when Shakespeare insistently links it with death.[7] Preparations for the wedding feast parallel those made for the party in the play's first part, so as to make more wrenching the contrast when Capulet must order,

All things that we ordained festival
Turn from their office to black funeral:
Our instruments to melancholy bells.
Our wedding cheer to a sad burial feast,
Our solemn hymns to sullen dirges change.

(IV.v.84–88)

The play's last scene shows how completely the comic movement has been reversed. It is inherent in that movement, as we have seen, that the young get their way at the expense of the old. The final tableau of comedy features young couples joined in love; parents and authority figures are there, if at all, to ratify with more or less good grace what has been accomplished against their wills. But here, the stage is strikingly full of elders – the Friar, the Prince, Capulet, Lady Capulet, Montague. Their power is not passed on. Indeed, there are no young to take over. If Benvolio survives somewhere offstage, we have long since forgotten this adjunct character. Romeo, Juliet, Tybalt, Mercutio, and Paris are all dead. In effect, the entire younger generation has been wiped out.

I have been treating these two worlds as separate, consistent wholes in order to bring out their opposition, but I do not wish to deny dramatic unity to *Romeo and Juliet*. Shakespeare was writing one play, not two; and in spite of the clearly marked turning point we are aware of premonitions of disaster before the death of Mercutio, and hopes for avoiding it continue until near the end of the play. Our full perception of the world-shift that converts Romeo and Juliet from instinctive winners into sacrificial victims thus comes gradually. In this connection the careers of two secondary characters, Friar Laurence and the Nurse, are instructive.

In being and action, these two belong to the comic vision. Friar Laurence is one of the tribe of manipulators, whose job it is to transform or otherwise get round seemingly intractable realities. If his herbs and potions are less spectacular than the paraphernalia of Friar Bacon or John a Kent, he nevertheless belongs to their brotherhood. Such figures abound in romantic comedy, as we have seen, but not in tragedy, where the future is not so manipulable. The Friar's aims are those implicit in the play's comic movement: an inviolable union for Romeo and Juliet and an end to the families' feud.

The Nurse's goal is less lofty but equally appropriate to comedy. She wants Juliet married – to anyone. Her preoccupation with bedding and breeding reminds us of comedy's ancient roots in fertility rites, and it is as indiscriminate as the life force itself. But she conveys no sense of urgency in all this. On the contrary, her garrulity assumes the limitless time of comedy. In this sense her circumlocutions and digressions are analogous to Mercutio's witty games and, for that matter, to Friar Laurence's counsels of patience. 'Wisely and slow', the Friar cautions Romeo; 'they stumble that run fast' (II.iii.94). The Nurse is not very wise, but she is slow. The leisurely time assumptions of both Friar and Nurse contrast with the lovers' impatience, to create first the normal counterpoint of comedy and later a radical split that points us, with the lovers, directly towards tragedy.

Friar Laurence and the Nurse have no place in the new world brought into being by Mercutio's death, the world of limited time, no effective choice, no escape. They define and sharpen the tragedy by their very failure to find a part in the dramatic progress, by their growing estrangement from the true springs of the action. 'Be patient', is the Friar's advice to banished Romeo, 'for the world is broad and wide' (III.iii.16). But the roominess he perceives in both time and space simply does not exist for Romeo. *His* time has been constricted into a chain of days working out a 'black fate', and he sees no world outside the walls of Verona (17).

Comic adaptability again confronts tragic integrity when Juliet is forced to marry Paris – and turns to her Nurse for counsel, as Romeo has turned to Friar Laurence. In the Nurse's response comedy's traditional wisdom of accommodation is carried to an extreme. Romeo has been banished, and Paris is after all very presentable. In short, adjust to the new state of things.

> Then, since the case so stands as now it doth,
> I think it best you married with the County.
> O, he's a lovely gentleman!
> Romeo's a dishclout to him.
>
> (III.v.217–220)

She still speaks for the life force, against barrenness and death. Even if Juliet will not accept the dishclout comparison, an inferior husband is better than no husband at all: 'Your first is dead, or 'twere as good he were / As living here and you no use of him' (225–226).

But her advice is irrelevant, even shocking, in this new context. There was no sense of jar when Benvolio, a spokesman for comic accommodation like the Nurse and the Friar, earlier advised Romeo to substitute a possible love for an impossible one. True, the Nurse here is urging Juliet to violate her marriage vows; but Romeo also felt himself sworn to Rosaline, and for Juliet the marriage vow is a seal on the integrity of her love for Romeo, not a separable issue. The parallel points up the move into tragedy, for while Benvolio's advice sounded sensible in Act I and was in fact unintentionally carried out by Romeo, the course of action that the Nurse proposes in Act III is unthinkable to the audience as well as to Juliet. The memory of the lovers' passionate dawn parting that began this scene is too strong. Juliet and her nurse no longer speak the same language, and estrangement is inevitable. 'Thou and my bosom henceforth shall be twain,' Juliet vows when the Nurse has left the stage.[8] Like the slaying of Mercutio, Juliet's rejection of her old confidante has symbolic overtones. The possibilities of comedy have again been presented only to be discarded.

Both Romeo and Juliet have now cast off their comic companions and the alternative modes of being that they represented. But there is one last hope for comedy. If the lovers will not adjust to the situation, perhaps the situation can be adjusted to the lovers. This

is the usual comic way with obstinately faithful pairs, and we have
at hand the usual manipulator figure to arrange it.

The Friar's failure to bring off that solution is the final definition
of the tragic world of *Romeo and Juliet*. There is no villain, only
chance and bad timing. In comedy chance creates that elastic time
that allows last-minute rescues. But here, events at Mantua and at
the Capulet tomb will simply happen – by chance – in the wrong
sequence. The Friar does his best: he makes more than one plan to
avert catastrophe. The first, predictably, is patience and a broader
field of action. Romeo must go to Mantua and wait

> till we can find a time
> To blaze your marriage, reconcile your friends,
> Beg pardon of the Prince, and call thee back . . .
> (iii.iii.150–52)

It is a good enough plan, for life if not for drama, but it depends on
'finding a time'. As it turns out, events move too quickly for the
Friar. The hasty preparations for Juliet's marriage to Paris leave no
time for cooling tempers and reconciliations.

His second plan is an attempt to *gain* time: he will create the
necessary freedom by faking Juliet's death. This is, of course, a
familiar comic formula. Shakespeare's later uses of it are all in
comedies.[9] Indeed, the contrived 'deaths' of Hero in *Much Ado*,
Helena in *All's Well*, Claudio in *Measure for Measure*, and Hermione
in *The Winter's Tale* are more ambitiously intended than Juliet's,
aimed at bringing about a change of heart in other characters.[10]
Time may be important, as it is in *Winter's Tale*, but only as it
promotes repentance. Friar Laurence, more desperate than his fellow
manipulators, does not hope that Juliet's death will dissolve the
Montague–Capulet feud, but only that it will give Romeo a chance
to come and carry her off. Time and chance, which in the other
plays cooperate benevolently with the forces of regeneration and
renewal, work against Friar Laurence. Romeo's man is quicker with
the bad news of Juliet's death than poor Friar John with the good
news that the death is only a pretense. Romeo himself beats Friar
Laurence to the tomb of the Capulets. The onrushing tragic action
quite literally outstrips the slower steps of accommodation before
our eyes. The Friar arrives too late to prevent one half of the tragic
conclusion, and his essential estrangement from the play's world is

only emphasized when he seeks to avert the other half by sending Juliet to a nunnery. This last alternative means little to the audience or to Juliet, who spares only a line to reject the possibility of adjustment and continuing life: 'Go, get thee hence, for I will not away' (v.iii.160).

The Nurse and the Friar show that one way comedy can operate in a tragedy is by its irrelevance. Tragedy is tuned to the extraordinary. *Romeo and Juliet* locates this extraordinariness not so much in the two youthful lovers as in the love itself, its intensity and integrity. As the play moves forward, our sense of this intensity and integrity is strengthened by the cumulative effect of the lovers' lyric encounters and the increasing urgency of events, but also by the growing irrelevance of the comic characters.

De Quincey saw in the knocking at the gate in *Macbeth* the resumption of normality after nightmare, 'the re-establishment of the goings-on of the world in which we live, [which] first makes us profoundly sensible of the awful parenthesis that had suspended them'.[11] I would say, rather, than the normal atmosphere of *Macbeth* has been and goes on being nightmarish, and that it is the knocking episode that turns out to be the contrasting parenthesis, but the notion of sharpened sensibility is important. As the presence of other paths makes us more conscious of the road we are in fact traveling, so the Nurse and the Friar make us more 'profoundly sensible' of the love of Romeo and Juliet and its tragic direction.

The play offers another sort of experiment in mingled genres that is less successful, I think. It starts well, in iv.iv, with a striking juxtaposition of Capulet preparations for the wedding with Juliet's potion scene. On the one hand is the household group in a bustle over clothes, food, logs for the fire – the everyday necessaries and small change of life. On the other is Juliet's tense monologue of fear, madness, and death. It is fine dramatic counterpoint, and its effect is stronger in stage production, as Granville-Barker observed, when the curtained bed of Juliet is visible upstage during the cheerful domestic goings on.[12] The counterpoint, of course, depends on the Capulets' ignorance of what is behind those curtains. It comes to an end when in scene v Nurse and the others find Juliet's body. But Shakespeare keeps the comic strain alive through the rest of the scene. The high-pitched, repetitive mourning of the Nurse, Paris, and the Capulets sounds more like Pyramus over the body of Thisbe than a serious tragic scene. Finally Peter has his comic turn with the musicians. What Shakespeare is attempting here is not counterpoint but the *fusion* of tragic and comic. It doesn't quite work. S. L. Bethell suggests that the mourners' rhetorical excesses direct the audience to remain detached and thus to reserve their tears for the real death scene that will shortly follow.[13] This makes good theatrical sense. It is also possible that the musicians' dialogue, modulating as it does from shock to professional shop to dinner, was meant to set off the tragic action by projecting a sense of the ongoing, normal life that is denied to Romeo and Juliet. Still, the scene tends to leave spectators uneasy – if, in fact, they get to see it at all: often the mourning passages are cut and the musicians' business dropped altogether.[14] Shakespeare's hand is uncertain in this early essay at fusing tragic and comic.

SOURCE: Extract from *The Comic Matrix of Shakespeare's Tragedies* (Princeton, 1979), pp. 57–69.

NOTES

1. Various critics have commented on the comic thrust of the early acts of *Romeo*, with interpretations ranging from H. A. Mason's somewhat lame and impotent conclusion, 'Shakespeare decided that in a general way the play needed as much comedy as he could get in' (*Shakespeare's Tragedies of Love* (London, 1970), p. 29), to Harry Levin's well-argued contention that the play invokes the artifices of romantic comedy in order to transcend them ('Form and Formality in *Romeo and Juliet*', *Shakespeare Quarterly*, 11 (1960), 3–11). Levin's essay is illuminating on the play's style; he does not speculate on what the transcendence-of-artifice theme (admittedly already used by Shakespeare in a comedy, *Love's Labour's Lost*) has to do with tragic structure. Franklin Dickey deals at some length with *Romeo* as 'comical tragedy' in *Not Wisely But Too Well* (San Marino, 1967), pp. 63–88. But Dickey's treatment of comedy is nonorganic, dwelling on such features as the witty heroine, the motif of lovers' absurdity, the debate on love's nature, the elaborate patterning of language, and the *commedia dell'arte* type-characters. He does not deal with why Shakespeare would want to present a tragic story this way or how the large comic element shapes the play as a whole. To explain the presence of that element, Dickey invokes the conventional association of love with comedy. J. M. Nosworthy thinks the comic admixture a mistake and blames it on Shakespeare's immaturity, as well as on the influence of Porter's *Two Angry Women of Abington*. 'The Two Angry Families of Verona', *Shakespeare Quarterly*, 3 (1952), 219–226.

2. Charlton, '*Romeo and Juliet* as an Experimental Tragedy', British Academy Shakespeare Lecture, 1939 (London, 1940), pp. 8–12.

3. Northrop Frye, *Anatomy of Criticism* (Princeton, 1957), p. 169. Although the younger generation participate in the feud, they have not created it; it is a habit bequeathed to them by their elders.

4. *Experimental Tragedy*, pp. 36–40.

5. Maynard Mack, 'Engagement and Detachment in Shakespeare's Plays', in *Essays on Shakespeare and Elizabethan Drama in Honor of Hardin Craig*, ed. Richard Hosley (Columbia, Mo., 1962), pp. 287–291.

6. i.iv.113; ii.ii.82–84. Later Mercutio hails the lovers' go-between, the Nurse, with 'A sail, a sail!' (ii.iv.98).

7. iii.vi.23–28; iii.v.201–202; iv.i.6–8, 77–85, 107–108, iv.v.35–39.

8. iii.v.241. In the potion scene Juliet's resolve weakens for a moment, but almost immediately she rejects the idea of companionship. The momentary wavering only emphasizes her aloneness: 'I'll call them back again to comfort me. / Nurse! – What should she do here? / My dismal scene I needs must act alone' (iv.iii.17–19).

9. Or in the comic part of a history, in the case of Falstaff's pretended death on the battlefield at Shrewsbury.

10. The same effect, if not intention, is apparent in the reported death of Imogen in *Cymbeline*.

11. 'On the Knocking at the Gate in *Macbeth*', in *Shakespeare Criticism: A Selection*, ed. D. Nichol Smith (Oxford, 1916), p. 378.

12. *Prefaces to Shakespeare* (London, 1963), iv, 62–63.

13. *Shakespeare and the Popular Dramatic Tradition* (London and New York, 1944), p. 111. Charles B. Lower agrees and argues as well for the more doubtful proposition that the audience needs to be reassured that Juliet is really still alive. Lower convincingly defends the authenticity of a Q1 stage direction, '*All at once cry out and wring their hand[s]*', which, by requiring the laments of Lady Capulet, the Nurse, Paris, and Capulet (iv.v.43–64) to be spoken simultaneously like an opera quartet, would increase the scene's burlesque quality. '*Romeo and Juliet*, iv.v: A Stage Direction and Purposeful Comedy', *Shakespeare Studies*, 8 (1975), 177–194.

14. Granville Barker wrote in 1930 that modern producers usually lowered the curtain after the climatic potion scene and raised it next on Romeo in Mantua, skipping the mourning and the musicians entirely. *Prefaces*, iv, 63–64. The most notable production of more recent years, by Franco Zeffirelli, omitted the musicians. J. Russell Brown, *Shakespeare's Plays in Performance* (London, 1966), p. 177.

T. J. L. Cribb   The Unity of *Romeo*
and Juliet   (1981)

Dryden thought Mercutio was Shakespeare's rather ill-bred idea of
a Gentleman.[1] Coleridge thought he was a man possessing 'all the
elements of a Poet'.[2] Between them they may be taken to establish
the two poles of preference, the one for the realistic, the other for
the poetic, between which criticism has since oscillated. Many critics
have settled the dilemma by sacrificing the play, for example Duthie,
who agreed with Charlton that 'as a pattern of the idea of tragedy
[the play] is a failure'.[3] Such critics excuse it as prentice work and
concentrate on deciding whether it is trying to be mainly a medieval
tragedy of the stars and Fortune, or a social tragedy, or a tragedy
of character. The most sophisticated attempt to reconcile the poetry
to the realism in defence of the play's unity is by Nicholas
Brooke, who argues: 'The play depends, then, very much on formal
patterning, like a sonnet; but explored, criticized, and penetrated,
so that the formal surface not only restrains but also reveals the
inner experience.[4] I say 'sophisticated', for the argument, brilliant
and illuminating though it is, verges on the sophistical in the way it
recruits the play's poetry against itself and so, in the last resort, into
the service of a kind of realism. My own view is that the play is
indeed a unity, but a unity founded not on 'poetry' as such, whatever
that might be, and still less on realism, another vexed term, but on
a particular set of values or ideas principally embodied in the lovers,
values which may indeed appear to be highly poetical. It is these
which are the source of doubts about the play's responsibility to
reality and viability in the theatre.

I can best begin my exposition of these ideas by calling attention
to Romeo's language in the balcony scene, the scene to which T. S.
Eliot paid remarkable tribute, and to which Harold Mason, seeking
to explain the predominance in it of a 'sense of the sacred', has also
devoted a sensitive if inconclusive study.[5] Romeo begins:

> But soft, what light through yonder window breaks?
> It is the East, and *Juliet* is the Sun.
>
> (II. ii. 2–3)

If we follow this image through we find that Romeo associates or actually identifies Juliet once with the moon, once with the stars, four times with the sun, and twice, climactically, with an angel. The effect is of a light shining through darkness with steadily increasing splendour. We must remember that in the context of the original performance in an outdoor theatre the play of reference between the audience's reality – day – and the imagined reality of the scene – night – would be peculiarly bewildering and disorienting, and contrived indeed to refer us to another reality beyond both – and that is Juliet. The logic of the syntax works to the same end, for Romeo's references to the sun, the moon, her eyes, the stars, lamps, her cheeks, daylight and darkness, earth and heaven are presented in a subtly confused structure of hypothetical statements, later taken as assumptions for further statements based on them. The subtlety is insidious, for the opening assertion that Juliet is the sun is not maintained, but changes to almost its opposite, as the thought of the moon being lost in the light of the sun makes Romeo think of Juliet's virginity as one of Diana's handmaidens. The idealizing transformation of Juliet is then renewed in:

> Two of the fairest starres in all the heaven,
> Having some busines do entreate her eyes,
> To twinckle in their spheres till they returne
> (II.ii.15–17)

and this time Romeo interrupts the fancifulness by his half-question, 'What if her eyes were there, they in her head'. Yet in the very act of dismissing the fancy he creates a new one, which, supported and as it were established by a lengthening of the phrasing, is even more transforming:

> The brightness of her cheek wold shame those stars,
> As day-light doth a lampe, her eyes in heaven,
> Would through the ayrie region streame so bright,
> That birds would sing, and thinke it were not night.
> (II.ii.19–22)

All is governed by the hypothetical condition, but at the end of the conceit that control is lost sight of and Juliet once again is the sun, transforming and vivifying all nature with her radiance. The cumulative effect of these liberties with logic and metamorphoses of imagery is to pass on us as real what begins as frank hyperbole or mere fancy.

All this is too specific, too insistent and too extraordinary to be encompassed in naturalistic terms, whether of atmosphere and scene-setting or of adolescent psychology. As Nicholas Brooke says of a sequence of images in *Macbeth*, it 'emerges from an acute psychological speech, but transposes into a mode that cannot be accounted for in psychological terms'.[6] When Romeo says that Juliet is the sun, since it is unsatisfactory to take him psychologically or pictorially and clearly impossible to take him literally, what then does he mean? In only one intellectual context do his images become intelligible, his feelings become principled, and his words make sense. Take for instance of that context the following:

The passion of a lover . . . desires the splendour of the divine light shining through bodies, and is amazed and awed by it . . , Certainly it is not a human passion which frightens them, which seizes and breaks them . . . but that glow of divinity, shining in beautiful bodies, like an image of God, compels lovers to awe, trembling, and reverence.[7]

The speaker is Giovanni Cavalcanti in Ficino's commentary on the *Symposium*. Awe and amazement are a good description of the feelings portrayed and evoked at the climax of Romeo's soliloquy:

> Oh speake againe bright Angel, for thou art
> As glorious to this night being ore my head,
> As is a winged messenger of heaven
> Unto the white upturned wondring eyes,
> Of mortalls that fall backe to gaze on him,
> When he bestrides the lazie puffing Cloudes,
> And sayles upon the bosom of the ayre.
>   (ii.ii.26–32)

Early on in his explanation of the difficult passages in Petrarch, Castiglione rather defensively admits that 'Many will say I want to make out that our poet was a Platonist, against his will.'[8] Such an attribution is not what is at issue here. We can rest content that our English poet is a poet and not a philosopher. However, as J. V. Cunningham observed of St Augustine, 'Experience never comes together except when ordered by some principles, implicit or explicit, and the principles are describable'.[9] Since Shakespeare's ordering

principles in *Romeo and Juliet* are certainly implicit, the issue is
whether or not we find Renaissance Platonism offers a satisfactory
explication of the evident features of the play. In the instance before
us, the master image of light, the peculiarly ideal nature of the
description and the climactic idea of beauty as a theophany are all
consistent and meaningful in the terms provided by the passage
from Ficino. Analysis couched in purely intellectual terms, however,
would omit the main quality, which is the feeling. Edgar Wind
pointed out long ago that the distinguishing feature of the attitude
to the world that Ficino represents is that the divine may be attained
by a *via amoris* that begins in passion.[10] It is true that at the end of
the way the world is left behind so that the divine may be
contemplated in pure intellection, but this, in its measure of
compatibility with traditional *contemptus mundi*, is not the novel
feature of the doctrine. What is striking is that the original motive
to this progress is love, and love of another, not for another, *eros* not
caritas. This revaluation of desire is quite explicit. Pico interprets the
figure of Janus to mean that some natures can contemplate both
intellectual beauty and the corporeal beauty that communicates
with it.[11] Indeed, the only way out from the deceptions of matter is
'the amatory life, which by sensible beauties, excites in the soul a
remembrance of the intellectual . . . by the flame of love refined into
an Angel'.[12] Castiglione, following Plato, presents the same idea in
the myth of the two Venuses, the vulgar leading to the heavenly.[13]
Such an attitude to life, with its emphasis on emotion and subjectivity,
can be called psychological, but it is a highly spiritualized psychology,
combining intense idealism with intense emotion founded on real
desire, and such is the quality of feeling demonstrated in Romeo's
speeches.

Guided by this peculiar orientation to life we can turn from the
language of the soliloquy to Romeo's role in the play and what he
represents. In her very interesting monograph on Shakespeare's play
in the context of the sonneteers Inge Leimberg has shown how the
revaluation of *eros* by the Florentine Academy led to a reinterpretation
of classical myths.[14] Hence Bruno can take the goddess Diana to
mean the beauty of the world reflecting 'the light shining through
the obscurity of matter and so resplendent in the darkness'.[15]
Consequently, Actaeon's seeing of Diana naked is not an act of
presumption or of reprehensible lust, as it had been interpreted in

the moralized Ovids of the Middle Ages, but a theophany achieved
by an eager hunter after beauty. His transformation into a deer
pursued by his own hounds is not a punishment but an apotheosis,
because 'he comes to apprehend that it is himself who necessarily
remains captured, absorbed, and united'.[16] To make of love rather
than reason the determining factor in one's account of the world
has the natural consequence of making a hero of the lover, and this
is what Bruno does with Actaeon. However, although 'there is no
man who does not have God within him'[17] yet 'very few are the
Actaeons to whom destiny gives the power to contemplate Diana
naked'.[18] To judge by his language Romeo would seem to be a
member of this elite, the new category of the heroic lover. Previous
critics have remarked Shakespeare's originality in taking the
unhappy story of the two young lovers as suitable for a serious stage
tragedy, but without perceiving the principles and implications.[19]
In the context of Renaissance Platonism the lovers and their fate
have the dignity of heroes *par excellence*.

Their fate, like Actaeon's, is death, and the manner in which it is
presented is as distinctively ideal, emotional and unnaturalistic as
their love. Inge Leimberg amply demonstrates from the sources in
Ficino and Pico and from the practice of the sonneteers in France
and England how widely diffused was the idea that death was a
symbol for the highest form of love or, as Edgar Wind has shown,
to be identified with love itself. In this latter case it was symbolized
by the kiss. Pico comments on Benivieni's poem that 'He who would
possess her [the heavenly Venus] more intimately . . . must be
separated from the body by the total separation of the second death,
and then . . . transfusing their souls into each other by kisses . . .
they will unite themselves together in perfection.'[20] This is the
meaning of Romeo's final pun: 'O true Appothecary: / Thy drugs
are quicke. Thus with a kiss I die' (v.iii.120–1). The whole of his
speech in the tomb is as surprising in the circumstances as his
speech in the garden. It is full of images of light, marriage, triumphs,
lanterns, feasts, laughter, lightning, love and beauty, all reminiscent
of earlier scenes in the play, particularly the one in which he first
met Juliet. This light shines through an opposite series of images of
darkness – the death of Paris, the pale flag, Tybalt's corpse and the
palace of night. Like the speech in the balcony scene, the climax to
the structure is a kind of theophany. Just as Juliet there became an
angel, so here death becomes her lover:

> Ah dear *Juliet*
> Why art thou yet so faire? shall I beleeve
> That unsubstantiall death is amorous,
> And that the leane abhorred monster keepes
> Thee here in darke to be his parramour?
> (v.iii.101–5)

This grisly medieval version of Pluto would triumph were it not that Romeo proves himself a more heroic lover than Orpheus by going to the extreme of death. The true climax is in Romeo's resolution 'For fear of that I still will stay with thee', and action. Juliet recapitulates the theme, language, and symbolically erotic act in her last words:

> I will kisse thy lips
> Happlie some poyson yet doth hang on them
> To make me dye with a restorative. . .
> O happy dagger
> This is thy sheath, there rust and let me dye.
> (v.iii.164–6, 169–70)

The effect therefore of the death of the lovers is not one of frustration or accident, but of the triumph of life in death, or of consummation.[21]

So much as this may perhaps be granted readily enough, for it concerns only the lovers and their values. It is when one turns to the play as a whole that disagreement is more likely. The most popular interpretations of the tragedy ascribe it either to society or, more commonly, to the stars, and both of these are of course deterministic readings.[22] It is my intention to argue that both are wrong, or at best partial, and I can best show this through an extended study of the role of Tybalt, since he is obviously crucial to the plot. If *Romeo and Juliet* is the tragedy of two young victims of social circumstances, then Tybalt is necessarily the agent of those circumstances. There are numerous objections to such an interpretation. The first is his complete lack of detailed characterization. He consequently offers absolutely no purchase for an attempt to relate him to a social background. Moreover, the feud between the families is explicitly renounced by old Capulet at the feast and Tybalt's rebellion against this prohibition is given no context of social causation beyond his own wilfulness. Again, at no point in the play are we able to connect its personae to any set of relations that could be called social process, however much we make of the realistic detail particularly associated with Capulet's household. Lastly, if the lovers are rebels against an oppressive society of which Tybalt is the voice, then we might expect them to refer to society in general terms, such as we find in *Titus Andronicus* or *Julius Caesar*. Instead, their references to the feud are summary, and in Juliet's famous reflections on Romeo's name the lovers immediately translate family relationships into the more abstract terms of nominalism and realism.[23]

Since the feud is clearly a prominent factor in the action of the play, and Tybalt is clearly a part of it, then we are still to seek a meaning for it, unless it is to be taken as a mere *donnée* of the story, having no tragic meaning in itself. Before accepting so trivializing a reading, let us turn to that other view of the play which sees it as the story of two lovers crossed by the stars. If *Romeo and Juliet* is a tragedy of this kind of fate, then, again because of his role in the plot, Tybalt must again be its agent. I cannot myself see the play quite in that way, but it does, I think, bring one closer to the truth; accordingly I shall now play devil's advocate for the view that the stars predominate, but, having done so, return to Tybalt, and try to show how his true role rises out of and above this particular pattern of meaning. J. W. Draper long since pointed out that Shakespeare is noticeably at pains to particularize the time of year, day, and days of the week when the events take place. His thoroughgoing astrological reading of the play can in fact be taken even further.[24] Juliet's birthday is on Lammas Eve, that is 31 July, and the play occurs a fortnight and odd days before then. Juliet was therefore born under Leo and the play takes place under Cancer and very likely during the dog-days. According to almanacs of the period the summer period of 23 June to 23 August is associated with youth, fire and yellow choler, which is hot and dry. In July one should avoid lechery, because 'then the braine and the humours are alwayes open' while the dog-days are 'of great daunger and perill'.[25] The other sign governing this season is Virgo and the organs affected by the three signs are the breast, lungs, back, ribs, heart and stomach. Love, violence, misfortune and hot weather are to be expected, therefore, at this period. In this context of medieval–Renaissance natural science the fiery Tybalt and his 'wilful choler' might perhaps signify the determining influence of the stars, which is indeed Draper's unqualified conclusion.

The fullest commentary on the zodiac which we know Shakespeare read is Barnabie Googe's translation of Palingenius, many phrases from which lodged themselves in his memory.[26] We there find that the book on Cancer or summer begins with a hymn to the sun, the 'starre divine' who 'partes in foure the yeare' and that the book is devoted to the subject of love – Venus, Cupid's rule, fire and social love.[27] The book of Leo asks why so few are wise and finds an answer in the subjection of most men to Nature by confluence of the stars or by genetically transmitted accidents of birth. Book VI moves into Virgo, opens with a grim description of Hell and Death, and deals with the troubles of man's estate, the chief of which is mortality. The three books may therefore be seen as corresponding to the three phases of the play: ardent love, rash error, and death, all presided over by the stars, although if Shakespeare did have such a scheme in mind he would have been conflating an astrological time-scale of four months with his own time-plot of four days. Palingenius lays as much emphasis on material causes as any author we know Shakespeare to have read and this, in addition to his anti-clericalism, may have been a heterodoxy that resulted in *The Zodiake of Life* being placed on the Index. Yet however materialist and determinist some of the arguments, the overall attitude to man's lot is traditional enough, if eclectic in a typically Renaissance way. The three books mentioned all conclude with the mind rising superior to adversity in a fashionably Stoic manner, which is consistent with the concern of the whole work to show how rationality can triumph over ignorance and matter. Thus book IV in fact opens with two hymns to the sun, first as governor of times and seasons and all things engendered in time, and second as source of the holy spirit which inspires the minds of poets to rise to immortal fame beyond time.[28] Similarly, two Venuses are distinguished, one a physical principle determining, for instance, erotic dreams, the other a spiritual principle preserving the world in harmony, like God's love for Creation.[29] There is thus already present in *The Zodiake* an Ancipient Platonism, as is explicitly avowed in the preface.[30]

Against this background we can perhaps get a clearer view of the parts played by determinism, chance and will in the play. When Romeo exclaims 'O I am fortunes foole' (III.i.141), he realizes that by killing Tybalt he has delivered himself over to a world of consequence and law which he had seemed triumphantly to sur-mount in his union with Juliet. When he later says 'Then I denie you starres' (v.i.24), he resolves to shake off that yoke by joining

Juliet in the tomb. When in Act I his mind misgives 'Some consequence yet hanging in the stars' (I.iv.107) his dream appears to be ironically reversed by his then meeting and falling in love with Juliet, yet the meeting does eventually lead as it happens to the bitter consequence of death. When in Act v his dreams presage 'some joyful newes at hand' (v.i.2) they seem to be ironically reversed with the news of Juliet's 'death', yet this news does in fact cause him to return from separation and exile to lie with her that night. The marked prophetic symmetry of the two dreams calls attention to the central paradox of the play, that their love is both destiny and choice. It is both presaged, and hence independent of individual will, and embraced, so that in fulfilling their love they rise superior to circumstances, including the stars. Pico expresses this metaphysically when he says that 'Every Creature consists of two Natures, Material, the imperfect (which we here understand by Necessity), and Formal, the occasion of perfection' and he makes the same point in mythical terms when he explains that Venus is said to command Fate because 'temporal, corporeal things only are subjected to Fate; the Rational Soul, being incorporeal predominates over it'.[31] A similar paralogical double standard may lie behind the seeming self-contradiction in Palingenius when he proceeds from an emphatic assertion that love is a mystery of destiny to the more mundane proverb that there's no love without luck.[32] Tybalt, then, is an agent not merely of the stars, but of the metaphysical paradoxes which present the lovers both as star-crossed by 'misadventur'd pittious overthrowes' (Prologue, 7) and as heroes of love who triumph over the stars through love itself, for Tybalt is the principle opposite to love: Tybalt is hate.

If we consider his role in the play from this point of view, character and plot unite in meaning. If we see him not as an intrinsically insignificant part of the mechanics of plot but as arising from the principles of the play, then a covert parallel between him and Romeo becomes apparent. He is equally youthful, equally impetuous – Mercutio considers him equally fantastic (II.iv.20). The same night and feast that reveal Juliet to Romeo reveal Romeo to Tybalt and he chooses Romeo for his enemy as immediately and absolutely as Romeo chooses Juliet for his love. His voice is insistently counterpointed against that of the lovers. We think of him in the orchard when Juliet tells Romeo the place is death if any of her kinsmen find him there. Directly after the Friar leaves to arrange the marriage we learn of his challenge, and directly after the marriage the challenge is effected. His name alternates bewilderingly with Romeo's as Juliet gathers the news of the duel from the Nurse, and she equivocates with the two names to her mother just after Romeo has left for Mantua. Capulet refers to him in conversation with Paris. Perhaps most striking of all are Juliet's references as she plucks up courage to take the potion. There are three, all coming after the thoughts of Romeo in the first part of the speech. As her imagination grows more fevered and the relatively ordered syntax disintegrates, he is displaced by Tybalt. 'Where bloudie *Tybalt* yet but greene in earth, / Lies fest'ring in his shrowde' (iv.ii.42–3) suggests a sinister life in him. A few lines later she thinks she may 'pluck the mangled *Tybalt* from his shrowde' and shortly after that he appears, together with Romeo:

> O looke, me thinks I see my Cozins Ghost,
> Seeking out *Romeo* that did spit his body
> Upon a Rapiers poynt: stay *Tybalt*, stay:
> *Romeo, Romeo, Romeo*, I drinke to thee.
>
> (iv.ii.55–8)

The ghost rises as an hallucination on the realistic psychological basis of her fear, but its role in the scene and its relation to Romeo in the structure of the speech go beyond realism. It is almost as if Romeo were metamorphosed into Tybalt. Juliet's words and action at the end anticipate Romeo's 'Heeres to my Love' (v.iii.119) when he drinks the poison in the tomb. There is a further point of resemblance in the startling and unexpected way that Tybalt occurs here too, this time in Romeo's description of Juliet:

> Thou art not conquerd, bewties ensigne yet
> Is crymson in thy lips and in thy cheeks,
> And deaths pale flag is not advanced there.
> *Tybalt* lyest thou there in thy bloudie sheet?
> O what more favour can I do to thee,
> Then with that hand that cut thy youth in twaine,
> To sunder his that was thine enemie?
> Forgive me Couzen.
>
> (v.iii.94–101)

Once Tybalt is dead these continuing references to him cannot be said to further a sense of doom gathering over the lovers' heads; rather, Tybalt's role in the play is akin to that of an image or theme as well as that of an agent or character. The curious association with Romeo weaves plot and poetry together as varying aspects of a single imaginative vision, and the principle uniting both is of course the *discordia concors* of Platonic theology. Bruno explains it psychologically:

The human heart contains two summits, which rise progressively from one root; and in the spiritual sense, from a single passion of the heart proceed the two contraries of hate and love. For Mount Parnassus has two summits rising from one foundation.[33]

Pico explains the same principle in aesthetic terms:

Beauty arises from contrariety, without which is no composition; it being the union of contraries, a friendly enmity, a disagreeing concord. . . . Thus in the Fictions of the Poets, Venus loves Mars: this Beauty cannot subsist without contrariety.[34]

Spenser pictures it iconographically when in the Temple of Venus Concord is mother of the two brothers Love and Hate, Hate the elder but Love the stronger.[35] It is typical of Florentine idealism that it is love which subsumes hate in the end. So the feud, and Tybalt's role as agent of the feud, should be understood ultimately in the context not of social causes, nor even of the stars, but of a metaphysic of opposites that informs both of these secondary causes, and indeed all of the human and natural world. Study of chance, destiny and Tybalt's role in the plotting of the play leads one to reaffirm that the death of the lovers is to be seen as a strange kind of triumph rather than defeat, and their status as a special kind of heroes is also confirmed.

From observation of the strange affinity between Romeo and Tybalt, then, follows the conclusion as to the meaning of Tybalt's role in the play and the subsidiary status of material causes. Once again such an interpretation may perhaps be conceded, as with the interpretation of Romeo's love, but this time on the ground that Tybalt is, after all, a character who makes relatively little impact on audience or reader. Now this is odd in itself, for there is something wrong about a play that does not make its dramatic emphases coincide with the main lines of its meaning. We are in fact returned to the critical disagreements about the play which were my point of departure, for, apart from Romeo and Juliet themselves, and indeed sometimes despite them, the characters who do make an impact on audiences and readers are surely Mercutio and the Nurse. Indeed, the question now arises as to what such robust realists can possibly have to do with a dramatic poem so idealistically Ficinan. I shall offer an answer to this presently, but, and this is the critical point, it is not necessarily an answer that will convince in the theatre. I am myself convinced of its intellectual coherence and that it answers to Shakespeare's design in this particular play, but that design, by its very supra-physical idealism, goes beyond the inherent possibilities of theatre. An actor playing Romeo has to overcome an audience's sense of mundane reality and the main resource he is given is the power of words; an actor playing Mercutio is given words that happily reinforce that sense of everyday reality. The one strives against natural limitations, the other revels in them – an unequal contest, although a Romeo who manages to win should sweep the board. This dramatic difficulty about the play is not a matter of one or two characters only, for a good deal of the texture of it is essentially realistic and comic.

The play's first scene begins comically with gross punning and although the entry of Tybalt makes a sudden change of tone and tempo, it is resolved in a serio-comic way. Montagues and Capulets slink off with their tails between their legs, very much like rebuked schoolboys, and it is an easy modulation from the self-consciously 'moved prince' who has to shout to get himself heard to old Capulet asserting his authority over young Tybalt:

> What goodman boy, I say he shall, go too,
> Am I the master here or you? go too.
>   (I.v.79–80)

Capulet and his household are the source and location of a good deal of the comedy in the play, a comedy that maintains itself not only in the face of the furious Tybalt, cutting him down to size, but also against choplogic Juliet in her 'peevish selfewield harlottry' (IV.ii.15). All his servants are comic, from Peter, played by Will Kemp, to the one who wants the porter to 'let in Susan Grindstone, and Nell, Anthonie and Potpan' at the same time as the gentlefolk, to, above all, the Nurse. Outside the household, she is reinforced by Mercutio, and the two of them supply the mixture of simple earthiness and cynical obscenity for which the play is also well known. Each of the two romantic lovers is pointedly coupled with a satiric counterpart embodying an attitude remote indeed from lyricism: 'This driveling love is like a great naturall that runs lolling up and downe to hide his bable in a hole' (II.iv.95–7). An important part of the play's tone and atmosphere is determined by domestic arrangements, bedrooms, adolescent joking, potmen, nurses, orchard walls, truckle beds, people sitting up late talking or returning from parties, cooks, parental tantrums and family scenes, worms pricked from the lazy fingers of maids. Proverbs are ready for every occasion and the busy surface of domestic normality is confidently maintained, supported in turn by the novella elements of the plot. The effect of all this is to set the Romeo and Juliet story, and also Tybalt's, in a world where Jove laughs at lovers' perjuries, because they have all happened before and are no more than youth and sex.

Now it is possible to reconcile all this to the ideals of the play by a simple reiteration of the principle that while such things as the stars, adolescent desire, comic family life and tragic family feuds do indeed have a standing in the play, their physicality is ultimately subsumed in a metaphysic which works in and through the natural towards the spiritual: *serio ludere*. Equally simply, however, a sort of Occam's razor of the theatre automatically applies, for all these physical elements are, as far as theatre goes, sufficient in themselves, and do not need the support of ulterior meanings to be entertaining, vivid and moving. Nor is such a view of the play a case of *Hamlet* without the Prince, for an audience may well be content to accept the story of Romeo and Juliet as simply a very sad and very human one, on a level with what one might read in the papers. That such a view is sensational, sentimental and indifferent to matters of intellectual and aesthetic coherence need be no obstacle to the play's success in the theatre. As I now turn, then, to analysis of the principal comic figures in relation to that aesthetic and intellectual coherence, it should be understood that it is something which exists at a poetic level that may not be fully appreciable on stage. In other words, in this play poet and playwright are not perfectly united.

It was H. C. Goddard who pointed out the interesting symmetry between Mercutio, the Nurse and the Friar as both advisers and opposites to the hero and heroine.[36] Inge Leimberg takes the idea a good deal further and reveals a quite elaborate system of parallelisms between characters, although she leaves her analysis at a purely formal level.[37] Taking up the analysis from this point, then, it is easy to see that just as Mercutio and the Nurse are supplanted as guides and confidants by the Friar, so he in turn is abandoned for the Apothecary, and the similarity of function is pointed up by verbal echoes. The effect of this can only be to divert our attention beyond the characters in themselves and towards the patterns, ironic correspondences and unconscious motives that they represent. Within the Ficinan scheme of things, the physicality of sex is not so much antithetical to ideal intellection as the first crude and yet indispensable impulse towards it. The bawdry for which the play is noted is not so much antithetical to the elevated lyricism for which it is famous as a lower version of the same thing. This was because, as André Chastel says of the arts in general:

The new idea which triumphed through the teaching of Ficino was that of the fundamental unity of all human activity . . ., and this affirmation of an *impulsus* common to all . . . transformed the mental horizons of the age.[38]

Ralegh gives a physical version of the same idea in the preface to his *History of the World* when he says that 'all things worke as they do . . . by an impulsion, which they cannot resist; or by a faculty, infused by the supremest power'.[39] Not everyone was prepared to go much further, or even so far. Burton, for example, sharply separates the perturbing passions from reason and prefers materialist explanations when they are to be had. He nonetheless faithfully reports the more heady and exciting doctrine, quoting Leone Ebreo to the effect that God's beauty 'draws all creatures to it' through the 'habit infused' into them, and he ruefully acknowledges of Eros that all must 'doe homage to him . . . and sacrifice to his altar'.[40]

Now the idea that Shakespeare had to kill Mercutio off to prevent him from stealing the play has proved a popular one ever since Dryden first gave it currency, but against the background of erotic theology we can see that his death has a meaning. His method is to 'be rough with love . . . and you beate love downe' (i.iv.27–8) and that is what he does in his famous speech.[41] Strangely, however, the very virtuosity with which he mocks dreams, dreamers and lovers and attempts to belittle them produces the opposite effect. He picks up a piece of idle superstition or rustic fancy to argue that dreams express merely the preoccupations of the dreamer, but having picked it up he seems unable to let go and the very circumstantiality with which he miniaturizes Queen Mab's state serves to authenticate and establish it. When he moves from charming description of her appearance to reporting her actions as she 'gallops night by night',

the wheels begin to take fire from their own motion, the pace
quickens, Mab reveals more and more powers, the syntax becomes
disordered, and we begin to feel that the fancy embodies something
real:

> Sometime she driveth ore a souldiers neck,
> And then dreames he of cutting forrain throates,
> Of breaches, ambuscados, spanish blades:
> Of healths five fadome deepe, and then anon
> Drums in his eare, at which he starts and wakes,
> And being thus frighted, sweares a praier or two,
> And sleeps againe.
>
> (i.iv.82–8)

By this stage we have lost sight of the supposed argument, that
men's dreams are merely the twitches of habitual thoughts during
sleep. Such an interpretation of our impression of the speech seems
as superficial as Theseus's of that other Dream:

> Or in the night, imagining some feare,
> How easie is a bush supposed a Beare?
> (v.i.21–2)

We have already seen that the play espouses the Platonic belief that
dreamers may prophetically dream 'things true' (i.iv.53).[42] Mercutio
professes a robust disbelief in such claims, yet the racing uncontrolled-
ness of this speech, and the suddenly dashed, veering rhythm of the
one following, undermine his position. The Mab he mocks is a
domestic, folkloric version of Titania–Diana, goddess of the moon,
childbirth and death. It is in *A Midsummer Night's Dream* that
Shakespeare gives us English folklore developed on Renaissance
principles of comparative mythology, but *Romeo and Juliet* may
anticipate it in this, as it is well known for doing in other ways.[43] If
Mab is Diana, to whom Mercutio bears unconscious witness through
the diminishing-glass of his scepticism, then his conscious intentions
are dangerously hubristic. The book of the *Metamorphoses* in which
Diana is called Titania is also the book telling the stories of Pentheus,
Semele, Narcissus and Actaeon, and Diana is shown to be a jealous
goddess.[44] Mercutio's scorn for her mystery is paralleled by his scorn
for Tybalt: 'The Pox on such antique lisping affecting phantacies'
(ii.iv.29), and this is a kind of madness. The *pulsus* of the world,
then, which exalts the lyrical rhythms of the lovers, also beats in

Mercutio's speeches, but dangerously *à travers*. Nicholas Brooke finds a shocking insensitivity when Romeo continues to speak in verse while Mercutio is dying in prose, and from a modern humanistic point of view this may be so.[45] The play, however, is not imagined from that point of view. It is much closer to the analysis of Mercutio offered by its most recent editor, who concludes that it is 'as if some unacknowledged premonition like Romeo's were inducing [his] train of thought'.[46] In its own Platonistic context, how appropriate that he should die in prose and that, according to Robert O. Evans, Mercutio's distinctive figures of speech are chiasmus and anaphora, whereas the characteristic figure for the rest of the play is oxymoron, ironically concealing truth behind apparent contradiction.[47] Mercutio is bound to die. Similarly the Nurse is bound to be excluded from the play's consummation, and excluded in the very definite terms that Juliet uses: 'Auncient damnation' (iii.v.235).

Any doubts about Shakespeare's comprehensive espousal of the Ficinan tradition in this particular play may be assuaged by comparing it with two other treatments of the same material, Arthur Brooke's in 1562, Shakespeare's main source, and Luigi Groto's in 1578. Brooke asserts that his purpose is to deter people from yielding to the excesses of passion by showing them the pitiful things that happen to those who do. He therefore represents the lovers as continually torn between the dictates of reason and the impulses of desire. This yields one of the principal interests of the poem, that is, a detailed psychological realism and a touching pathos as the lovers wallow in their conflicting feelings after their successive misfortunes. Brooke, like Fenton later, thus helps to bring England up to date with the interests of the Italian novellas. There is a further conflict between Romeus who, as a man, can sometimes muster a degree of rational self-restraint, and Juliet who, as the weaker vessel, has to be lectured by Romeus: 'Wherefore represse at once, the passions of thy hart'.[48] At the end, Romeus kneels in the tomb and prays to Christ:

> Take pitty on my sinnefull and my poore afflicted mynde.
> For well enough I know, this body is but clay,
> Nought but a masse of sinne, to frayle, and subject to decay.[49]

In contrast, Shakespeare introduces Tybalt at the beginning, omits the long complaints to Fortune, and above all discards the rational,

moralizing framework to concentrate on the lovers' passion as an
end and value in itself. To discard rationality of the moralizing kind
as an ultimate criterion was, in the English context, a poet's radical
stroke.

Where Brooke's poem is interesting but not informed by any
principle grasped comprehensively enough to confer unity on the
work, Groto's drama is boring but systematically elaborate. As such
it shows what the learned of the age were capable of seeing in the
story. The social status of the lovers is elevated to royalty, thus
underlining the doctrine of heroic love that the celestial arrow strikes
only 'materia alzata ad alto'.[50] The Friar becomes a Magus and the
presence of a Chorus shows that the story is to be treated on the
level of classical tragedy. The lovers are self-consciously compared
with the classical myths of Orpheus, Persephone and Cupid and
Psyche, which Shakespeare hauntingly assimilates by subtle echoes.
The two forces of love and hate are developed by setting the love
story in a city under siege and the Magus gives an exposition of
how frequently marriage is the father of war, changing the pipe to
the trumpet, invoking Mars instead of Hymen, changing garlands
to helmets, and torches to swords – all simultaneously and emblemati-
cally present in the tomb scene of *Romeo and Juliet*. Hadriana dies
asserting the union of the lovers in death: 'O stay, husband, that I
may follow thee',[51] thus demonstrating the Prologue's equation of
the arrow of 'Amor' with the arrow of 'Morte',[52] just as Ronsard
had asserted in his final sonnet that 'l'Amour et la Mort n'est qu'une
mesme chose'.[53] In sum, Groto's version is academic and frigid, but
he does display the meanings his age found in the story and may
thus alert us to many details of Shakespeare's treatment.

Romeo and Juliet, then, is up-to-date, perhaps even avant-garde in
the English theatre of its day. Both in over-all design and local
detail it is informed by a 'single energy', which Coleridge detected
in his notes on the play but did not follow through in his lectures.[54]
To say this is to accept the play on its intellectual, ideal and
poetic level. In the physical medium of theatre, concreted in the
personalities of actors and responding to an audience in all its
humanity, the Ficinan aspirations may well fade in the light of
common day, or haunt the play with a sense of the strained and
unachieved. This however is not because of something lacking in its
design but more because of an excess of purpose, almost an
overdetermination of meaning. Those who mislike, for example, the

death of Mercutio, or the dismissal of the Nurse, or the unrealistic elevation of the language, should not explain these features as the accidental immaturities of an apprentice writer, but rather fasten their objections on the principles of which the features are consequences. It was a kind of religion and a very unorthodox one. Having strong feelings and principles of his own about such matters, Dr Johnson grasped this in one of his notes, which, thwart and opposite to the yearning beauty of the play though it may be, is of the essence:

Juliet plays most of her pranks under the appearance of religion; perhaps Shakespeare meant to punish her hypocrisy.[55]

SOURCE: 'The Unity of *Romeo and Juliet*', *Shakespeare Survey, 34* (Cambridge, 1981), pp. 93–104.

NOTES

All quotations from *Romeo and Juliet* are taken from the 1599 Second Quarto, ed. Greg (Oxford, 1949), except for I.iv.54–91, where I introduce verse lineation; II.ii.16, where I adopt the First Quarto's *do* instead of *to*; IV.iii.58, where I adopt Dr Johnson's emendation; and V.iii.102–3, where I delete the redundant 'I will beleeve' and relineate accordingly.

1. John M. Aden, *The Critical Opinions of John Dryden* (Nashville, 1963), p. 237.
2. R. A. Foakes (ed.), *Coleridge on Shakespeare* (1971), p. 78.
3. G. I. Duthie and J. D. Wilson (eds), *Romeo and Juliet* (Cambridge, 1955), p. xxvi.
4. Nicholas Brooke, *Shakespeare's Early Tragedies* (1973), p. 87.
5. H. A. Mason, *Shakespeare's Tragedies of Love* (1970), pp. 42–55.
6. Brooke, 'Myth and Naturalism: *Merchant to Macbeth*' in Bevington and Halio (eds), *Shakespeare, Pattern of Excelling Nature* (Newark, 1976), p. 141.
7. Sears R. Jayne (trans.), *Marsilio Ficino's Commentary on Plato's 'Symposium'* (Columbia, 1944), p. 140.
8. Giovanni Battista da Castiglione, *I Luoghi Difficili del Petrarcha nuovamente dichiarati* (Venice, 1532), p. 5ʳ.
9. J. V. Cunningham, *Tradition and Poetic Structure* (Denver, 1960), p. 22.
10. Edgar Wind, *Pagan Mysteries of the Renaissance* (rev. edn, 1967), 'Virtue Reconciled with Pleasure', pp. 81–96.
11. Giovanni Pico della Mirandola, *A Platonick Discourse upon Love*, trans. Thomas Stanley (1651), ed. Edmund Gardner (1914), p. 45.
12. *Ibid.*, p. 17.

13. Castiglione, *I Luoghi Difficili*, pp. 44^v–45^r.

14. Inge Leimberg, *Shakespeare's 'Romeo und Julia'. Von der Sonnettdichtung zur Liebestragödie* (Munich, 1968). The reinterpretation is shown to have been accomplished by the sonneteers in England by 1590. Daniel's *Complaint of Rosamund* is echoed at v.iii.92–6 and 112–15.

15. Giordano Bruno, *The Heroic Frenzies*, trans. Paul E. Nemmo (Chapel Hill, 1964), p. 225.

16. *Ibid.*, p. 225.

17. *Ibid.*, p. 165.

18. *Ibid.*, p. 225.

19. E.g., H. B. Charlton, '*Romeo and Juliet* as Experimental Tragedy', British Academy Shakespeare Lecture (1939); Harry Levin, 'Form and Formality in *Romeo and Juliet*', *Shakespeare Quarterly*, 11 (1960), pp. 3–11; Paul N. Siegel, 'Christianity and the Religion of Love in *Romeo and Juliet*', *Shakespeare Quarterly*, 12 (1961), pp. 371–92.

20. Quoted by Wind, *Pagan Mysteries*, 'Amor as a God of Death', p. 155, n. 7.

21. This is Leimberg's well supported conclusion, in flat contradiction to D. R. C. Marsh, *Passion Lends Them Power* (Manchester, 1976), pp. 83–8.

22. E.g., Duthie (ed.), *Romeo and Juliet*; Irving Ribner, ' "Then I denie you starres": A Reading of *Romeo and Juliet*' in *Studies in English Renaissance Drama*, ed. J. W. Bennett (New York, 1959); Virgil Whitaker, *The Mirror up to Nature* (San Marino, 1965).

23. See James L. Calderwood, *Shakespearean Metadrama* (Minnesota, 1971), pp. 81–91.

24. J. W. Draper, 'Shakespeare's "Star-Crossed Lovers" ', *Review of English Studies*, 15 (1939), pp. 16–34. In contrast Whitaker judges that 'the metaphysics of the play is not particularly sophisticated, and it is nowhere clear whether the stars symbolize blind fate or chance or . . . natural forces', *The Mirror up to Nature*, p. 111.

25. 'Erra Pater'. *A Prognostication for ever* (n.d., *c.* 1565), Bodleian Library, Douce A 55(4), Sigs. A7^v, B2^2.

26. See T. W. Baldwin, *William Shakespere's Small Latine and Lesse Greeke*, 2 vols. (Urbana, 1944), vol. 1, pp. 652–81, and John Erskine Hankins, *Shakespeare's Derived Imagery* (Lawrence, 1953), *passim*.

27. [Marcellus Palingenius Stellatus,] *The Zodiake of Life*, trans. Barnabie Googe, new edn (1588), pp. 40–1.

28. *Ibid.*, p. 41.

29. *Ibid.*, pp. 46–8, Sig. D2^r (mispaginated as p. 62).

30. *Ibid.*, π4^r.

31. Pico della Mirandola, *A Platonick Discourse*, pp. 39–40.

32. Palingenius, *The Zodiake of Life*, p. 49. There may be interesting echoes in Romeo's speeches at II.ii.82–4 and v.iii.116–18 of the comparison in this passage between venturers and lovers when crossed by stars. Muir links Romeo's imagery here to Sidney and (following Whiter) Brooke, in *The Sources of Shakespeare's Plays* (1977), pp. 43–5.

33. Bruno, *The Heroic Frenzies*, p. 86.

34. Pico della Mirandola, *A Platonick Discourse*, p. 26.

35. Spenser, *The Faerie Queene*, IV.x.31–6.
36. H. C. Goddard, *The Meaning of Shakespeare* (Chicago, 1951), pp. 120–4.
37. Leimberg, 'Romeo und Julia' in *Das englische Drama*, ed. Dieter Mehl (Düsseldorf, 1970), pp. 60–78.
38. André Chastel, *Marsile Ficin et l'art*, Travaux d'humanisme et renaissance 14 (Geneva and Lille, 1954), p. 61.
39. Ralegh, *The History of the World* (1614), Preface, Sig. c3^r.
40. Burton, *The Anatomy of Melancholy*, 'Religious Melancholy', III.4.i.1. and 'Love Melancholy', III.2.v.5.
41. I am encouraged in my reading of this speech by my closeness to the analysis by Brian Gibbons in his new Arden edition (1980), pp. 67–8.
42. 'Dream', *New Catholic Encyclopaedia* (Washington, D.C., 1967), vol. 4, p. 1054b. Marjorie Garber's discussion of *Romeo and Juliet* in *Dream in Shakespeare* (New Haven and London, 1974), does not grasp the issues.
43. See Frank Kermode, 'The Mature Comedies' in *Early Shakespeare*, ed. J. R. Brown and B. Harris, Stratford-upon-Avon Studies, 3 (1961), and Glynne Wickham, *Shakespeare's Dramatic Heritage* (1969), pp. 180–90.
44. Ovid, *Metamorphoses*, III.1.173.
45. Brooke, *Shakespeare's Early Tragedies*, p. 83.
46. Gibbons (ed.), *Romeo and Juliet*, p. 69.
47. Robert O. Evans, *The Osier Cage. Rhetorical Devices in 'Romeo and Juliet'* (Lexington, 1966). See also Leonid Arbusow, *Colores Rhetorici* (Göttingen, 1963), p. 88.
48. Arthur Brooke, *The Tragicall Historye of Romeus and Juliet* in G. Bullough (ed.), *Narrative and Dramatic Sources of Shakespeare*, 8 vols. (1957–75), vol. 1, p. 329, l. 1683.
49. *Ibid.*, p. 354, ll. 2678–80.
50. Luigi Groto, *La Hadriana. Tragedia nova* (Venice, 1599 edn), p. 6^v.
51. *Ibid.*, p. 70^r.
52. *Ibid.*, Prologo, p. 5^v.
53. Ronsard, *Sonnets Pour Hélène*, ed. M. Smith (Geneva, 1970), p. 195, cited by Leimberg, *Das englische Drama*, pp. 73–4.
54. Coleridge, *Shakespearean Criticism*, ed. T. M. Raysor, 2 vols (1930; repr. 1960), vol. 1, p. 5.
55. Quoted from *Johnson on Shakespeare*, ed. Arthur Sherbo, 2 vols (New Haven and London, 1968), vol. 2 p. 953.

SELECT BIBLIOGRAPHY

The following books and articles are recommended.

GENERAL READING

M. C. Bradbrook, *Shakespeare and Elizabethan Poetry* (London, 1951).

A. C. Bradley, *Shakespearean Tragedy* (London, 1904).

A. R. Braunmuller, 'Early Shakespearean Tragedy and Its Contemporary Context: Cause and Emotion in *Titus Andronicus, Richard III*, and *The Rape of Lucrece*', in J. R. Brown and B. Harris (eds.), *Shakespearean Tragedy*, Stratford-upon-Avon Studies, vol. 20 (London, 1984), pp. 96–128.

N. Brooke, *Shakespeare's Early Tragedies* (London, 1968).

H. B. Charlton, *Shakespearian Tragedy* (Cambridge, 1948).

Jonathan Dollimore, *Radical Tragedy: Religion, Ideology and Power in the Drama of Shakespeare and His Contemporaries* (Brighton, 1984).

Huston Diehl, 'The Iconography of Violence in English Renaissance Tragedy', *Renaissance Drama*, NS 11 (1980), pp. 36–8.

W. Farnham, *The Medieval Heritage of Elizabethan Tragedy* (Berkeley, 1936).

A. C. Hamilton, *The Early Shakespeare* (San Marino, California, 1967).

G. K. Hunter, 'Seneca and the Elizabethans', *Shakespeare Survey 20* (Cambridge, 1967), pp. 17–26.

G. K. Hunter, 'Seneca and English Tragedy', in C. D. N. Costa (ed.), *Seneca* (London and Boston, 1974), pp. 166–204.

E. Jones, *The Origins of Shakespeare* (Oxford, 1977).

Kenneth Muir, 'Shakespeare and the Tragic Pattern', *British Academy Shakespeare Lecture* (1958).

Ruth Nevo, *Tragic Form in Shakespeare* (Princeton, New Jersey, 1972).

Irving Ribner, *Patterns in Shakespearean Tragedy* (London, 1960).

E. M. W. Tillyard, *The Elizabethan World Picture* (London, 1943).

R. Weimann, *Shakespeare and the Popular Tradition in the Theatre* (Baltimore and London, 1978 edition).

R. Williams, *Modern Tragedy* (London, 1966; revised edition 1979).

H. S. Wilson, *On the Design of Shakespearean Tragedy* (Toronto, 1957).

RICHARD III

J. P. Brockbank, 'Shakespeare's Histories, English and Roman', in C. Ricks (ed.), *English Drama to 1710* (Sphere History of Literature in the English Language) (London, 1971).

Lily B. Campbell, *Shakespeare's Histories: Mirrors of Elizabethan Policy* (Cambridge, 1947).

W. H. Clemen, *A Commentary on Shakespeare's 'Richard III'* (London, 1968 edition).

M. French, *Shakespeare's Division of Experience* (London, 1982).

Andrew Gurr, 'Richard III and the Democratic Process', *Essays in Criticism* 24 (1974), pp. 39–47.

M. Krieger, 'The Dark Generations of Richard III', *Criticism* 1 (1959), pp. 32–48.

M. M. Miner, ' "Neither mother, wife, nor England's queen": The Roles of Women in Richard III', in C. R. S. Lenz, G. Greene and C. T. Neely (eds.), *The Woman's Part: Feminist Criticism of Shakespeare* (Urbana, Illinois, 1980).

John Palmer, 'Richard of Gloucester', in *Political Characters of Shakespeare* (London, 1945), pp. 65–117.

Moody E. Prior, *The Drama of Power: Studies in Shakespeare's History Plays* (Evanston, Illinois, 1973).

Irving Ribner, *The English History Play in the Age of Shakespeare* (Princeton, 1957).

Kristian Smidt, *Unconformities in Shakespeare's History Plays* (London, 1982), pp. 53–71.

B. Spivack, *Shakespeare and the Allegory of Evil* (New York, 1958).

E. M. W. Tillyard, *Shakespeare's History Plays* (London, 1944), pp. 141–47.

J. Wilders, *The Lost Garden* (London, 1978).

TITUS ANDRONICUS

J. L. Calderwood, *Shakespearean Metadrama: The Argument of the Play* (Minneapolis, Minn., 1971), pp. 23–51.

Lawrence Danson, *Tragic Alphabet: Shakespeare's Drama of Language* (New Haven, 1974), pp. 1–21.

A. V. Ettin, 'Shakespeare's First Roman Tragedy', *English Literary Renaissance* 37 (1970), pp. 325–41.

A. L. Fawcett, 'Arms/Words/Tears: Language and the Body in *Titus Andronicus*', *English Literary Renaissance* 50 (1983), pp. 261–78.

Ann Haaker, '*Non Sine Causa*: the Use of Emblematic Method and Iconology in the Thematic Structure of *Titus Andronicus*', *Research Opportunities in Renaissance Drama* 12–14 (1970–1), pp. 143–68.

A. C. Hamilton, '*Titus Andronicus*: the Form of Shakespearean Tragedy', *Shakespeare Quarterly 14* (1963), pp. 206–07.

R. F. Hill, 'The Composition of *Titus Andronicus*', *Shakespeare Survey 10* (Cambridge, 1957), pp. 60–70.

S. Clark Hulse, 'Wresting the Alphabet: Oratory and Action in *Titus Andronicus*', *Criticism* 21 (1971), pp. 106–18.

G. H. Metz, 'The Stage History of *Titus Andronicus*', *Shakespeare Quarterly* 28 (1977), pp. 154–69.

Ruth Nevo, 'Tragic form in *Titus Andronicus*', in A. A. Mendilow (ed.), *Further Studies in English Language and Literature* (Jerusalem, 1975), pp. 1–18.

D. J. Palmer, 'The Unspeakable in Pursuit of the Uneatable: Language and Action in *Titus Andronicus*', *Critical Quarterly* 14 (1972), pp. 320–39.

J. E. Reese, 'The Formalization of Horror in *Titus Andronicus*', *Shakespeare Quarterly* 21 (1970), pp. 77–84.

Alan Sommers, ' "Wilderness of Tigers": Structure and Symbolism in *Titus Andronicus*', *Essays in Criticism* 10 (1960), pp. 275–89.

T. J. B. Spencer, 'Shakespeare and the Elizabethan Romans', *Shakespeare Survey 10* (Cambridge, 1957).

Rudolf Stamm, 'The Alphabet of Speechless Complaint: A Study of the Mangled Daughter in Shakespeare's *Titus Andronicus*', in J. G. Price (ed.), *The Triple Bond* (Pennsylvania and London, 1975), pp. 255–73.

A. H. Tricomi, 'The Mutilated Garden in *Titus Andronicus*', *Shakespeare Studies* 9 (1976), pp. 89–105.

Eugene M. Waith, 'The Ceremonies of *Titus Andronicus*', in J. C. Gray, *The Mirror up to Shakespeare* (Toronto, 1983), pp. 159–70).

Eugene M. Waith, 'The Metamorphosis of Violence in *Titus Andronicus*', *Shakespeare Survey 10* (Cambridge, 1957), pp. 39–49.

ROMEO AND JULIET

J. R. Brown, *Shakespeare's Plays in Performance* (London, 1966).

H. B. Charlton, '*Romeo and Juliet* as an Experimental Tragedy', *British Academy Shakespeare Lecture* (1939).

F. M. Dickey, *Not Wisely But Too Well: Shakespeare's Love Tragedies* (San Marino; California, 1966).

R. O. Evans, *The Osier Cage: Rhetorical Devices in 'Romeo and Juliet'* (Lexington, Ky., 1966).

B. Everett, '*Romeo and Juliet*: the Nurse's Story', in C. B. Cox and D. J. Palmer (eds.), *Shakespeare's Wide and Universal Stage* (London, 1984), pp. 134–45.

F. Granville-Barker, '*Romeo and Juliet*', in *Prefaces to Shakespeare* series ii (London, 1930; 1958 edition), pp. 300–49.

G. Holderness, '*Romeo and Juliet*: Empathy and Alienation', *Shakespeare-Jahrbuch*, 123 (1987), pp. 118–29.

J. Lawlor, '*Romeo and Juliet*', in J. R. Brown and B. Harris, *Early Shakespeare* Stratford-upon-Avon Studies 3 (London, 1961), pp. 122–43.

Harry Levin, 'Form and Formality in *Romeo and Juliet*', *Shakespeare Quarterly* 11 (1960).

D. C. Marsh, *Passion Lends Them Power* (Manchester, 1976), pp. 46–88.

H. A. Mason, *Shakespeare's Tragedies of Love* (London, 1970).

P. N. Siegel, 'Christianity and the Religion of Love in *Romeo and Juliet*' *Shakespeare Quarterly* 12 (1961), pp. 371–92.

G. R. Smith, 'The Balance of Themes in *Romeo and Juliet*', in G. R. Smith (ed.), *Essays on Shakespeare* (London, Pa., 1965).

M. B. Smith, *Dualities in Shakespeare* (Toronto, 1966), pp. 79–109.

Caroline Spurgeon, *Shakespeare's Imagery and What It Tells Us* (Cambridge, 1935), pp. 309–16.

NOTES ON CONTRIBUTORS

T. J. L. CRIBB is a fellow of Churchill College, Cambridge. In addition to works of criticism, he has published translations of Romanian poetry.

IRENE G. DASH is Assistant Professor of Literature at Hunter College, City University, New York. She has written extensively on feminist approaches to literature.

MICHAEL HATTAWAY is Professor of Literature at Sheffield University. He has published extensively in the field of Elizabethan drama.

G. K. HUNTER is Professor of Literature at Yale University. His numerous publications include *Shakespeare: the Later Comedies* and the new Arden edition of *All's Well that Ends Well*.

M. M. MAHOOD is Professor Emeritus, Kent University. Her publications include *Poetry and Humanism*.

PETER REYNOLDS is a lecturer in Drama at the Roehampton Institute. His publications include *Drama: Text into Performance* and *As You Like It: a Critical Study*.

A. P. ROSSITER was a Fellow of Jesus College, Cambridge, until his death in 1957. His publications include *English Drama from Early Times to the Elizabethans*.

SUSAN SNYDER is Professor of English at Swarthmore College. Her publications include an edition of Joshua Sylvester's translation of Du Bartas' *Divine Weeks and Works*.

E. M. W. TILLYARD, who died in 1962, was Master of Jesus College, Cambridge, from 1945 to 1959. His many books include *Shakespeare's Problem Plays* and *The Elizabethan World Picture*.

ALBERT H. TRICOMI is Associate Professor of English at the State University of New York, Binghampton. He is the author of numerous critical studies dealing with Elizabethan drama.

ACKNOWLEDGEMENTS

The editors and publishers wish to thank the following for permission to use copyright material: T. J. L. Cribb, extract from 'The Unity of *Romeo and Juliet*', *Shakespeare Survey*, 34, Cambridge University Press (1982), by permission of the author; Irene G. Dash, extracts from *Wooing, Wedding and Power: Women in Shakespeare's Plays* (1981). Copyright © 1981 by Columbia University Press, by permission of Columbia University Press; M. Hattaway, extract from '*Titus Andronicus*: Strange Images of Death' in *Elizabethan Popular Theatre* (1982), by permission of Routledge and Kegan Paul; G. K. Hunter, extract from 'Shakespeare's Earliest Tragedies: *Titus Andronicus* and *Romeo and Juliet*, *Shakespeare Survey*, 27, Cambridge University Press (1974), by permission of the author; M. M. Mahood, extract from chapter on *Romeo and Juliet* in *Shakespeare's Wordplay* (1957), by permission of Methuen & Co.; A. P. Rossiter, extract from 'The Unity of *Richard III*' in *Angel With Horns, and Other Shakespearean Lectures* (1961), by permission of Longman Group Ltd.; Susan Snyder, extract from 'Beyond Comedy: *Romeo and Juliet*' from *The Comic Matrix of Shakespeare's Tragedies: Romeo and Juliet, Hamlet, Othello, and King Lear* (1979). Copyright © 1979 by Princeton University Press, by permission of Princeton University Press; E. M. W. Tilliard, extract from *Shakespeare's History Plays* (1944), by permission of Chatto and Windus; Albert H. Tricomi, extract from essay 'The Aesthetics of Mutilation in *Titus Andronicus*', *Shakespeare Survey*, 14, Cambridge University Press (1961), by permission of the author.

Every effort has been made to trace all the copyright holders but if any have been inadvertently overlooked the publishers will be pleased to make the necessary arrangement at the first opportunity.

INDEX